July 7, 1988

To Howard + ♡

With best wishes and the hope
for future time (and conversations)
together.

Sandy

CONSTITUTIONAL FAITH

SANFORD LEVINSON

Constitutional Faith

PRINCETON

UNIVERSITY PRESS

Copyright © 1988 by Princeton University Press

Published by Princeton University Press, 41 William Street,
Princeton, New Jersey 08540

In the United Kingdom: Princeton University Press,
Guildford, Surrey

All Rights Reserved

Library of Congress Cataloging in Publication Data will be found on
the last printed page of this book

ISBN 0-691-07769-X

This book has been composed in Linotron Caledonia

Clothbound editions of Princeton University Press books are printed
on acid-free paper, and binding materials are chosen for strength and
durability. Paperbacks, although satisfactory for personal collections,
are not usually suitable for library rebinding

Printed in the United States of America by Princeton University
Press, Princeton, New Jersey

Illustrations by Zevi Blum

DESIGNED BY LAURY A. EGAN

To Cynthia,
for everything

A MATURE
COW FAITH IN
A WORLD COME
OF AGE

A SOBER
FAITH FILLED
EMPOWERING
BOOK for
A WORLD
come of age
NO PLATITUDES
To SHORE
UP COMMIT
IT through
CONVERSA,
INVITES

FOR SOME IT
WON'T BE ENOUGH
BUT THEY WILL
NOT BE ABLE
TO REFRESH/
Retire easily
for the
encounter
they will
have had
PUSHING as
A TRUE
TEACHER?!
WILL DO!
To CRITIQUE
I CHOOSE!

C O N T E N T S

ACKNOWLEDGMENTS

OVER THE MANY YEARS during which this book was gestating, one of the incentives for its completion was the opportunity I would then have to write an acknowledgments page that would convey my thanks for help to an ever-increasing number of friends and associates. Now the time has come, and I want to take full advantage of that opportunity. With completion has come as well chastening knowledge of the reality undergirding what had, as I read other writers' acknowledgments, always seemed to me the cliche that those acknowledged were not responsible for any remaining weaknesses. Along with advice gratefully accepted there remain other suggestions that were unwisely rejected. (The problem, of course, is that I am not wise enough to know *which* of the rejected suggestions are in that category.) In any event, I am immensely grateful both for the opportunity to work with these many individuals and to the institutions that provided the setting for collaboration.

I begin with the institution that most directly contributed to my completing this work, the Institute for Advanced Study in Princeton, New Jersey, which honored me with membership, half of which was funded by the National Endowment for the Humanities, during 1986-87. The remaining funding came from the University Research Institute of the University of Texas. Without denigrating the importance of the funding, I want to register special gratitude for the almost literally incredible work environment provided at the Institute for Advanced Study; it made the writing of this manuscript a joy. In addition to the institution, I am grateful to several of its members, including Elizabeth Hill Boone, William Connolly, Clifford Geertz, Albert Hirschman, Joan Scott, and Barbara Herrnstein Smith, all of whom read drafts of chapters and discussed them with me. Encouraging words from Carl Schorske and Barbara and Dennis Tedlock early in the year were much appreciated.

One member of the Institute, Michael Walzer, deserves separate mention. He could be listed under almost all of the institutional references to follow: I first met him at Harvard; it was as a teaching fellow in his course at Harvard that I first became obsessed by the problem of pluralism, which in this book is the focus of Chapter

Three. Equally important has been my participation with him in a continuing study group organized by the Shalom Hartman Institute on Jewish philosophy. I have never failed to benefit from his insights and ideas for the two decades I have been privileged to know him.

Having begun with my latest institutional debts, I now turn to my earliest one. Though it is now a full quarter-century since I arrived at Harvard as a graduate student in government, I remain under the influence of at least three individuals with whom it was my pleasure to study. Two, sadly, are now dead: Robert McCloskey and Louis Hartz. McCloskey provided an invaluable lesson in how to mix the study of constitutional law and more general American political and social thought. (He was also an extraordinarily decent man who contributed to my having an unusually happy experience as a graduate student.) Hartz provided a model of visionary thinking and absolute fearlessness in making comparisons and connections among thinkers and ideologies. Some worked, some did not, but there was never any doubt that one was stimulated by whatever he said. The third, happily, is still actively contributing to scholarship and intellectual life: Judith Shklar, too, has provided a model of absolute intellectual intensity and integrity that inspires even as it sometimes overwhelms.

After leaving Harvard, I was fortunate to receive a fellowship from the Russell Sage Foundation that allowed me to attend the Stanford Law School. The Law School provided me with both intellectual succor and good fellowship. It also provided me with the opportunity to deepen a personal and professional friendship with Paul Brest, whose traces run especially throughout Chapter One below.

My former colleagues at Princeton University, where I taught between 1975 and 1979, also left tracks that can be found in this book. In particular I wish to thank James Fleming, Amy Gutmann, Will Harris, Stanley Katz, Walter Murphy, Martin Sherwin, and Dennis Thompson. I also benefitted from the counsel of three new members of the Politics Department—Jennifer Hochschild, Anne Norton, and Jeff Tulis—whom I got to know during my stay at the Institute.

Another Institute, far removed from the United States, must also be mentioned, for this book reflects in many ways my connection with the Shalom Hartman Institute for the Study of Jewish Philosophy, in Jerusalem, Israel. The director of the Institute, David Hartman, and its members all combine a blazing intellectual seriousness with personal decency and moral commitment. What relatively little I know about my own Jewish tradition I owe to the patience of my teachers at the Institute, including, in addition to the inimitable David Hartman, David Dishon, Moshe Halbertal, Menachem Lorberbaum, Zvi Marx, Noam Zion, and Noam and Zvi Zohar. It is also through the Institute and meetings in the United States, Canada, and Israel that I have gotten to know, and benefit from, Sidney Morgenbesser, Michael Sandel, and Alan Silver. The initial draft of Chapter Three was originally prepared for a conference on community membership that was held in Jerusalem in December 1985. One of the participants at that conference was the late Robert Cover, whose work is reflected at points in this book and whose passionate wisdom I, like so many others, will miss for the rest of my life.

The primary institution with which I have been associated over the past eight years is the University of Texas Law School, which has been extremely generous in every way in providing support for my work. I am particularly grateful to its dean, Mark Yudof, and to my colleagues Douglas Laycock, Scot Powe, and Bill Powers, all of whom read multiple drafts of practically every chapter. Philip Bobbitt, an important conversational partner, deserves special thanks for his quick acquiescence in permitting me to give my own book a title extremely close to that of his own stimulating book, *Constitutional Fate*. (To any readers who thought they were asking for his book but received mine instead, my apologies!) Fortunately, the University of Texas consists of more than a law school, and I have benefitted from the encouragement and advice of colleagues from other parts of the University, including James Fishkin, Betty Sue Flowers, and Susan Heinzelman.

Several law schools over the years have invited me to give lectures or speak to faculty colloquia at which I have presented one or another of the chapters of this book. Without exception, the responses were valuable, and the differences between what they heard and what is printed below are tribute to those responses. The law schools include those at Campbell College, Hamline University, Harvard, University of Iowa, Oklahoma City University, University of Puerto Rico, Saint Louis University, Tulane, William and Mary, Yale, and Yeshiva University (the Cardozo Law School). In addition, I profited from the opportunity to speak at the University of North Carolina-Charlotte in 1986 and Princeton University in 1987.

The community of scholars-friends is itself an institution, from whose help I have benefitted. In particular I want to thank Milner Ball, Joseph Carens, Walter Dellinger, John Dzienkowski, Booth

ACKNOWLEDGMENTS

Fowler, Ron Garet, Leslie Goldstein, Don Herzog, Randall Kennedy, Frank Michelman, Victor Navasky, Gene Nichol, Robert Post, Jeff Powell, John Rosenberg, Fred Schauer, Tom Shaffer, Ellen Shrecker, Rogers Smith, Werner Sollors, John Stick, Mark Tushnet, Howard Vogel, and Michael Zuckerman. Special mention should be made of one friend, Richard Rabinowitz, whose depth of knowledge about and insight into the mysteries of American culture is unmatched. For fifteen years Richard has offered me personal and intellectual support and unstinting encouragement, even when he has been most skeptical about some of my ideas.

Writing is one thing; publication is another. I was helped by advice and encouragement received from an old friend, Bobbie Bristol, and a new one, Naomi Schneider. Sandy Thatcher, of the Princeton University Press, is another old friend whose comments through the years have been very important to me. It was therefore a special pleasure to work with him on the publication of this book. Sherry Wert, my editor at the Press, was consistently helpful and made enjoyable what could have been a trying process. I am also grateful to the Press for arranging to have Zevi Blum illustrate this book. Ten years ago he drew amazingly insightful illustrations for an article I published in *Harper's*. (They are reproduced here as the frontispiece and at the head of each chapter.) I very much appreciate his willingness to use some of his scarce time to contribute the cover.

Cynthia Yenkin Levinson not only generally supported, well beyond the call of any duty, the writing of this book, but also read, and made valuable comments on, an entire draft of the manuscript. My daughters, Meira and Rachel, provided no specific help on the book, but they nevertheless deserve mention as altogether splendid human beings.

To everyone above, as to anyone whom I have inadvertently forgotten, my deepest thanks.

CONSTITUTIONAL FAITH

If you take the faith out of Religion, you have a wasted Sunday morning. If you take the belief out of Law, all you have is litigation. And if you take the Ritual out of celebration, all you have is Presidents' Day.

—DAVID MAMET, *Writing in Restaurants*

INTRODUCTION

WHAT POLITICAL COMMITMENTS, if any, does a foreign-born person make upon joining the American polity by taking on the formal status of citizen? That question, among others, was raised by a case decided by the United States Supreme Court in 1943. It was an unusually volatile case, and Justice Felix Frankfurter, during the Court's consideration of the case on December 5, 1942, articulated what can only be described as a personal testament of faith by way of answering the question.[1] Naturalization is a process whereby, in Frankfurter's words, one must "shed old loyalties and take on the loyalty of American citizenship." What made his remarks so personal was his own status as an American by choice rather than by birth. Born in Vienna, he came to the United States in 1894, at the age of 12. He was unique among the justices in having become an American by process of naturalization, and he tried to convey to his fellow justices the meaning of becoming an American.

"I was at college when my father became naturalized and I can assure you that for months preceding it was a matter of moment in our family life, and when the great day came it partook for me of great solemnity." Frankfurter described himself "[a]s one who has no ties with any formal religion," his commitment to Jewish belief or observance of Jewish rituals long since having ceased.[2] He admitted, however, that "perhaps the feelings that underlie religious forms [for others] for me run into intensification of my feelings about American citizenship."

He went on to read his colleagues a letter he had received from Professor Salvemini of Harvard, which referred to the "grand function" Salvemini had performed in taking the oath of citizenship. "[Y]ou are asked to give allegiance to the Constitution of your adopted country, that is, to an ideal life. Thus I took the oath with a joyous heart, and I am sure I will keep it with the whole of my heart as long as I am alive." The justice then concluded his homily by stating that "American citizenship implies entering upon a fellowship which binds people together by devotion to certain feelings and ideas and ideals summarized as a requirement that they be attached to the principles of the Constitution."

It is tempting to identify the intense feelings about American citizenship displayed by Frankfurter and Salvemini with ordinary patriotism—love of country. Patriotic Frankfurter surely was,[3] and for many persons of my generation (I came to adulthood in the 1960s), the meaning of patriotism was permanently sullied by its joinder with American involvement in Vietnam. The "new patriotism" promoted later by President Reagan only served to confirm one's doubts about such "love" of country. But the sentiments expressed by Frankfurter and Salvemini are in fact more complex. After all, their devotion to country comes through identifying it with what one would hope to be its highest ideals. There is something terribly naive about describing the Constitution as incarnating "an ideal life." But might there not be something equally distorting in denying (and refusing to share wholeheartedly) its aspirational vision, revealed most clearly in the Preamble, of a "more perfect Union" where "domestic Tranquility" is achieved because the "Blessings of Liberty" are used in behalf of "the general Welfare" in order to "establish Justice"?

This book is written out of the ambivalence registered in the last paragraph, where "patriotism," measured as commitment to constitutional ideals, struggles against a wariness about a too-eager willingness to celebrate one's own country, including the celebration of its Constitution. The book is intended to make clearer the ambiguities of "constitutional faith," i.e., wholehearted attachment to the Constitution as the center of one's (and ultimately the nation's) political life. I write not in the belief that I can resolve these ambiguities—there will be many more questions than answers in the pages to come—but out of a conviction that there is an important conversation to be initiated about what it means to be "an American" in the late twentieth century. Of course, that is not a new question. J. Hector St. John Crevocoeur, writing two centuries ago in *Letters from an American Farmer*, asked, "What is the American, this new man?" Our status as a country of immigrants has made the United States especially obsessed with self-referential questioning. One can converse across the generations with Calvinist ministers, Thomas Jefferson, Henry David Thoreau, Herman Melville, Frederick Douglass, and Abraham Lincoln, to name only some of the most distinguished contributors to American self-consciousness.

It is my obvious conviction, though, that the conversation is not merely "historical," to be safely distanced somewhere in the past.

Though my own concerns are no doubt linked in some ways to details of personal autobiography, I assume that in fact my persona is not so idiosyncratic that its concerns are without resonance in at least some of my readers. In particular, I assume that there are many persons who share a very strong sense of "being" American, but are without an equally confident sense of what that means, especially in regard to what, if any, political commitments that identity entails.

Consider, for example, the vivid words of Frances Wright, described recently as "an Americanized Englishwoman of the 1820s":

> For what is it to be an American? Is it to have drawn the first breath in Maine, in Pennsylvania, in Florida, or in Missouri? Pshaw! . . . Hence with such paltry, pettifogging . . . calculations of nativities! *They* are American who, having complied with the constitutional regulations of the United States . . . wed the principles of America's Declaration to their hearts and render the duties of American citizens practically in their lives.[4]

Wright's citation to "constitutional regulations" suggests one way of answering Crevocoeur's (and her) question. Indeed, only twenty years ago Whittle Johnson—after asking, "What, then, does it mean to be an American?"—responded confidently: "To be an American means to be a member of the 'covenanting community' in which the commitment to freedom under law, having transcended the 'natural' bonds of race, religion, and class, itself takes on transcendent importance."[5] The central "covenant" of the community, from this perspective, is the Constitution. Indeed, the neoconservative writer Irving Kristol, adopting Johnson's argument, has recently cited the Constitution as part of the holy "trinity" of the American civil religion, along with the Declaration of Independence and the Flag.[6] Pledging faith in the Constitution, therefore, presumably defines one as a "good American," a full member of our political community.

As a professor of constitutional law (a term whose ambiguities will be explored in Chapter Five below), I have significant reservations about defining "Americanism" in terms of constitutional fidelity. Too many problems emerge to allow such ebullient answers as are given even by serious scholars like Johnson or Kristol. Indeed, the central aim of this book is to identify and discuss the problems that emerge if one seriously grapples with the Constitution's role as what might be termed the "constituent agent" of our identity as Americans. My concern is not so much to make a linear argument aimed at moving the reader toward some purportedly ineluctable conclusions (e.g., "this, and this alone, is the one best way to perceive the Constitution") as to attempt what I hope will become a common exploration of what is at stake in taking the Constitution seriously as a presence in one's life or, conversely, in rejecting that presence and relegating it instead to the status of any other legal document that occasionally imposes itself, through a court, into one's personal life but is not otherwise of genuine significance.

Frances Wright speaks of "wedding" principle to heart. A central feature of weddings, of course, is the exchange of vows in which the "meaning" of marriage, in some sense, is reduced to a set of propositional utterances outlining what duties one is in theory taking on. Similarly, we have on many occasions tried to simulate such vows within the polity through the particular form of pledges of allegiance or political loyalty oaths whose implicit message is that the commitments of community membership (citizenship) can be reduced to words. Perhaps the most famous example of such a reduction is the Pledge of Allegiance, which includes a commitment "to the republic for which it stands." As we shall see in both Chapters Two and Four, it may be no small matter to pledge one's allegiance to maintaining a "republic" or to assert one's "attachment" to the principles of the Constitution. In any case, this is an age that finds the taking of (and adhering to) such categorical oaths, or the making of unequivocal attachments, increasingly difficult, whether in one's "personal" life, as in marriage, or in one's "public" life, as in citizenship. Chapter Three therefore is devoted to an extended treatment of our feelings about a variety of oaths and affirmations.

One of the things we all now know about marriage is that there is no guarantee that it will endure through time. Early passion may turn into hollow form or outright desertion. We are more reticent in regard to the endurance of political communities. Yet of course history is a relentless tale of the rise, decline, and fall of such communities. Hegel's comment is all too relevant: "How blind they are who may hope that institutions, constitutions, laws . . . from which the spirit has flown, can subsist any longer; or that forms in which intellect and feeling now take no interest are powerful enough to be any longer the bond of a nation!"[7] To try to discover what bonds us (or could bond us) into a coherent political community, especially after the triumph of a distinctly (post)modernist sense of the contingencies of our own culture and the fragility of any community memberships, is the core of this book. To treat this theme fully would require a much different (and longer) book than the one now in your hands. It will be enough if I can establish with some clarity the importance of the general question—What, indeed, does it mean to be an American?—and indicate the role of more specific questions about the Constitution in answering the larger one.

I hope that the ensuing discussion will be helpful to lawyers and social scientists in the detached analysis of social orders across time and space. Indeed, the central thesis of Chapter One, which elaborates a variety of "constitutional faiths," is that the typology there presented helps to illuminate the entire structure of American constitutional discourse over the past 200 years. But the major point of this preface is to embed the abstractions that will follow in a decidedly more personal concern about what it means to live in *this* social order at this time—the United States as it careens toward the twenty-first century. Can we speak cogently to one another about this, so that the inevitable imperfection of language nonetheless works to join us in common conversation (and, ultimately, political community)? This concern explains why I devote the final chapter to inquiring about the possibility of one's signing the Constitution in our time as an act of "personal ratification" of what is presumptively embedded within it.

Every text has a subtext, and perhaps the subtext of this book is a paraphrased version of the title of a Raymond Carver collection of stories on modern life and love, "What we talk about when we talk about law." One of the things we talk about is our own difficulty in defining (or recognizing) law, so "sophisticated" (or merely cynical) have we become about the ambiguities and outright contradictions connected with the concept. And *how* we talk about law (or love), at the end of the twentieth century, is suitable to our ambivalences and confusions, for the conversations are often halting and ineloquent, with silences that become independent parts of the conversation. But even some of the refugees from Carver-land find themselves entering relationships and enunciating wedding vows, with whatever self-conscious irony, as a means of fending off the end of conversation itself, what Clifford Geertz has recently described as a life "marooned in a Beckett-world of colliding soliloquy."[8]

I hold open the possibility that the ultimate conclusion of these meditations on "constitutional faith" might be that we indeed live in such a "Beckett-world." Yet I take it that most of us prefer to believe that some kind of dialogue remains more or less possible, the question being whether we can find a common language in which to speak and ask our questions. This book is written in the belief that such a dialogue is worth attempting.

CHAPTER ONE

THE "CONSTITUTION" IN AMERICAN CIVIL RELIGION

INTRODUCTION: THE CONSTITUTION
AS SACRED OBJECT

 WRITING IN 1816, Thomas Jefferson commented acerbically that "[s]ome men look at constitutions with sanctimonious reverence and deem them like the ark of the covenant, too sacred to be touched."[1] This complaint is reminiscent of an argument that Jefferson had had with his great friend and colleague James Madison some quarter-century earlier concerning the advisability of recurrent constitutional conventions, where the people could consider the relationship between their current needs and the document drafted in Philadelphia in 1787. After all, as Jefferson characteristically phrased it in his 1816 letter, "[I]nstitutions must advance also, and keep pace with the times. We might as well require a man to wear still the coat which fitted him when a boy, as civilized society to remain as under the regimen of their barbarous ancestors."[2] An ever-changing (and presumably progressing) society should with some frequency check its wardrobe and cast out that which no longer fits.

Madison had a different perspective. As he wrote in the 49th Federalist Paper, "[Because] every appeal would carry an implication of some defect in the government, frequent appeals would in great measure deprive the government of that veneration, which time bestows on every thing, and without which perhaps the wisest and freest governments would not possess the requisite stability."[3] What for Jefferson was "sanctimonious reverence," and thus the object of our critical capacity, was for Madison a wonderful "veneration" that guaranteed the stability of our (presumably wise and free) political order.

Although one of Madison's letters indicates that "I am not one of the number if there be any such who think the Constitution lately adopted a faultless work," such sentiments were better reserved for private discourse than the public realm.[4] More typical of his public commentary is a short essay on "Charters" published in the *National Gazette* on January 19, 1792. There Madison emphasized that the "complicated form of [the American] political system . . . requires a more than common reverence for authority," with the *"great charters"* of government as the worthiest objects of such reverence. These "instruments" in "every word . . . decide[] a question between power and liberty," and he concluded that public opinion "should guarantee with a holy zeal, these political scriptures from every attempt to add to or diminish from them."[5]

Indeed, Washington's Farewell Address, given to coincide with the ninth anniversary of the adoption by the Philadelphia Convention of the constitutional draft, included the plea that "the Constitution be sacredly maintained."[6] And a later president-to-be, Abraham Lincoln, in his own way as much a Founder as Washington, Madison, or Jefferson, would summon the populace to adopt the principle of "reverence for the laws" as the "political religion of the nation." "Every American, every lover of liberty, every well wisher to his posterity," Lincoln asserted, must "swear by the blood of the Revolution, never to violate in the least particular, the laws of the country; and never to tolerate their violation by others." All laws should be "religiously observed."[7]

What is important is not only the substantive disagreement between these seminal founders of the American republic, but the rhetoric within which their debate was conducted. Jefferson recognized, albeit with some apparent disdain, the key role that the Constitution played within the structure of the American "civil religion," that web of understandings, myths, symbols, and documents out of which would be woven interpretive narratives both placing within history and normatively justifying the new American community coming into being following the travails of the Revolution.[8] Jefferson feared an ossification of the polity similar to the ossification he could readily detect in most traditional religion. To prevent such ossification would require, presumably, an ultimate "irreverence" toward the Constitution that would keep it in its place as a *creation* of the polity (rather than its creator and judge) to be supplemented—if not supplanted— whenever the polity thought it useful to do so.

Though it is Jefferson, and not Madison, whom we have honored by building a memorial in Washington, it cannot truly be said that he has prevailed, at least in regard to the issue of constitutional veneration. "Veneration" of the Constitution has become a central, even if sometimes challenged, aspect of the American political tradition. Irving Kristol typifies this strand of our tradition, and its accompanying rhetoric, in his lead article in a special issue of *The Public Interest* devoted to the Constitution. "The Flag, the Declaration, the Constitution—these," according to Kristol, "constitute the holy trinity of what Tocqueville called the American 'civil religion.' "[9] These formal symbols—and the historical experiences that they condense—evoke, for some, what the late Alexander Bickel once termed "the secular religion of the American republic," in which "we find our visions of good and evil."[10]

The Constitution, of course, is intimately linked in a symbolic way with the American Revolution, as we have already seen in Lincoln's paean to law. "To those . . . whose lives it touched the Revolution was a miracle, a sign of God's grace, a reminder of the covenant."[11] For Kristol, in turn, the Constitution in particular is the "covenanting document" that defines the American community.[12]

The Protestants who settled the New World, revolted against England, and "ordained" the Constitution were imbued with the heritage of covenant. Anne Norton recently described the Puritans in particular as "children of the covenant, of a long series of covenants between man and God, and man and man: God and Noah, God and Abraham, the new covenant of the New Testament, the Magna Carta, [and] the Mayflower Compact," to which their descendants would add "the Constitution";[13] and she went on to describe America itself as "bound up in a continuous history that stretched from Abraham to the Constitution in a concatenation of covenants. . . ."[14] Historically intrinsic to the notion of covenant has been the notion of writing, which establishes the covenant. "The written possesses the qualities sought in covenant; it endures and endures unaltered." Although the author is preserved in the writing, it is also the case that "once written [the compact] is no longer subject to his will." It is the process of writing that "creates communities removed from the will, and enduring beyond the lives of their authors."[15]

As Norton indicates, covenants can take overtly religious or formally secular forms. It should be no surprise that a culture so suffused with Protestantism would transfer some of the same attitudes (and, as

we shall see, controversies) found in the former to the latter covenants of governance. Thus, in a classic article, Max Lerner pointed to
the role of the United States Constitution in what later analysts would
term America's civil religion. "Every tribe," said Lerner, "clings to
something which it believes to possess supernatural powers, as an instrument for controlling unknown forces in a hostile universe." The
American tribe is no different. "In fact the very habits of mind begot-
ten by an authoritarian Bible and a religion of submission to a higher
power have been carried over to an authoritarian Constitution and a
philosophy of submission to a 'higher law'; and a country like America, in which its earlier tradition had prohibited a state church, ends
by getting a state church after all, although in a secular form."[16]

It is this framework of covenantal civil religion that provides a ready
basis of understanding for the following advice delivered by John
Quincy Adams on the occasion of the fiftieth anniversary of the Constitution and repeated in Williamsburg, Virginia in February 1987 by
former Chief Justice Warren Burger:

> Teach the [Constitution's] principles, teach them to your chil-
> dren, speak of them when sitting in your home, speak of them
> when walking by the way, when lying down and when rising up,
> write them upon the doorplate of your home and upon your
> gates.[17]

Anyone familiar with the liturgy of Judaism instantly recognizes this
as taken from Deuteronomy 6:7-9, which many congregations read
aloud immediately after the central confession of faith, the She'ma,
with its affirmation of belief in the one God who gave the Torah to the
people of Israel. It is, of course, the commands of Torah that are to
be taught to the young and constantly evoked within one's life. To
this day observant Jews place *mezzuzahs* on the doorposts, containing
within them the She'ma. The analogue, presumably, would be to
place on our "doorplates" copies of the Preamble to the Constitution
as a constant reminder of our national faith.

There is a special fittingness to former Chief Justice Burger repeating Adams's earlier message, for Burger gave as his reason for step-
ping down from the Supreme Court his desire to serve as an active
chairman of the Constitution's bicentennial celebration and to help
instill in the citizenry a deeper appreciation of its meaning. Although
Burger calls for "examination" of the Constitution, I think it safe to
say that for him the Bicentennial should ultimately be an occasion for

confirmation, for renewed veneration. Thus the operative assumption of the Adams passage, as with the Biblical setting from which it is taken, is essentially hierarchic or catechismic. That is, the Constitution is essentially good (whether or not "perfect") and thus a fit object to be inculcated in the young and accepted by adults. Burger does not raise the possibility that the Constitution's "principles" might themselves be objectionable and unworthy of being taught or accepted. There is no suggestion, for example, that this might be a particularly suitable time, to take perhaps the most drastic counterexample, for a Jeffersonian convention in which we could truly examine, with a skeptical eye, the adequacy of our constitutional structure and perhaps suggest alternatives to the framework inflicted upon us by the Founders.

Consider, within this context, the most important exhibit celebrating the Bicentennial. It is located, appropriately enough, in Philadelphia, where the Constitution was written in the summer of 1787. The exhibition, placed in the Second Bank of the United States, is titled "Miracle at Philadelphia." "Miracle" can, of course, have a secular meaning, but both the dictionary and our ordinary language evidence its decidedly sacred connotations. And as visitors climb the steps of the small but elegant Bank, modeled after a temple—the Greek Parthenon—they can well be developing a suitable frame of mood and mind attendant on entering more traditional temples of faith. Any such feelings will be reinforced by an early encounter with the view of Philadelphia's Dr. Benjamin Rush concerning the origins of the Constitution.

Rush is one of the more fascinating of the "minor" Founders. A signer of the Declaration of Independence and one of the two key figures, with James Wilson, of the pro-Constitution party in the Pennsylvania convention that ratified the extremely controversial handiwork of that Philadelphia summer of 1787, Rush was as well a committed "New Light" Presbyterian who took religion with the utmost seriousness. It is therefore illuminating to read his comment about the Constitution: Though rejecting the belief that the Constitution was "the offspring of inspiration," Rush nonetheless pronounced himself "perfectly satisfied that the Union of the States, in its *form* and *adoption*, is as much the work of a Divine Providence as any of the miracles recorded in the Old and New Testament were the effects of a divine power."[18] One did not have to be conventionally religious to adopt such imagery. Even James Madison, one of the most secular of the framers, in the 37th Federalist Paper was moved to suggest, whether out of conviction or for rhetorical effect, that the ability of the Constitution's authors to surmount the many difficulties placed in their way was so astonishing that "[i]t is impossible for a man of pious reflection not to perceive in it, a finger of the Almighty hand which has been so frequently and signally extended to our relief in the critical stages of the revolution."[19] And the equally secular Thomas Jefferson perhaps contributed to the veneration of which he was otherwise suspicious when he referred, in a letter to John Adams, to the Philadelphia Convention as "an assembly of demigods."[20]

Such views are not confined to a founding generation that was perhaps both overeager to sanctify its handiwork and the product of a much less secular society than our own, for they can be found even in our own century: George Sutherland, nominated in 1922 to the Supreme Court, believed the Constitution to be a "divinely inspired instrument."[21] Nor is such sentiment absent even today: National Public Radio reported that Arizona Governor Evan Mecham joins Sutherland in declaring that the Constitution was indeed inspired by God, even if recent judicial interpreters have sadly strayed far from divine intention.

Indeed, the belief in some kind of transcendent origin of the Constitution obviously contributes to according it utmost devotion. Edward Corwin once noted that "the *legality* of the Constitution, its *supremacy*, and its claim to be worshipped, alike find common standing ground on the belief in a law superior to the will of human governors."[22] The negative pregnant, of course, is that disbelief in such origins will serve in some sense to delegitimize the Constitution as we view it as simply an all-too-human artifact with attendant imperfections.

In any event, what Corwin termed "worship of the Constitution" is a thread running through much American political rhetoric.[23] A nationwide radio audience in 1928, for example, heard Louis Marshall refer to the Constitution as "our holy of holies, an instrument of sacred import."[24] Not all of this rhetoric was approving: Thus James Beck in 1930 criticized the "sacerdotal conception of law" that placed the Constitution with the Bible as "infallible and onmipotent";[25] but such critics have almost always been swimming against the tide.

Some of our most eloquent American political rhetoric specifically evokes an imagery of constitutional faith. Perhaps the most powerful example in our recent history was provided during the deliberations regarding the potential impeachment of Richard Nixon. What viewer of the Nixon impeachment hearings can ever forget Barbara Jordan's affirmation, just before she cast her vote to impeach the president? "My faith in the Constitution," said the representative from Texas, "is whole. It is complete. It is total. I am not going to sit here and be an idle spectator to the diminution, the subversion, the destruction of the Constitution."[26] It was not only Representative Jordan's eloquence and magnificent voice that etched her remark in the memory of its listeners. Her status as a black carried with it as well the unspoken message that black and white together can unite (and ultimately overcome our divisions) if only we have sufficient faith in the vision imparted by the Constitution.

Barbara Jordan's manifestation of "faith in the Constitution" served as the binary opposition to what Theodore H. White, perhaps the most widely respected journalist of the postwar period, labeled Richard Nixon's "breach of faith" in his book of that name detailing the misdeeds that led to Nixon's unique humiliation.[27] The title of this book—*Constitutional Faith*—is intended to convey the utmost seriousness with which I take the notion of constitutional faith so stunningly conveyed by Ms. Jordan and alluded to by White, for I believe that its continued presence in our late-twentieth-century culture is both revealing and significant.

What it reveals—and therefore its significance—is, of course, controversial. Those historians and sociologists who have revived interest in the study of civil religion usually follow Rousseau's lead by emphasizing its integrative function.[28] Thus Robin Williams refers to the fact that certain "symbols can supply an overarching sense of unity even in a society otherwise riddled with conflict."[29] It therefore becomes tempting to see the Constitution as a means of providing either a "sense" or even the reality of "unity" for an otherwise fractious United States. For some the news that constitutional faith is alive and well is "good," manifesting the continuing "veneration" called for by Madison that will help us maintain a free and wise republic.

Other observers, however, might see Representative Jordan's comments—and the widespread applause they generated—as an almost willed attempt to maintain belief in a heritage that cannot in fact withstand a confrontation with the "postmodernist" elements in our contemporary culture. From this perspective, what is remarkable about use of the metaphor of "civil religion" to explain social unity is the way it overlooks the fact that religion, especially over the past 500 years, has served much more as a source of deep cleavage than of unity.

It is not merely that what Max Weber termed the "disenchantment" engendered by modern thought has corroded the tenets of most "traditional" religious thought. That is true enough. What is also central, however, is the remarkable fragmentation *within* the world of religious communities, where the maintenance of strong faith has as often led to division (and, on occasion, bloodshed) as to joinder in an inclusive community. Schism has been a part of the history of Christianity from its beginning, culminating in the Protestant Reformation and the flowering of a multiplicity of denominations and sects. Similar developments have occurred within the Jewish community and, indeed, within all major religious systems. A complacent use of the term "civil religion" that ignores the ubiquity of religious division will be more often misleading than helpful as a tool for social analysis.

If the metaphor of civil religion might evoke more complexity than first appears, it seems uncontroversial that our stance toward the Constitution—our ability to use it as the center of a genuine community of faith—is relevant to a much wider set of questions about the meaning of the American polity as we enter its third century. The title of Lerner's article—"The Constitution and Court as Symbols"—directs us, moreover, not only to a possible analogy between Bible and Constitution; it also points to the essential role assigned by many to the United States Supreme Court as the principal keeper of the religious flame, the definer of constitutional "orthodoxy." As Professor Alpheus T. Mason once wrote, "In our tripartite constitutional system, it is the Holy of Holies."[30] One is therefore not at all surprised to discover William Howard Taft's yearning for appointment to the "sacred shrine" of the Supreme Court, a wish fulfilled by Warren Harding in 1921.[31] William Yandell Elliot offered a similar, even if much less affirmative description. After laconically noting that "lawyers . . . have been our rulers for most of our national history," Elliott went on to describe the Supreme Court, through its power of judicial review, as having "become the 'epic symbol' of the whole [national social] myth" surrounding the Constitution.[32] There is more than one theorist who views the Supreme Court as the authoritative "church" built upon the "rock" of the Constitution, and the Court's pronouncements therefore as "the keys to the kingdom" of the heavenly status of a country ruled "by law" instead of people.[33] Perhaps the most poignant example, given his generally radical skepticism, is Henry Adams. Though "driven, like the rest of the world, to admit that American society had outgrown most of its institutions," Adams nonetheless confessed that "he still clung to the Supreme Court, much as a churchman clings to his bishops, because they are his only symbol of unity; his last rag of Right."[34]

Of course the most fundamental schism in Western religious history came precisely from disputes over the interpretation to be given "the rock" upon which Christianity was to be built, for the claim of the Roman Catholic Church, and more particularly of papal supremacy within the Church, rests in significant measure upon this passage. A key element of the Protestant Reformation was the rejection of the Church's authority, and even in this "post-Christian" age, we have not yet left behind the implications of Luther's momentous revolt and its denial of the duty of institutional orthodoxy as defined by the Catholic Church. Adams's own metaphor of a "churchman cling[ing] to his bishops" requires an almost willful ignorance of the fact that the Protestant era saw wholesale rejection by many loyal "churchmen" of the claims of bishops in favor of a radically new understanding of the role of individual congregants. Anyone seeking to examine the operation of the Constitution within the American polity must come to terms with the implications and traces left over from the Reformation era. Whatever "miracle" occurred at Philadelphia, the product of that Convention presents perplexities fitting its divine analogue.

To summarize, then, there is a double message contained within the analogy of the Constitution to a sacred text or the Supreme Court to a holy institution. The first, emphasizing unity and integration, is the one with which we tend to be most familiar. I propose here, however, to examine the alternative message, which is the potential of a written constitution to serve as the source of fragmentation and *dis*-integration. Indeed, many classic constitutional controversies have their parallels within the religious disputes of the sixteenth and seventeenth centuries, among others. The object of this analysis is not only to present a somewhat different perspective from which to look at the Constitution, but also to attack by implication any confidence that having "the Constitution" as a common symbol guarantees meaningful national political unity. As Professor Bruce notes, "The possession of a common holy book . . . does not guarantee religious unity. The interpretation of the holy book . . . is important; and divergent interpretations tend to produce religious divisions."[35]

CATHOLICISM AND PROTESTANTISM:
ESSENTIAL TENSIONS IN
WESTERN RELIGIOUS THOUGHT

Two aspects of the Protestant Reformation are central to my argument. The first concerns the dispute over the source of Christian doctrine. The second concerns the institutional nature of Christianity, even assuming agreement on its doctrinal basis. The two are interrelated, of course, but they can be analytically separated.

It is well known that the Protestant reformers, especially the followers of Martin Luther, emphasized the centrality of Scripture to Christianity. *Sola scriptura* were the great watchwords; an authentic Christianity must be based on the Scriptures alone. "The BIBLE, I say, the BIBLE only, is the religion of Protestants," said a seventeenth-century reformer, describing *The Religion of Protestants: A Safe Way to Salvation*.[36] Not the least important program of the reformers was their insistence on translation of the Bible into vernacular languages, so that the divine word could be known directly to readers untrained in Latin.[37]

What were the "reformers" rejecting within Catholicism? The Catholic Church did not reject Scripture. How could it? One of the principal bases of its institutional authority was the passage from Matthew. Yet it supplemented reliance on Scripture with the independent authority of oral tradition as mediated through the *magisterium*—the teaching authority—of the Church. As declared at the Council of Trent—the 1546 counterattack against Protestant heresies—unwritten traditions were coequal in stature to Scripture, and these traditions were stated to be those "which were received by the apostles from the lips of Christ himself, or by the same apostles at the dictation of the Holy Spirit and were handed down and have come down to us." The key to the authoritativeness of tradition was its preservation "by unbroken succession in the Church."[38] According to one commentator, "the Council could fairly claim that Bible and Tradition were to be received *pari affectu*, with an equal reverence from believers."[39]

Frank Kermode points out, moreover, that it had been seriously proposed by some members of the Council that tradition be accorded supremacy: "[F]or since scripture was always subject to the superior traditional knowledge of the Church, it could be called redundant and, in the hands of ignorant outsiders, a source of error."[40] Even if what some termed the "inutility" of Scripture was rejected, its linkage to tradition remained central. As Cardinal Bellarmine argued in his treatise *The Word of God*, Lutherans were mistaken in asserting that "everything necessary for faith and behavior is contained in the scriptures," for "as well as the written word of God we require the unwritten word, that is the divine and apostolic traditions." Because Scripture is often "ambiguous and perplexing," said Bellarmine, there are "many places in which we shall be unable to reach certainty" unless the text is supplemented "by accepting the traditions of the Church."[41]

The traditional Catholic emphasis on the capacity of human reason to supply the teachings of natural law should also be mentioned, because this source provided yet another means by which the necessity of reliance on the written text could be limited.[42] Early Protestants, on the other hand, by returning to a much more Augustinian emphasis on human depravity, rejected right reason as well as the Church's institutional traditions.[43] One vital difference, then, between the initial reformers—particularly Luther—and the Church concerned the exclusivity of Scripture as the basis of Christian doctrine and behavior. It must be emphasized that there is nothing uniquely "Christian" in this struggle. Thomas Grey has noted in an important article that every one of the major Western religions—Judaism, Christianity, and Islam—has featured similar struggles. Within Islam, for example, there is a distinct split between the Sunnis, who hold that the Koran is supplemented by the *sunnah*, the custom of the Prophet passed on by oral tradition and eventually written down as *hadith* ("reports"), and their opponents, who wish to return to the Koran alone as the source of Islamic doctrine.[44]

Grey also points to the initial conflict within Judaism between Pharisees and Sadducees. In the words of F. E. Peters, the Pharisees accepted the "oral legal tradition that enabled them to extend Torah precepts into new areas of behavior," whereas the Sadducees were, according to Josephus, "literal interpreters of the Law who rejected all Pharisaic appeals to the 'traditions of the Fathers,' and so could be at the same time stricter in their exegesis of scriptural prescriptions and more permissive where the Torah had not explicitly spoken."[45]

As Marcel Simon observes, "What the *Catholic Encyclopedia* writes . . . could just as well have been written by a rabbi: 'Holy Scripture is . . . not the only theological source of Revelation made by God (to his Church [or People]). Side by side with Scripture there is tradition, side by side with the written revelation there is the oral revelation.' "[46] The rabbis, and the rabbinic tradition that has historically triumphed within Judaism, emphasize the existence of *two* Torahs, fidelity to which serve to constitute the Jewish community. One was written, the other oral. For the rabbinic tradition, the *Torah shebe'al peh*—"the Torah that is memorized"—was of equal significance with the written Torah found in the Bible.[47] And, as in the Catholic Church, there was self-conscious historical connection from Moses to the latest "sages" who claimed authority to invoke the "traditions" of Judaism. It is, for example, essential to the claims of authority of Moses Maimonides, the greatest Jewish scholar of medieval times, that he name, at the beginning of his commentary on the Torah, the line of sages that began with Moses and ran through his own teachers.[48]

A taste of the emphasis on (and legitimacy of) the oral Torah is provided by an excerpt from a rabbinic *midrash*, or discussion:

> After he had taught Moses the oral Torah, the Holy One— blessed be He—said unto him: teach it to Israel. Moses answered: Lord of the Universe, I shall write it down for them. But God replied, saying: I do not want you to write it down, for I know that the nations of the world will rule over Israel and attempt to take it from them. I give Israel *mikra* [reading] in written form, but I give them *Mishna*, Talmud and Agada orally, and thus will Israel be distinguished from all other nations.[49]

An emphasis on tradition, moreover, is linked with a specifically "historical consciousness" rooted in "concrete historical experience."[50] As Gershom Scholem, the great student of Jewish mysticism, phrased it, awareness of "[t]radition as a living force produces in its unfolding another problem. What had originally been believed to be consistent, unified and self-enclosed now becomes diversified, multifold and full of contradictions." Yet, paradoxically, "[i]t is precisely the wealth of contradictions, of differing views, which is encompassed and unqualifiedly affirmed by tradition."[51] This position drew from Scholem's adversary, the great German-Jewish theologian Franz Rosenzweig, the designation of "nihilism," inasmuch as Scholem seemingly rejected any essentialist definition of Judaism in favor of the existential development of tradition(s) through time.[52] As we shall see below, in Chapter Five, this controversy, and the charge of nihilism, is present in contemporary controversy about the meaning of law and the Constitution.

Across all of the great Western religions, therefore, there occur significant disputes about the relationship between "written" and "unwritten" foundations of doctrine and, ultimately, especially in Judaism and Islam, conduct. And, as the earlier quotation from Cardinal Bellarmine indicates, there may be a special connection between the perception of an authoritative unwritten tradition and the need for a specific institutional authority that can articulate its claims, especially if one is fearful of the pluralism evoked by Scholem's understanding of tradition. To this day, after all, defense of the authority of the Catholic Church emphasizes the relative subordination of "Scripture and the subsequent documents of the tradition" to "a living magisterium that articulates universal Christian meanings."[53]

Thomas Grey, in his review of some significant modern theological literature, aptly points out that many contemporary theologians reject "the very distinction between one-source and two-source theories." The reason for this partly lies in a rejection of what might be termed "propositional" religion, that is, the view of God as revealing a "collection of . . . truths" that must be assented to (or obeyed). Instead, says Grey, the modern trend is to emphasize "encountering" God rather than the holding of cognitive beliefs about God.[54] Thus the Catholic theologian David Tracy rejects the notion that Christianity (or, for that matter, Judaism) is "strictly a religion of the book. Like Judaism but unlike Islam, Christianity considers the scriptures not the revelation itself but the original witness to the revelation." However important these "witnessing texts" undoubtedly are, "[i]t is the revelatory event and not the witnessing texts that must play the central role in Christian self-understanding."[55]

In addition, there is a greater emphasis on the basic inability of language to capture knowledge about God. For these Christian theologians, "revelation is neither the written scripture nor the oral traditions; but scripture and tradition are only human accounts of the true revelation, which is the 'Christ-event,' the 'Word made flesh.' "[56] A Jew could as easily cite the recent theology of David Hartman, for example, who emphasizes the encounter between God and human beings as the central aspect of the "living covenant" of Judaism.[57]

Moreover, Grey emphasizes the impossibility of truly distinguishing between written text and unwritten tradition, for what we recognize as a religious text in the first place is mediated by complex traditional sources. S.G.F. Brandon notes that "the authority that endorses the sacred character of the Book must clearly be the recognized embodiment or exponent of the Holy Tradition within the com-munity concerned." Thus, Brandon reaches the "significant conclu-sion that the Holy Tradition precedes the Holy Book, and that the Holy Tradition inheres in, and is interpreted by, a person or persons, whose supernatural character or status is already established and ac-cepted."[58] The easiest example of Brandon's point lies in the history of "canonical" judgment, the ascription to only *some* books of suffi-ciently sacred quality to become part of the "Scriptures." Both Juda-ism and Christianity include in their histories the making of such de-cisions.[59] One author notes that "[t]he inclusion of the cynical Book of Ecclesiastes in the Hebrew canon shocked many philosophically con-servative Jews; the battle over whether or not the weirdly apocalyptic and magical Second Esdras was inspired raged among Christians until the Renaissance."[60] "Holy Books," he observes, are not "self-se-lected." (What could that possibly mean?) They are selected by dis-tinctly human beings with their own inevitable "prejudices."

Grey's points are all well taken; my comments that follow do not indicate my agreement with the theoretical arguments required to sustain a hard-and-fast distinction between written text and unwritten tradition. Indeed, I agree that this distinction has been exploded by certain modern developments. Still, even David Tracy, with his de-nunciation of turning "Christianity into a strict religion of the book on the model of the place of the Koran in Islam," nonetheless points to "[t]he opposite danger—removal of an authoritative role for the text in favor of a contemporary experience of the Christ-event alone—[which] can be equally devastating for Christian self-understand-ing."[61]

Moreover, one of the central points of this book is to explore the tensions between our "traditional" or "conventional" understanding of the Constitution—the way ordinary (and some quite extraordinary) Americans have spoken about the covenant—and "modernist" sensi-bility. It remains a mistake, even in a world almost 500 years removed from the early Reformation, to underestimate the importance of the Scripture-tradition distinction as a barrier to Christian unity. Grey is discussing important developments within a branch of Christian the-ology, but it can scarcely be said that the melding of Scripture and tradition has become truly "ordinary language." (Indeed, had that oc-curred, the last sentence would be quite odd, for there would be no distinction between "Scripture" and "tradition" that the reader could grasp and understand.)

Still, even if the distinction between the two sources were completely overcome, that would not suffice to bring about Christian
unity. For there is more at the root of the schism that occurred between Protestants and Catholics within Christianity, or between similar groups within the other faith communities. Inevitably, the argument about *what* speaks to the community—text or tradition—is
linked with *who* in the mundane world speaks to (and has authority
over) the community. "The reformers dethroned the pope and en-
throned the Bible. This," says the standard *Cambridge History of the
Bible*, "is the common assertion; but when so stated it is not valid,
because a book cannot replace a man. A book has to be interpreted.
This was the main reason why authority had come to be ascribed to
the pope in faith and morals."[62]

The problem of institutional authority presents itself even if one
agrees that Scripture alone is the proper guide. From very early in
the history of organized Christianity, a recurrent problem was the
ability of "heretics" to quote Scripture. Tertullian in about 200 C.E.
wrote *De praescriptione haereticorum* denouncing the legitimacy of
such interpreters (and not only their interpretations). Acknowledging
that "[t]hey put forward the scriptures and by their audacity make an
immediate impression on some people," he made an appeal to the
legal authority of the Church, through apostolic succession, to fix the
meaning of Scripture and therefore resolve the disputes. In the institutional Church, and there alone, will there "be the true scriptures,
the true interpretations, and all the true Christian traditions."[63] Thus
it is possible to proclaim the authority of Scripture while assigning the
duty of interpretation to a particular institution whose decisions about
disputed passages are to be accepted as final by all members of the
denomination.[64]

Similarly, Nachmanides, a great thirteenth-century rabbi in Spain,
analyzed Deuteronomy 17:11—"Thou shalt not depart from the word
which they shall tell thee, to the right nor to the left"—as an exceedingly necessary commandment requiring obedience to a judge of the
Great Sanhedrin, "[e]ven if," in the words of the eleventh-century
rabbi Rashi, "he tells you of the right that it is the left or about the
left that it is the right." According to Nachmanides, "the need for this
commandment is very great, for the Torah was given to us in written
form and it is known that not all opinions concur on newly arising
matters." The absence of an institutional structure to still disputation
would ultimately mean that "the one Torah would become many To-

rahs. Scripture, therefore, defined the law that we are to obey the Great Court . . . with respect to the interpretation of the Torah, whether they received its interpretation by means of witness from witness until Moses [who heard it] from the mouth of the Almighty, or whether they said so based on the implication [of the written words] of the Torah or its intent."[65]

The full import of Martin Luther's attack on Roman Catholicism, after all, can be understood only against this background assumption concerning the need for institutionally definitive interpreters capable of holding back the onrush of interpretive multiplicity. After all, Luther's critique of the Church was not confined simply to its use of unwritten tradition as a supplement to *Scripture*. He attacked its basic legitimacy as an authoritative institution. In his 1520 *Open Letter to the Christian Nobility of the German Nation*, Luther denounced what he termed the "second wall" of the Church's defense of its own authority: "[W]hen the attempt is made to reprove them out of the Scriptures, they raise the objection that the interpretation of the Scriptures belongs to no one except the pope."[66] Luther, of course, disagreed, and he moved quickly to try to bring down this wall. "And if it were true," he asked, "where would be the need or use of the Holy Scriptures?" He went on, after quoting from Scripture, to make an argument concerning the ability of any true Christian to offer a "true understanding" of the text: "[A]n ordinary man may have true understanding; why then should we not follow him? Has not the pope erred many times? Who would help Christendom when the pope errs, if we were not to believe another, who had the Scriptures on his side, more than the pope?"[67]

As to the passage from Matthew, about the keys of the kingdom, Luther responded that "it is plain enough that the keys were not given to Peter alone, but to the whole community." Moreover, Luther quoted an article of the traditional Christian creed: "I believe [in] one holy Christian Church."[68] He argued that subscription to this article established that "it is not the pope alone who is always in the right," for then the prayer "must run: 'I believe in the pope at Rome,' and so reduce the Christian Church to one man—which would be nothing else than a devilish error." He then concluded his attack on the wall by evoking the powerful image of the priesthood of all believers: "[I]f we are all priests . . . and all have one faith, one gospel, one sacrament, why should we not also have the power to test and judge what is correct or incorrect in matters of faith?"[69]

Luther pointed out that even the patriarch "Abraham had to listen to Sarah, although she was in more complete subjection to him than we are to anyone on earth." Indeed, "Balaam's ass, also, was wiser than the prophet himself. If God then spoke by an ass against a prophet, when should He not be able even now to speak through a righteous man against the pope?" It therefore "behooves every Christian" to "rebuke all errors," wherever found. "[W]hen the pope acts contrary to the Scriptures, it is our duty to stand by the Scriptures, to reprove him, and to constrain him."[70]

This argument can easily enough be read as rejecting the institutional competence of any organized church to proclaim its sole authority over interpretation of Scripture.[71] Protestantism has had an extremely complex historical reality, including organization into institutional churches, and a complete understanding of even radical Protestants like the Baptists requires one to recognize the ways by which religious communities are formed and exercise authority over their members. "Reformers themselves were by no means inclined to let the Church become a debating hall for all possible types of belief," and Hans Küng, who quotes this comment, goes on to say that "the brutal reality" of institutional Protestantism "forms for the Catholic theologian the historical evidence for the fact that the alternative to the authoritarian Roman doctrinal system," of which Küng is extremely critical, "certainly cannot be Protestantism which protests against all authority in the Church (it scarcely exists in Protestantism anyway)."[72]

Nonetheless, if one focuses on the logic of certain Protestant arguments, there is a strong push to a radically deinstitutionalized relationship between the individual believer and the God revealed in Scripture. Here, again, there is a Jewish analogue of sorts in the ill-fated history of the ninth-century Karaite community, which rebelled against both the rabbinic embrace of the oral Torah and the rabbinic claim to interpretive authority. "Search well in the Torah and do not rely upon my opinion," said Anan ben David, the founder of the sect.[73] Rabbinic Judaism successfully suppressed its "protestant" opponents, although the rabbinic tradition contains within itself the potential for remarkable variety in interpretations.

It cannot be stressed too much that rejection of institutional authority is not at all the equivalent of antinomianism, which is rejection of the binding authority of the Word (or Law) itself. Instead, the most radical protestant might hold, it is up to each member of the faith community who feels touched by God's saving grace to decide what the Word actually requires. This version of the Protestant tradition was explicated in America by Roger Williams: "In vain have English Parliaments permitted English Bibles in the poorest houses, and the simplest man and woman to search the Scriptures, if yet against their souls' persuasion from the Scripture, they should be forced (as if they lived in Spain or Rome itself without the sight of the Bible) to believe as the Church believes."[74] This emphasis on individual competence served as an essential underpinning of Williams's theory of qualified religious toleration, though the intra-Protestant struggles of the seventeenth and eighteenth centuries should serve as reminders that toleration was the historical exception rather than the rule.

The deinstitutionalization of authority could also have volatile implications for political structure, especially when that structure was viewed as under an obligation to follow divine law. Initially, of course, many Protestants emphasized Paul's injunction in the Book of Romans to acquiesce to the commands of earthly political rulers, whose authority was God-given. But Protestants who viewed themselves as having the authority to "constrain" the pope soon extended their authority to the political realm.[75] Almost inexorably, the "divine right of kings" fell victim to both religious and secular onslaught. The English Revolution itself, in which the king was slain, was warmly backed by many Protestant militants, few of whom were heard quoting Paul in behalf of the hapless Charles I. Political authorities became subject to popular judgment about the performance of their duties.

As Christopher Goodman, one of the most radical Puritan theorists, argued, God's law was "not geven onely to the Rulers and Governors (thoghe I confesse it chieflie apperteyneth to their office to see it executed, for which cause they are made Rulers) but also is common to all the people, who are likewise bownde to the observation of the same."[76] This meant that "if the Magistrates would whollye despice and betraye the justice and Lawes of God, you which are subjects with them shall be condemned except you mayntayne and defend the same Lawes agaynst them."[77] A conscientious Protestant under Goodman's formulation may therefore have a religious duty to commit what is perceived by the corrupt magistrates as civil disobedience rather than acquiesce in the magistrate's misapplication of God's law.

It is obviously true that there are many rooms within the vast house of Protestantism, and no description of Protestantism per se captures the subtleties of specific denominations. Nor is Catholicism a simple monolith, as it is sometimes caricatured by its opponents. The analysis sketched above, however, captures two fundamental differences between Protestantism (or Karaite Judaism) and Roman Catholicism (or some varieties of rabbinic Judaism) that will be the basis for the following analysis of the Constitution. Thus, "protestantism" herein refers to either (1) an emphasis on the exclusivity of written Scripture or text as the basis of doctrine, or (2) the legitimacy of individual (or at least relatively nonhierarchical communitarian) interpretation as against the claims of a specific, hierarchically organized institution. "Catholicism" herein refers to either (1) the legitimacy of unwritten tradition in addition to Scripture, or (2) the authority of a particular institution, hierarchically organized, to give binding interpretations of disputed aspects of relevant materials.

"Protestant" and "Catholic" Strains in Constitutional Interpretation

With this brief excursus into religious history behind us, I return to my principal subject: the implications of religious analogies for understanding the role of the Constitution within the American civil religion. I propose to take seriously an epithet once hurled at Christopher Langdell, who became dean of the Harvard Law School in 1870—that he was "the greatest living legal theologian."[78] For what could be a more appropriate vocation than that of theologian in any culture organized around sacred texts or traditions? Indeed, if sociologists and anthropologists are correct, we cannot escape membership in some civil faith even if we wish to, for the alternative to organizing belief is chaos.

In any case, it is obvious to anyone observing American political culture that much of our disputation is in some sense organized around constitutional categories. What in most other political systems is described simply as a "political" *contretemps* in our system tends to take on "constitutional" overtones, precisely because the Constitution is viewed as a way of structuring politics, of setting rules for the activity.

Any discussion of methods of constitutional interpretation carries with it a threat of political instability. Indeed, to talk about a "method" inevitably suggests a way of differentiating correct from incorrect interpretations. To talk about "correct" decisions requires coming to terms with those decisions which are "incorrect." The great merit of constitutionalism is that it provides a way to hold even government officials to standards of judgment. The potential danger, at least for these same officials and their supporters, is that ordinary citizens may justify disobeying what these officials define as "the law" in the name of the higher law of the Constitution. As Louis Hartz pointed out many years ago, "consensus" on the Constitution as the basis of authority did not guarantee stability to the United States, for the South could make cogent recourse to the same Constitution available to Lincoln during the crisis of 1860-61.[79] The very ambiguity of the written Constitution (which was inevitable because of the nature of language) helped to legitimize civil war.[80]

It is therefore in the interests of the State—presumably only the "creature" of the Constitution—to meld with its creator and become the interpreter of the Constitution. The Supreme Court plays this role. For all the talk of its status as an "umpire," the Court is, as Madison recognized in the Virginia Report of 1799-1800, an intimate part of the structure of the new national government established by the Constitution.[81] Indeed, Daniel Webster, in a speech quoted by Justice Joseph Story in his extraordinarily influential *Commentaries on the Constitution*, candidly admitted that, "[h]aving constituted the government, and declared its powers, the people have further said that since somebody must decide on the extent of these powers, the government shall itself decide."[82] A significant role of the Court throughout our history has been to legitimize highly controversial governmental actions by trying to assure the populace that such activity is indeed constitutional (for the Court would surely strike it down if it were not).[83]

Both Story and Webster were concerned to establish the Court as what later would come to be called the "ultimate interpreter" of the Constitution in order to forestall the prospect of multiple interpretations by state courts, who were made subject to the Constitution (and thus became its interpreters) in Article VI of the document.[84] As Story wrote in the extremely important case *Martin* v. *Hunter's Lessee* in 1816, appellate authority over state supreme courts was justified by the "necessity of *uniformity* of decisions throughout the whole United States, upon all subjects within the purview of the constitution. Judges of equal learning and integrity, in different states, might differently interpret . . . the constitution." In the absence of a "revising authority to control these jarring and discordant judgments, and harmonize them into uniformity, . . . the constitution of the United States would be different in different States, and might perhaps, never have precisely the same construction, obligation, or efficacy in any two states. The public mischiefs that would attend such a state of things would be truly deplorable."[85]

It is vital to recognize, as Robert Cover so brilliantly argued, that one of the central tasks of those who purport to have final authority to establish the content of the law, such as the Supreme Court, is not so much to "make" law as to "kill it." That is, "[c]onfronting the luxuriant growth of a hundred legal traditions," all of which can draw on the authoritative materials of the culture, "[judges] assert that *this one* is law and destroy or try to destroy the rest."[86]

There are, however, conflicting concepts of constitutionalism paralleling the varied concepts of Christianity (and other religions) discussed above. One must first decide, for example, what "the Constitution" is even prior to deciding what "it" means. Does "the Constitution" refer only to the specific text of the document written in 1787 and amended infrequently thereafter, or does it include as well a significant unwritten component derived from implicit assumptions of American political traditions? Second, one must confront the separate question of institutional authority to interpret the Constitution. Is the Constitution institutionalized ("incarnated" as the "Word made flesh") in the specific humans who fill judicial office?

There are, therefore, two separate variables for each of what I have labeled the "catholic" and "protestant" positions. As to source of doctrine, the protestant position is that it is the constitutional text alone (A), while the catholic position is that the source of doctrine is the text of the Constitution plus unwritten tradition (B). As to the ultimate authority to interpret the source of doctrine, the protestant position is based on the legitimacy of individualized (or at least nonhierarchical communal) interpretation (C), while the catholic position is that the Supreme Court is the dispenser of ultimate interpretation (D). It is not necessary that one be "protestant" or "catholic" along both dimensions. There is no logical connection between Constitution-identity and who is to be the authorized interpreter of the Constitution. It is therefore possible to generate four intellectually plausible positions: (1) "protestant–protestant" (A + C); (2) "protestant–catholic" (A + D); (3) "catholic–protestant" (B + C); and (4) "catholic–catholic" (B + D). It is my central argument that a significant number of constitutional debates can be organized under one or another of these four categories. It is to the explication of these elements that I now turn.

Scripture Versus Tradition as Sources of Constitutional Doctrine

I begin with the problem of the source of American constitutional law. What is "the Constitution" whose authority binds us together in a common polity? Consider, for example, the advice offered by Franklin Roosevelt during one of his "fireside chats" to the nation in March 1937: "Like the Bible, [the Constitution] ought to be read again and again."[87] By now, of course, we should find such an analogy altogether familiar. But note the assumption: The Constitution is a discrete document that can be taken off the shelf, like the Bible, and perused. Its writtenness supplies a tangibility, an ability quite literally to take the Constitution into one's own hands and read it with one's own eyes.

The special nature of the American Constitution as a writing is a prominent theme in American political thought. In *Marbury* v. *Madison*, John Marshall, after noting the "reverence" with which Americans viewed written constitutions, went on to label such creations the "greatest improvement on political institutions" made by the citizenry of the new country.[88] And Marshall deftly asserted the power of the "obvious meaning" of the constitutional text to undergird his claim for the primacy of judicial review: "The powers of the legislature are defined, and limited; and that those limits not be mistaken, or forgotten, the constitution is written." Indeed, he goes on to ask in an almost plaintive tone, "To what purpose are powers limited, and to what purpose is that limitation committed to writing, if these limits may, at any time, be passed by those intended to be restrained."[89]

The rhetoric of *Marbury*—and much constitutional rhetoric thereafter—cannot be understood apart from its emphasis on the alleged power of a writing. "The physical presentation of a text," the literary theorist Jonathan Culler points out, "gives it a stability. . . . Writing has something of the character of an inscription, a mark offered to the world and promising, by its solidity and apparent autonomy, meaning which is [only] momentarily deferred."[90] In a more ominous vein, the late French critic Roland Barthes described writing as "a hardened language," which "manifests an essence and holds the threat of a secret."[91] In any case, we feel the power of the written word. To "get it in writing" is viewed as the mark of a serious deal; the ability to refer to the writing will presumably provide the means of resolving any future disputes that might arise.

One of the most remarkable evocations of a textual Constitution is that of Frederick Douglass, the former slave who became a leading abolitionist.[92] Douglass freely conceded that many of the framers supported slavery and, indeed, probably intended to "secure certain advantages in [the Constitution] for slavery." Moreover, it was obvious that the Supreme Court had, in a number of important decisions before 1860, the date of his speech, issued opinions protective of the institution. Yet he "den[ied] that the Constitution guarantees the right to hold property in man"[93] and proposed to his audience an approach to the Constitution that would vindicate his otherwise startling assertion.

His first move was to "ascertain what the Constitution itself is." The answer was simple: "[I]t is a plainly written document, not in Hebrew or Greek, but in English. . . . The American Constitution is a written instrument full and complete in itself. No Court in America, no Congress, no President can add a single word thereto, or take a single word therefrom." Douglass insists "that the mere text, and only the text, and not any commentaries or creeds written by those who wished to give the text a meaning apart from its plain reading was adopted as the Constitution of the United States." As for the "intentions of those who framed the Constitution, be they good or bad, for slavery or against slavery, [they] are to be respected so far, and so far only, as we find those intentions plainly stated in the Constitution."[94]

Part of Douglass's argument therefore involves the appeal to textuality and the concomitant ability of any reader of the English language to grasp the meaning of "the simple text of the paper itself." Douglass repeated that "the paper itself, and only the paper itself, with its own plainly-written purposes, is the Constitution. It must stand or fall, flourish or fade, on its own individual and self-declared character and objects." That, after all, is the "advantage of a written Constitution," which allows us to seek "its meaning in its words."[95]

In the modern era, the great proponent of a "protestant" Constitution was clearly Justice Hugo Black. On the very first page of his aptly titled *A Constitutional Faith*, he stated, "It is of paramount importance to me that our country has a written constitution."[96] Black was famous for carrying a copy of the Constitution in his coat pocket. Like the radical protestants from whom he sprang—he had been raised as a member of the Clay County, Alabama, Primitive Baptist

Church[97]— he wanted the sacred text instantly available so as to be able to resolve disputes by pointing to the text. Eric Sevareid once asked Black about this habit, saying, "Mr. Justice, I would think you'd know the Constitution by heart at this time. Why do you always carry that little book of the Constitution?" Black responded, "Because I don't know it by heart. I can't—my memory is not that good. When I say something about it, I want to quote it precisely."[98] It is this faith that precise quotation of constitutional text is conclusive that additionally identifies Black as a legal protestant. For Black the Constitution meant the relatively easily understood text, and nothing else. Another example of his protestantism was his belief that nonlawyers could serve on the Supreme Court. Better the contribution of a conscientious fellow citizen who shared Black's self-described "constitutional faith" than the sophistic interpretations—so often departing from the text—of allegedly well-trained lawyers like his great adversary, the former Harvard Law School professor Felix Frankfurter.

It has become a staple of much contemporary thought that "everything is interpretation," for there is no such thing as an "unmediated" text. Words never speak for themselves; understandings are therefore "constructed" by the "reader-interpreter." Black would be profoundly suspicious of such a view, for "interpretation" would too easily become "invention" and thus a "straying" from the text. One can easily imagine his subscribing to the sentiment of Gerrard Winstanley, a radical "Digger" in seventeenth-century England: "And so though the Laws be good, yet if they be left to the will of a Judge to interpret, the Execution hath many times proved bad." The history of the "Laws" provides occasion for suspicion. Just as "the scriptures of *Moses*, the Prophets, Christ, and his Apostles, [have] been darkened and confounded by suffering Ministers to put their Inferences and Interpretations upon them," so have "Judges for the Law" been "unfaithful servants" by feeling free "to expound and interpret [i.e., distort] that Rule which they are bound to yield obedience to, without adding to, or diminishing from."[99]

Justice Black's textualism manifested itself, for example, in regard to the constitutional basis for a so-called right to "privacy." He rejected the existence of such a constitutional right and therefore dissented when the Supreme Court invalidated a Connecticut law preventing the use of contraceptives by married couples.[100] He later defended his vote by proclaiming that he "refuse[d] to go farther than a specific provision [could] be taken . . . ," and he could "find in the

Constitution no language which either specifically or implicitly grants to all individuals a constitutional 'right to privacy.' " Thus, he stated, "even though I like my privacy as well as the next person, I am nevertheless compelled to admit that the states have a right to invade it unless prohibited by some specific constitutional provision."[101] Like others of this orthodox persuasion, Black was unwilling to recognize the shifting needs of society as a warrant for supplementing or overriding the bare bones of a sacred text.

The most recent restatement of such "protestantism" has come from President Reagan's attorney general, Edwin Meese, who has used his office in part to level a full-scale attack on the legitimacy of many contemporary judicial decisions. He has claimed that the courts have not followed Black in resisting the temptation to go "beyond" the text. Their duty is to enforce the Constitution, which for Meese "is a document of our most fundamental law," beginning with the first words of the Preamble, "We the People . . . ," and ending "some 6,000 words later, with the 26th Amendment."[102] As we shall see below, one effect of this definition of the Constitution is to set up a contrast with mere "constitutional law," which is "what the Supreme Court says about the Constitution," and, in turn, to question the authority of the Supreme Court as the "ultimate interpreter" of the Constitution.

The invocation of Marshall, Douglass, Roosevelt, Black, and Meese, among many others who could be brought to bear, should indicate that there is no "political" unity within the "protestant" constitutional denomination. One finds analysts on all points of the political spectrum using this particular rhetoric of justification, as is true of their "catholic" counterparts.

The antithesis of the documentary emphasis of Justice Black is found in the comment by a fellow justice, Felix Frankfurter, that the Constitution "is most significantly not a document but a stream of history,"[103] with its meaning presumably coming from the silt deposited by historical experience over the years. Frankfurter was fond of quoting Marshall's dictum in *McCulloch* v. *Maryland* that "it is a *constitution* we are expounding,"[104] the point of which is to underscore that the Constitution is "not a detached document inviting scholastic dialectics,"[105] but rather "a living framework within which the nation and the States could freely move through the inevitable growth and changes to be wrought by time and the great inventions."[106]

Already in 1890, Christopher G. Tiedman, an important participant in the constitutional debates of that era, had written a volume entitled *The Unwritten Constitution of the United States*,[107] and Harvard Professor of Government W. B. Munro called a set of lectures that he gave in 1929 *The Makers of the Unwritten Constitution*.[108] It can therefore be no surprise that when Thomas Grey asked in 1975, "Do We Have an Unwritten Constitution?" the answer was a resounding "yes."[109]

For Justice Frankfurter, recognition of the unwritten Constitution served mainly to legitimize locating power in legislative institutions. Thus he scoffed at the use by "an anointed priesthood [of judges] removed from knowledge of the stress of life"[110] of "finicky or textual arguments to interpose the Constitution as a barrier" to legislative decisionmaking.[111] It should be clear, though, that emphasis on the organic, "living" (and at least somewhat "nondocumentary") Constitution can also serve as the basis of judicial decision itself.

If Justice Black can be recognized as a quintessential "protestant" in the sense of emphasizing the written text and denouncing the legitimacy of going beyond the text, then perhaps the great exemplar of "catholicism" in the modern era was his colleague John Marshall Harlan. Justice Harlan joined in invalidating the Connecticut anticontraception law, a position presaged in a classic dissent several years earlier when the Court refused to decide a substantially similar case.[112] Harlan's "catholicism" emerges there with special clarity. He firmly rejected the argument that the meaning of the Due Process Clause of the Fourteenth Amendment was restricted to those rights which can be read from the words of the constitutional document. Instead, Harlan posited the availability of tradition as a source of valid constitutional doctrine. Here was an analogue to the Council of Trent, for Harlan did not reject the text so much as he supplemented its teachings with an equally valid, albeit unwritten, constitutional tradition:

> Due process has not been reduced to any formula; its content cannot be determined by reference to any code. The best that can be said is that through the course of this Court's decisions it has represented the balance which our Nation, built upon postulates of respect for the liberty of the individual, has struck between the liberty and the demands of organized society. . . . The balance of which I speak is the balance struck by this country,

having regard to what history teaches are the traditions from which it developed as well as the traditions from which it broke. That tradition is a living thing.[113]

"Tradition" is not found floating in the air, of course. It is presumably manifested in such central cultural documents as the Declaration of Independence and the Gettysburg Address, as well as, more controversially, Martin Luther King's "I have a dream" speech to the multitudes assembled in Washington in 1963. There will obviously be significant disagreement about what counts (or should count, assuming that that is a separate question) as part of our tradition; the point is simply that the "catholic" constitutionalist will seek to discover the tradition and to be informed by it.

Only a "protestant" could confuse Harlan's argument with an assertion of a right of judges to "roam at will in the limitless area of their own beliefs as to reasonableness."[114] But just as much to the point is the fact that only a "catholic" would accept without caviling Harlan's assurances that "[i]f the supplying of content to this Constitutional concept has of necessity been a rational process, it certainly has not been one where judges have felt free to roam where unguided speculation might take them."[115]

Here, too, there is a linkage between Harlan's arguments of 1962 and those offered at a much earlier stage of our constitutional history. In 1798, Justice Chase, considering the limits of legislative power, indicated, "I cannot subscribe to the omnipotence of a state legislature, or that it is absolute and without control; although its authority should not be expressly restrained by the Constitution, or fundamental law, of the State [or of the United States]." In addition to the express commands of the Constitution, a judge can have recourse to "certain vital principles in our free Republican governments, which will determine and overrule an apparent and flagrant abuse of legislative power." Chase refuses to concede that "[a]n ACT of the Legislature (for I cannot call it a law) contrary to the great first principles of the social compact, cannot be considered a rightful exercise of legislative authority." The maintenance of a view that government, whether state or national, possesses unlimited power unless it has "been expressly restrained" by the text "would, in my opinion, be a political heresy, altogether inadmissible in our free republican governments."[116]

Justice Iredell played Black to Chase's Harlan. He emphasized the necessity for the existence of textual "constitutional provisions" clearly limiting legislative power. In the absence of such clear text, "the Court cannot pronounce [a law] to be void, merely because it is, in their judgment, contrary to the principles of natural justice" or, presumably, "Republican governments."[117]

Within the world of contemporary jurisprudence, Ronald Dworkin is an especially influential proponent of a "catholic" notion of Constitution-identity. He invites anyone engaging in constitutional interpretation to reflect on the changing moral structure of society, including its background unwritten "principles," rather than to rely on written text. (Indeed, Dworkin would certainly agree with the views alluded to earlier that one cannot in fact "rely" on a written text if that is taken to mean that the text does not need to be "interpreted" in light of standards that by definition must come from outside the text.) Dworkin is especially critical of that branch of textualism that gives to the text the meaning allegedly desired by its drafters.[118]

The debate now raging between those who, like Meese, define "the Constitution" as the text of a specific document and those who argue that reference to an "unwritten Constitution" is necessary to make sense of the entire enterprise of American constitutionalism[119] is significantly similar to that which took place during the Reformation four centuries ago. And not the least of the similarities is the tone of frustration, and sometimes anger, that pervades the debate. The comparison between religious and legal disputation illuminates this bitter tone. Constitutionalism, like religion, represents an attempt to render an otherwise chaotic order coherent, to supply a set of beliefs capable of channeling our conduct. However much traditional religion may have lost its power to structure reality for most Western intellectuals, analogues present themselves in the guise of various civil religions. Yet recourse to "the Constitution" as a source of guidance within our own polity simply begs the question of what counts as "the Constitution," not to mention what interpretive guidelines must be followed.

Because questions of Constitution-identity are metatheoretical, moreover, all suggested answers inevitably are circular. There is simply no way of referring *to* "the Constitution" for a criterion of *what* "the Constitution" is. Whatever the process by which understandings of concepts like "the Constitution" emerge, it is doubtful that logical argumentation plays a crucial role.

Is the Constitution Institutionally Anchored?

The possibility of radical indeterminacy in regard to God's law or the Constitution is, of course, one of the sources of a search for some visible institution that will provide firm answers to those questions which might otherwise tear us apart. The primary Roman Catholic position has emphasized the magisterium of the organized Church, with an ultimate focus on papal supremacy, including, in very rare circumstances, infallibility.[120] Similarly, the United States Supreme Court has been quite willing, especially over the past quarter-century, to reward itself with the title of "ultimate interpreter of the Constitution."[121] To know what "the Constitution" means, therefore, in practice it is enough to know what a specific institution—the Supreme Court—has said about it. Even more to the point is the linked injunction to obey the Court's judgment. One need not agree with the Court's decision, but one must do what the Court says if one is to demonstrate respect for the Constitution, or so it is argued by judicial "catholics."[122]

This argument in its purest form is found in a letter by Leo Pfeffer denouncing a bill that would give tax credit to families with children in private (including parochial) schools. "Under our system," asserts Pfeffer, "the ultimate responsibility for interpreting the Constitution rests with the Supreme Court." People are free to disagree with the decisions and to promote constitutional amendments overruling them. "What they may not do is to disregard the judgments of the Court and proceed as if they had never been handed down or, indeed, as if the Court had reversed itself." For Congress to embark on such a path "is particularly unfortunate, for each of its members does take an oath to support the Constitution as interpreted by the Supreme Court." Thus, asks Pfeffer, "If Congress does not follow the Constitution, how can we expect the people to respect and obey it?"[123]

Pfeffer's understanding of "our system" may be a widely shared one. However, it is certainly not the only understanding available to a good-faith citizen of the American polity.[124] There is a rich "protestant" response that can be made and whose claims must be seriously assessed.

William Nelson has pointed out that colonial juries often exercised authority to make their own determinations of "the law" as well as to decide "factual" disputes. [125] Indeed, he notes that there are instances in which juries were charged by more than one judge—who gave conflicting instructions. And John Adams entered into his diary the observation that it was "not only . . . [every] juror's right but his Duty . . . to find the Verdict according to his own best Understanding, Judgment and Conscience, tho in Direct opposition to the Direction of the Court." [126] It is true that the nineteenth century saw a systematic effort to minimize discretionary authority of juries by enhancing judicial power. [127] But "protestant" argumentation survived the preconstitutional era.

Both Andrew Jackson and his great protagonist, John Calhoun, rejected judicial supremacy insofar as that meant judicial authority to give binding interpretations of the Constitution. [128] In his message accompanying his veto of the renewal of the charter of the Second Bank of the United States, whose constitutionality had been upheld by John Marshall in the great case of *McCulloch* v. *Maryland*, [129] Jackson limited the "authority" of Supreme Court opinions only to "such influence as the force of their reasoning may deserve." [130] In *Ableman* v. *Booth*, a justice of the Wisconsin Supreme Court explicitly denied that it was obligated to follow an earlier case of the United States Supreme Court, [131] stating that "duty and obligation require a departure from such precedent and authority, in obedience to a paramount law—*the fundamental law*, to which each and all are usually bound." [132]

Moreover, the speech of Frederick Douglass quoted earlier can hardly be understood without recognizing its doubly "protestant" aspect. Not only was the textuality of the Constitution its central reality, but Douglass, in blithely ignoring a host of Supreme Court decisions running counter to his thesis, was also clearly inviting his audience to use their own ability to read English as a means of rejecting the legitimacy of those decisions. As William Wiecek has argued, "Antislavery constitutionalism developed from nontechnical, popular origins that lay outside courts and legislatures. Constitutional development was (and is) not a monopoly of a hieratic caste of judges and lawyers. It has its beginnings in the American people, and its first expressions are to be found in documents less formal than decisions and statutes." [133] Indeed, William Howard Day, a delegate to the 1851 State Convention of Colored Citizens of Ohio, specifically accused proponents of a proslavery Constitution of falling into the error "of making the construction of the constitution of the United States, the same as the constitution itself."[134]

Perhaps the most notable rejection of judicial supremacy had come in 1858, in the great debates between Abraham Lincoln and Stephen Douglas in their campaign for the Senate. Lincoln, the proponent of "reverence for law" as our "political religion," rejected the legitimacy of the *Dred Scott* decision and announced that he would not feel bound by it should he be elected to the Senate. "If I were in Congress, and a vote should come up on a question whether slavery should be prohibited in a new territory, in spite of that Dred Scott decision [which held such prohibition unconstitutional], I would vote that it should."[135] Indeed, Lincoln taunted Douglas with references to his own erstwhile heroes, Jackson and Jefferson, and turned to his own advantage Jackson's comments in the Veto Message and an 1820 letter by Thomas Jefferson accusing his correspondent of "consider[ing] the judges as the ultimate arbiters of all constitutional questions—a very dangerous doctrine indeed and one which would place us under the despotism of an oligarchy."[136] And when Lincoln himself became president in 1861, he used his first inaugural address to argue, "[I]f the policy of the Government upon vital questions affecting the whole people is to be irrevocably fixed by decisions of the Supreme Court, the instant they are made in ordinary litigation between parties in personal actions the people will have ceased to be their own rulers, having to that extent practically resigned their Government into the hands of that eminent tribunal."[137]

Not surprisingly, no endorsements of such institutional "protestantism" can be found in the writings of Supreme Court justices, but that is no warrant for ignoring their presence in many other desk drawers of our historical cabinet. And this, too, is not simply a historical point. Attorney General Meese, whose "protestant" approach toward identifying the Constitution has already been noted, drew a very sharp "distinction between the Constitution and 'constitutional law' " in his speech delivered at the Tulane Law School.[138] If the Constitution is the unadorned text, then constitutional law is simply "what the Supreme Court says about the Constitution in its decisions resolving the case and controversies that come before it." Meese went on to cite the historian Charles Warren, who had said, "It is still the Constitution which is the law, not the decisions of the Court."[139]

What made Meese's speech both newsworthy and controversial was his insistence that Supreme Court decisions bind only the specific parties in a given case. "[A] decision does not establish a supreme law of the land that is binding on all persons and parts of government henceforth and forevermore."[140] He noted that the Court does not regard its own previous decisions as binding; he offered as an example the Court's 1896 decision in *Plessy* v. *Ferguson* upholding racial segregation,[141] which, he added, "finally and fortunately was struck down"[142] fifty-eight years later by *Brown* v. *Board of Education*,[143] What is good for the Court should be good throughout the polity. "[C]onstitutional decisions need not be seen as the last words in constitutional construction"; instead, it is "the business of all branches of government," and presumably the citizenry at large, to participate in giving meaning to the text.[144] As a modern analogue to Abraham Lincoln, with his rejection of *Dred Scott*, Meese offered Daniel Manion, a Reagan appointee to the federal judiciary who had, while an Indiana legislator, sponsored a bill authorizing the posting of the Ten Commandments in the public schools despite a 1980 Supreme Court decision invalidating a basically identical Kentucky statute. The attorney general described Manion as having "responded to a Supreme Court decision with which [he] disagreed."[145]

As one might imagine, given Meese's place on the political spectrum and the fears many had about his particular political agenda, the speech provoked immediate controversy.[146] Much of the reaction was highly critical. Eugene C. Thomas, the president of the American Bar Association, asserted that Supreme Court decisions are indeed the law of the land and that "public officials and private citizens are not free simply to disregard" their status as law. To imply the legitimacy of such disregard is to "shake the foundations of our system."[147] Ira Glasser, the executive director of the American Civil Liberties Union, described Meese's speech as "an invitation to lawlessness" and "a call to defiance and to undermining the legitimacy of abiding by decisions that you disagree with."[148] And Laurence Tribe, the Tyler Professor of Constitutional Law at Harvard and the author of the most distinguished treatise on constitutional law since Story's appeared 150 years ago, said that Meese's position "represents a grave threat to the rule of law because it proposes a regime in which every lawmaker and every government agency becomes a law unto itself, and the civilizing hand of a uniform interpretation of the Constitution crumbles."[149] Anthony Lewis, in *The New York Times*, described Meese's position as "invit[ing] anarchy."[150]

Some less critical commentators were disquieted by the apparent scope of Meese's speech. Gerald Gunther of the Stanford Law School agreed that the Supreme Court cannot "quiet a constitutional debate simply by issuing a particular ruling," but he warned that "the system would break down if every mayor, every state and local official insisted on being dragged into court" before recognizing that a Supreme Court decision was binding. Even Bruce Fein, a conservative constitutional theorist affiliated with the Heritage Foundation, said he wished that the attorney general had "qualified" his argument by conceding that "the rule of law" required that persons accept the authority of precedents that the Court itself has demonstrated no interest in reconsidering.[151]

The difficulty, though, was in finding a firm Archimedean point from which to lambaste Meese. As Lloyd Cutler, who was President Carter's White House counsel, noted, there was little in the speech with which Homer Cummings, F.D.R.'s attorney general prior to the 1937 "revolution" in the Court, would have disagreed. Indeed, in 1935, in anticipation of a possible ruling by the Supreme Court invalidating the suspension of the "gold clause," which had required the right to receive payment of certain obligations in gold, F.D.R. had prepared a speech announcing his refusal in effect to obey the decision. The Court in fact upheld the suspension, so the speech became unnecessary, but some of its passages are illuminating. After quoting the Lincoln passage from the First Inaugural, Roosevelt went on to state, "It is the duty of the Congress and the President to protect the people to the best of their ability. . . . To stand idly by and to permit the decision of the Supreme Court to be carried through to its logical, inescapable conclusion would so imperil the economic and political security of the nation" that the government must look beyond "the narrow letter of contractual obligations" as construed by the Court.[152]

By 1937, Roosevelt, whom we earlier saw encouraging us to read our Constitution-as-Bible, was defending his court-packing plan by arguing that the United States had "reached the point as a Nation where we must take action to save the Constitution from the [Supreme Court] and," he paternalistically added, "the Court from itself. We must find a way to take an appeal from the Supreme Court to the Constitution itself." Applying a spatial metaphor, Roosevelt called for "a Supreme Court which will do justice under the Constitution—not over it."[153] Nor was Roosevelt's antagonism toward the judiciary stilled by his success in naming a new majority of the Supreme Court by 1941. Francis Biddle, who was attorney general during World War II, reported Roosevelt's potential unwillingness to obey the courts following his establishment of a special military commission to try eight saboteurs who had attempted to land in the United States from a German submarine: "I want one thing clearly understood, Francis. I won't give them up. . . ." Repeating Lincoln's earlier defiance of Roger Taney during the Civil War,[154] Roosevelt simply informed Biddle, "I won't hand them over to any United States marshal armed with a writ of habeas corpus. Understand?"[155]

The unsteadiness of Meese's critics was exemplified by an editorial in *The Washington Post* titled "Why Give That Speech?" Having stated at the outset that Meese's overt argument—that the Supreme Court is not "immune from challenge"—is "self-evident," it focused on the "subtle, unspoken" message of his "very troublesome" remarks. The *Post* called on Meese to reject any implication that decisions of the Supreme Court have "no general applicability and that citizens may choose to ignore rulings at will." This implication, said the *Post*, would be "an invitation to constitutional chaos and an expression of contempt for the federal judiciary and the rule of law."[156]

It is bad enough, from one perspective, that Meese can count Jefferson, Jackson, Lincoln, and Roosevelt among his predecessors. But it is also the case that the leading contemporary writer on jurisprudence, Ronald Dworkin, has articulated a position that bears at least a family resemblance to the cruder argument made by the attorney general. As already noted, Dworkin is far removed from Meese's protestant identification of the Constitution as discrete text, but he moves far closer when the discussion turns to the relationship between the Constitution and specific institutions.

Although Dworkin refers to his ideal adjudicator, Hercules, as if he were necessarily a judge, Hercules could just as easily be an ordinary citizen as a justice of the United States Supreme Court. All that Dworkin requires is that this adjudicator be someone seriously committed to the Constitution (as opposed to someone simply seeking to maximize his individual welfare or the welfare of those particular groups with which he identifies).

One of Hercules' functions is to discover when courts can be said to have made mistakes or errors in interpretation. The true Constitution is not necessarily to be found in judicial opinions. "We cannot assume . . . that the Constitution is always what the Supreme Court says it is."[157] Although Dworkin would give judicial decisions respectful consideration, he argues that the American version of constitution-alism "does not make the decision of any court conclusive. Some-times, even after a contrary Supreme Court decision, an individual may still reasonably believe that the law is on his side."[158] Like Justice Frankfurter (not to mention Edwin Meese), Dworkin might agree that although "[j]udicial exegesis is unavoidable . . . the ultimate touchstone of constitutionality is the Constitution itself and not what we have said about it."[159] Under this formulation, judicial decisions, far from being ultimate interpretations, are simply *suggested* inter-pretations of the sacred document (or document plus tradition), inter-pretations that can be rejected if, like Jackson, one finds them "un-reasonable."

One must realize that Dworkin's formulation of the problem, like the other arguments in this vein, is not at all the same as positing the validity of morals or conscience *against* the demands of law. That way of stating the problem begs a central question: Who gets to determine what counts as "law"? Here it is clear that a person can speak of law independently of the statements found in judicial decisions. One need not assert the rejection of law in the name of a "higher" morality. Instead, the citizen can assert, like Christopher Goodman 400 years ago, that the magistrate—the institutional official—is the one who has betrayed the law, while the ostensibly "disobedient" citizen is in fact being faithful to the law's demands. To reject the ultimate authority of the Supreme Court is not in the least to reject the binding authority of the Constitution, but only to argue that the Court is to be judged by the Constitution itself rather than the other way around.

Dworkin argues, "A citizen's allegiance is to the law, not to any person's view of what the law is, and he does not behave unfairly so long as he proceeds on his own considered and reasonable view of what the law requires." As if frightened by the implication of his com-ment, Dworkin immediately goes on to insist "that this is not the same as saying that an individual may disregard what the courts have said," a reservation that can mean no more than that an individual must at least consider the merits of a judicial interpretation rather than flinging it unread into the trash. In any case, after this slight bow toward judicial authority, Dworkin returns to his central theme: "But if the issue is one touching fundamental personal or political rights, and it is arguable that the Supreme Court has made a mistake, a man is within his social rights in refusing to accept that decision as conclu-sive."[160] Thus it is ultimately the conscientious individual, and not the

Supreme Court, who is the ultimate interpreter of the Constitution. It is the province and duty of the citizen to declare what the law is.

A "protestant" Constitution is a deinstitutionalized, or at least, given the ubiquity of our life within institutional contexts, nonhierarchical, Constitution. It is vital to recognize that what I am terming a deinstitutionalized Constitution is not synonymous with the Beckett-like soliloquies mentioned at the very outset of this book. The model of "protestant" interpretation I have in mind is *not* the isolated individual joined in anguished communication with her personal God, but rather the community joined together in basically egalitarian discussion of the meaning (and demands) of the relevant materials.[161]

Assertions of institutional protestantism, however described, did not go unanswered. Frederick Douglass, for example, was attacked most strongly by his erstwhile abolitionist allies like Wendell Phillips, strongly ensconced in the Garrisonian movement.[162] Phillips heaped ridicule on arguments like Douglass's. He pointed to the "unanimous, concurrent, unbroken practice of every department of government," not to mention the "acquiescence of the people for fifty years," as proof of "the true construction" of the Constitution. According to Phillips, "If the people and the courts of the land do not know what they themselves mean, who has authority to settle their meaning for them?"[163] Americans "may well take the Constitution to be what the courts and nation allow that it is, and leave the hair-splitters and cobweb spinners to amuse themselves at their leisure."[164]

As already made clear in the reaction to Meese, the "catholic" embrace of judicial supremacy remains alive and well.[165] Perhaps the most important judicial articulation of this aspect of "catholicism" was made by Justice Harlan. Several cases in the late 1960s involved the legitimacy of Congress's engaging in its own interpretation of the Fourteenth Amendment, where the answers given by Congress sometimes differed from those given by the Court. Thus, for example, Congress in the Voting Rights Act of 1965 commanded that states extend the right to vote to persons educated in Spanish-language schools in Puerto Rico, even if these persons were unable to pass English-language literacy tests, which were a prerequisite for voting in many states. A majority of the Court upheld the statute.[166] Justice Harlan, however, dissented.

The Court, in a unanimous decision in 1959,[167] had upheld the legitimacy of state literacy tests as a prerequisite for voting, against a Fourteenth Amendment challenge that they violated equal protection of the laws; to this day, the Court has never formally overruled this decision. Still, the majority in the 1966 case accepted the legitimacy of the congressional statute in question, under the power assigned to Congress by Section 5 of the Amendment to "enforce" its terms. Justice Harlan suggested in his dissent that the decision could be purchased only "at the sacrifice of fundamentals in the American constitutional system,"[168] including the primacy of the role of the Court in defining constitutional requirements applicable to the states.

A later case involved the ability of Congress to require states to allow 18-year-olds to vote even though no court had held (or would hold) that the denial of the franchise violated the Equal Protection Clause.[169] Again, the basis of congressional power was Section 5 of the Fourteenth Amendment, and again the majority upheld the statute. Harlan dissented, once more registering his strong view that "[t]he role of final arbiter [of the meaning of Equal Protection] belongs to this Court."[170]

One other example of a strong emphasis on judicial supremacy is worth mentioning. Whatever their other differences, both Justice Black and Justice Harlan exhibited little patience with those who deviated from judicial mandates. The most dramatic example is almost undoubtedly *Walker* v. *City of Birmingham*,[171] where several black civil-rights demonstrators were jailed for violating a patently unconstitutional state-court injunction against a march on Easter Sunday.[172] The time of the march was obviously symbolically important, and to have delayed it in order to appeal would have been in effect to have foregone the point that was being made. The Court was unanimous in finding the injunction unconstitutional, but five members, including Black and Harlan, agreed with the legitimacy of punishing the demonstrators for contempt of court. Why "contempt of court" is so much worse than, say, "contempt of city council," which can occur when demonstrators choose to violate an unconstitutional city ordinance (and are protected in that violation), was not explained. No one reading the opinion can doubt the special sanctity that the Court awarded its fellow members of the judiciary.

Nor is it only judges who are so solicitous of judicial authority. Anthony Lewis, whom we have earlier seen denouncing Attorney General Meese as licensing "anarchy," has, as a *New York Times* columnist who often writes on the Constitution, been perhaps the most distinguished popular articulator of a "papalist" Constitution. He therefore believes that *Walker*, "for all its oddity, was correctly decided." America, says Lewis, "is bursting with diversity; I do not think it could have survived under one Constitution without the final voice it has had." Preserving the authority of that "final voice" requires that persons obey "decisions that we do not like" at pain of being cited for contempt of court.[173]

Toward Individual Authority to Interpret the Constitution

The rejection of hierarchical "authoritative" interpretation has implications not only for the Supreme Court's pronouncements, but also for the more ordinary pronouncements of the everyday lawyer or, for that matter, law professor. To put the matter most starkly: Is a lawyer's primary obligation to "the law" or to judges who make claims to incarnate the law? If a lawyer accepts the notion of a deinstitutionalized Constitution, then it becomes altogether possible that conflicts will arise between the lawyer's duty to the court and the duty to maintain the Constitution. At the very least, a lawyer would be bound to present a more pluralistic notion of "the law" than a prediction of judicial behavior.

Consider the following possibility. A client wishes to know whether he can refuse induction into the armed forces on grounds of selective conscientious objection. The client informs his lawyer that he has considered many of the classic arguments concerning the relationship between law and personal morality and has concluded that, in case of conflict, law ought to prevail. What the client wants from his lawyer is her considered judgment as to the possibility of both resisting induction and yet remaining the faithful legalist he wishes to be.

If the lawyer accepts the Supreme Court as ultimate interpreter, then the client should be advised that, as a result of the decision in *Gillette* v. *United States*,[174] there is no constitutional right to selective conscientious objection. But consider a "protestant" lawyer's answer to that question. Instead of taking down the relevant volume of the *United States Reports* and pointing to the dispositive written words of the Supreme Court decision, the lawyer might wish to note that some commentators criticize the decision as a "mistake." The lawyer surely is ethically bound to point out that the client might well go to jail for refusing induction, but this is not the equivalent of "breaking the law," at least from the perspective of the client. For he is the only person who can truly determine whether or not the law is being broken, after conscientiously reflecting on his own motivation and activity. If the client is persuaded that the Supreme Court was correct in *Gillette*, then, given his legalism, he must accept induction. If, on the other hand, he believes that the Court erred, then he becomes licensed, even within the terms of his own legalism, to reject the decision and to refuse induction. That is, *Gillette* becomes legal dross when placed next to the "touchstone" of the Constitution itself.

The final decision is the client's and not the lawyer's. A protestant constitutionalism that is true to itself would not substitute a priesthood of lawyers for a pontifical Court. And Dworkin, though recognizing the role of the legal community in assessing decisions, specifically rejects the view that only the legally trained can criticize courts.[175] The reason he gives relates to his other, more "catholic" methodological point that the law is intertwined with the ordinary moral understandings of the given social order.

Justice Jackson once made his own play on the notion of a "papal" Court: "We are not final because we are infallible, but we are infallible only because we are final."[176] But the question of finality is more open than Jackson recognized, at least if one accepts the basic structure of "protestant" constitutionalism, including the Dworkinian version.

It is also worth noting that the model I am describing (and, in fact, endorsing) does not imply only that one can on occasion "disobey" judicial decrees. It also has the much more important function of legitimizing, indeed requiring, lawyers to view their function vis-à-vis clients as something other than merely predicting what a court would do if presented with their cases. Imagine, for example, a city attorney faced with a particular city ordinance in regard to, say, freedom of speech. Should the city close off one of its public parks to those who would like to pass out political leaflets? It may be that such an ordinance could be successfully defended, given certain developments in contemporary judicial doctrine. But imagine as well that the attorney strongly, and with good reason, believes that these developments constitute a deviation from, if not outright betrayal of, the vision of the First Amendment or maintenance of the republican form of government commanded by Article IV of the Constitution. Could she not, *should* she not, argue vigorously that the ordinance is unconstitutional, even as she must also admit to her client that it could probably be sustained?

Ultimately it will be up to the city council and mayor to decide, but a central tenet of my argument is that *their* decision also should be based on conscientious analysis of what fidelity to the Constitution requires, rather than a mere assessment of their odds of winning in court. Ironically, it is the emphasis on judicial supremacy that has served to legitimize a debased notion of the Constitution as being, in effect, whatever can get the approval of a court. This may exemplify a touching faith in the judiciary, but it says little for the willingness of ordinary political officials to take seriously the responsibility placed upon them by their oaths of office to assess their activities in light of their duties to support and protect the values of the Constitution.

Consider, as a distinctly nonhypothetical example, the great controversy that occurred several years ago when the Minneapolis City Council passed an ordinance that would have severely restricted the distribution of material that was sexually explicit (though nonpornographic under the standard legal tests). The ordinance was passed at the behest of a coalition that included feminists who protested vigorously against the degradation of women found in the materials that would have been regulated.[177] The mayor of Minneapolis, Donald Fraser, vetoed the ordinance, on the grounds that it violated the First Amendment. Fraser's action triggered a remarkable letter by Laurence Tribe. Writing to the president of the Minneapolis City Council, Tribe expressed his "dissent and dismay" about the veto. Although he stated as well that he was "sympathetic" to the view that officials ought not "pass[] the buck to the courts," he castigates the veto as "an abuse of the fundamental structure of our system of government," for the mayor "has acted unilaterally to deprive the court of their unique Constitutional function: to pass on legislation that is not obviously unconstitutional." Indeed, Tribe accuses Fraser "[h]iding behind the First Amendment" and "usurp[ing] the judicial function."

Not everyone from Harvard shared Tribe's view: Professor Alan Dershowitz wrote Fraser congratulating him for his "courageous" veto. That letter in turn triggered a letter from Tribe to Fraser elaborating the critique of Fraser's veto:

> [W]hile I am prepared to assume that you acted from a good faith assessment of your constitutional duty, I cannot share Professor Dershowitz' admiration for the role you chose to play in *interposing yourself so pre-emptively* between those who believe their rights are violated by anti-female pornography, and the

courts—which *alone* can fairly decide whether this proposed protection of those alleged rights can be reconciled with the transcendent importance of free speech in an open society.[178]

One cannot imagine a stronger articulation of what I have been terming the "catholic" view of institutional supremacy. There is an absolutely fundamental divide between those who would view Fraser as
"courageous" in deciding for himself what it means to live up to the
oath—required by the Constitution of the United States—to be faithful to the Constitution and those who would see him as a "usurper"
challenging the unique authority of courts to decide what the Constitution means.

Perhaps the strongest argument for judicial oversight should be labeled "judicial view," rather than "judicial review." As Charles Black
has pointed out, in many situations courts are examining activity
where no one has engaged in thoughtful contemplation of constitutional requirements prior to acting.[179] (As argued above, simple cal-
culation of the prospects of winning does not count as "thoughtful
contemplation.") It is surely a prerequisite of constitutionalism that
officials take due regard of the constraints upon them before acting.
In the absence of such regard, judicial oversight provides the only
guarantee that "the Constitution" will be considered at all.

The critical problem arises when other individuals or institutions
do purport to have considered what the Constitution requires of
them. If a local police chief, argues Black, "did not in good faith consider the federal constitutional problem, his judgment on it is non-
existent. If he did consider it, his judgment, I think it is not too un-
kind to say, is worthless. When the accused person appeals to the
Court on the federal constitutional ground, he is appealing to the very
first official authorized or competent—or, for that matter, likely—to
consider his claim."[180] One may well be wary of Chief Doe's capacities
in all too many given instances, but Black slides much too quickly
over the problem of comparative competence. The very notion of
competence suggests the presence of privileged techniques of interpretation that can be recognized and transmitted (in law schools);
moreover, these techniques are peculiarly usable by members of a
particular institution, the judiciary. But this suggestion begs the central question, and it is an enduring contribution of Protestantism to
Western democratic theory to emphasize the capacity of ordinary men
and women, assuming their conscientious commitment to a shared

faith, to engage in their own reflection about the implications of sacred texts.

Because courts can view only a very small portion of official acts, it is crucial to the maintenance of a constitutional order that individuals believe themselves obligated to be conscientious adjudicators even in the absence of coercive constraints provided by courts.[181] Moreover, insofar as one is wary of Chief Doe, the United States Congress, or the president, the reasons for the wariness may apply as well to courts, since they are ultimately the creatures of the local, state, and national political structures that generate legislative and executive officials. So "citizen review" is a vital necessity of any polity that purports to call itself constitutional, as opposed to those regimes that, as Max Lerner suggests, simply use "the Constitution" as an ideological symbol to legitimize their own exercises of power.

This discussion of institutional authority is important only because there is disagreement about what constitutes correct interpretation of "the Constitution." But "the Constitution" is no different from other pieces of writing, and much recent discussion of literary interpretation has focused on the problem of validity. Interestingly enough, some critics counterpose the plurality of literary interpretations with a presumably different situation in the law. Thus E. D. Hirsch notes that "in legal questions, changed interpretations can be institutionalized by a pronouncement from the highest court. . . . No one, for example, would hold that a law means 'what the judges say a law means' if there were not a supreme tribunal to decide what, after all, the judges say." According to Hirsch, though, "[t]here could never be such arbitrary tribunals in the domain of knowledge and scholarship."[182] Elsewhere, Hirsch has referred to two "institutions that control interpretation"—the Supreme Court of the United States and the *Instituto Biblico* of Rome—both of which have 'controlling force.' "[183]

What is most interesting about Hirsch's formulation is the implicit denial that legal analysis involves "knowledge." His perception of the Court is ultimately quite Hobbesian insofar as he emphasizes its essentially "arbitrary" stance relative to the material it is interpreting. In any case, on Hirsch's account, it presumably makes no sense to say that the Supreme Court, or the *Instituto Biblico* for that matter, has made a "mistake." But the brunt of this chapter is to make such a use of language quite sensible, whether or not the reader is persuaded that it is attractive as well.

Summary

I have reached the end of the elaboration of the parallels between Protestant and Catholic approaches to Christian doctrine and "protestant" and "catholic" modes of approaching the United States Constitution. It may be helpful by way of summary to try to briefly fill in the categories set out above.

Justices Black and Harlan easily fit, respectively, into the designations of "protestant–catholic" and "catholic–catholic." Neither challenged judicial supremacy, but they disagreed fundamentally about what constituted "the Constitution," with Harlan rejecting the emphasis on "writtenness" that characterized Black's approach. Ronald Dworkin, as we have seen, is quintessentially "catholic–protestant." Like Harlan, he is willing to go well beyond the text in order to derive constitutional understandings. Unlike most judges, however, he radically rejects the notion that Supreme Court decisions are necessarily final in the sense of requiring obedience by conscientious citizens.

The extraordinarily odd couple of Frederick Douglass and Edwin Meese are both candidates for the category of "protestant–protestant." Both emphasize a highly textual Constitution, though they would strongly disagree on the specific method of interpreting the text, which has not really been a focus of this chapter. Neither accords "ultimate authority" to Supreme Court decisions as articulations of the "Law of the Land." Both radically separate Court and Constitution and, understandably enough if one accepts the separation in the first place, grant supremacy to the latter.

It should be clear by now that the ability of "the Constitution" to provide the unity so desperately sought as a preventive against disorder depends on the resolution of the same issues that split Judaism, Christianity, Islam, and, indeed, all other religions that have texts as a central part of their structure. "With a numinous document like the Constitution or the Bible, the principles and methods of correct interpretation are as important as they are problematical."[184] Only if there is widespread agreement on "principles and methods of correct interpretation" can a written Constitution be said to be a source of stability. Or, alternatively, only if an institution is accorded absolute supremacy in the interpretation of the creed will disorder be prevented. But sophisticated legal theorists agree on none of these premises. We are not sure of what "the Constitution" consists, or how it is to be interpreted, or who is to be the authoritative interpreter.

It is unlikely, moreover, that any of the participants in the debates about constitutional theory are going to have their minds changed by reading anything by a person of another sect, any more than Baptist theologians are likely to convert to Catholicism when presented with a "refutation" of their position. If Attorney General Meese was treated ungently by some of his critics, who refused to see the possible merits of his position, it may be because he and others within the Justice Department have been notably ungentle in pronouncing anathemas upon views with which *they* disagree.

The religious wars of the sixteenth and seventeenth centuries came to an end only when religion became sufficiently privatized so as not to remain an essential element of public order. New conceptions of the nation-state, and of constitutionalism, were called upon to provide order. Part of the apparatus of these new states was a "civil religion" to replace as an anchoring structure the divisive sectarian religions. Perhaps we can now understand a bit better Frankfurter's comment, quoted at the outset of this book, concerning his almost "religious" "feelings about American citizenship."

It is ironic that a culture that has experienced what Matthew Arnold over a century ago described as a "melancholy, long-withdrawing roar" from traditional religious faith can assert the continuing reality of a collectivity of citizens organized around a constitutional faith. The "death of constitutionalism" may be the central event of our time, just as the "death of God" was that of the past century (and for much the same reason). Many in our culture have neither belief in the persuasive force of detached reason nor the ability to make a "leap of faith" upon reaching the barriers of rational assent. The fact that the public rhetoric of American political culture remains organized, in substantial ways, as a faith community centered on the Constitution may mislead us as to the health of that culture. After all, as the senior Oliver Wendell Holmes reminded us in the "One-Hoss Shay," a thinly disguised parable about classical Calvinism, a once-strong, indeed culturally dominant, mode of thought can collapse almost literally overnight.

One ultimately can believe only in that which one can also respect. Tertullian could indicate that he believed in Christianity because it was absurd, but the "absurdity" was merely epistemological. One can presumably be skeptical of the knowledge claims of any given religion while nonetheless manifesting great respect for the vision of life it contains. The more pressing tension comes when one perceives in a particular vision not only a doubtful epistemology but also a conflict with one's central moral notions. A religious system that requires human sacrifice is, for most of us, harder to respect than one whose tenets accord with our fundamental moral propositions. What is true of religious systems is true also of legal ones, and I turn now to the relationship between the Constitution and moral norms.

THE MORAL DIMENSION OF CONSTITUTIONAL FAITH

INTRODUCTION: THE MORAL PREDICATE OF "RESPECT FOR THE LAW"

THE AMERICAN BAR ASSOCIATION in its Code of Professional Responsibility describes as a basic ethical duty of lawyers the promotion of "respect for the law."[1] Such respect should, of course, extend to the Constitution, the very fountainhead of the American legal system. This might appear to be a thoroughly uncontroversial premise, at least until one asks an all-important question: Is there anything built into the definition of law (or, more crucially, of the Constitution) that guarantees that it will necessarily be *worthy* of respect? For only if the answer is "yes" will one unhesitatingly agree to become "attached" to it and promote "respect" for it. Otherwise, both attachment and respect are at best problematic, and at times actually repugnant. In either case, unthinking devotion to the Constitution—or promotion of respect for it—might prove a Faustian bargain.

Thomas Grey has pointed out a very important—though often ignored—structural feature of the Constitution's mention of oaths of office in Article VI of the document. Although loyalty oaths will be the central focus of Chapter Three below, it is relevant to note here that Clause Three of Article VI requires that all political officials of the new country, both state and federal, "be bound by Oath or Affirmation, to support this Constitution; but no religious Test shall ever be required as a Qualification to any Office or public Trust under the United States." Yet, as Grey notes, the constitutional oath "is a ritual of allegiance, requiring officers to affirm their primary loyalty" to the values and commands presumably contained within the document.

And, he goes on, "[t]he 'but' suggests that the framers considered the constitutional oath a *substitute* for the religious tests the colonists were familiar with under the English established church. To push the point a bit: America would have no national church . . . , yet the worship of the Constitution would serve the unifying function of a national civil religion."[2]

Fittingly enough, some of the ratifiers considered the oath to be a genuine *religious* oath. Thus Oliver Wolcott, at the Connecticut Ratifying Convention, argued against the requirement of a specific religious oath on the grounds that the oath enjoined in the Constitution "upon all the officers of the United States" constitutes "a direct appeal to that God who is the avenger of perjury. Such an appeal to him is a full acknowledgement of his being and providence."[3] Similarly, the South Carolina Ratifying Convention suggested amending the Constitution by "inserting the word 'other' between the word 'no' and 'religious.' "[4]

The constitutional oath may not be a "religious Test" for those who define religion as necessarily including affirmations of supernatural beings and theological propositions, but it is surely a test establishing one's devotion to the civil religion as a predicate condition for the ability to hold office. It affirms, among other things, that any conflicts felt by office-holders between the demands of their religion and those of the law will be decided in favor of the law. This may be no idle—or unproblematic—promise. A dramatic example of this general point is found in an oath required by the Territory of Idaho—and upheld by the Supreme Court—of voters.[5] Part of an anti-Mormon campaign, the oath specifically required the person to swear "that I am not a bigamist or polygamist" or a member of any organization that promotes the doctrine of "plural or celestial marriage," as well as a promise not to "teach, advise, counsel or encourage any person to commit the crime of bigamy or polygamy, or any other crime defined by law, either as a religious duty or otherwise."[6] What is most striking, though, is the last part of the oath, which requires a declaration "that I do regard the Constitution of the United States and the laws thereof and the laws of this Territory, as interpreted by the courts, as the supreme laws of the land, the teachings of any order, organization or association to the contrary notwithstanding, so help me God."[7] The drafters of this oath presumably did not perceive any conflict between its extraction of constitutional faith and the final oath before God, though the obvious point of the Mormons' rejection of antipolygamy laws, at least at the time, was their belief that God required (and re-warded) plural marriage, in appropriate circumstances.[8]

One need not look to the past for evidence of the privileged status of constitutional faith as against the demands of one's religious faith. In 1986, as he began his thirtieth year on the Supreme Court, Justice William Brennan submitted to an interview. Asked if he had "ever had difficulty dealing with [his] own religious beliefs in terms of cases," the justice responded that he had, upon his appointment in 1956, "settled in my mind that I had an obligation under the Consti-tution which could not be influenced by any of my religious princi-ples." Although he would "as a private citizen" do "what a Roman Catholic does, . . . to the extent that that conflicts with what I think the Constitution means or requires, then my religious beliefs have to give way."[9] This assurance of constitutional supremacy echoes an ear-lier statement by Justice Joseph Story upon being assailed in the Northern press for an opinion giving legal succor to slavery: "I shall never hesitate to do my duty as a Judge, under the Constitution and laws of the United States, be the consequences what they may. That Constitution I have sworn to support, and I cannot forget or repudiate my solemn obligations at pleasure."[10]

Some readers, I suspect, take this subordination of religion (or "personal morality") to the Constitution as a *sine qua non* of what it means to be judge—or perhaps even a citizen. Indeed, many of us have come to expect as part of the ritual of Senate confirmation assur-ances by a nominee to the judiciary that he or she will subordinate "private" moral or religious visions to the "public" commands of the Constitution. One can observe the enactment of this most subtle deg-radation ceremony in the confirmation process of nominees to the United States Supreme Court, especially where the potential judges are Catholic, as with Antonin Scalia and Anthony Kennedy.

Other readers, however, may feel distinctly less comfortable at the privileging that lies beneath such assurances. This discomfort might well be strongest among those who identify "religious beliefs" as the knowable words (or commands) of a divine presence rather than either idiosyncratic metaphors concerning an ineffable mystery or, more likely, psychological or sociological projections of all-too-human anxieties or social structures. These more "God-oriented" readers, with whom many of us do not identify, might sympathize, for exam-ple, with the remark by Professor Paul Simmons of the Southern Bap-tist Theological Seminary: "Identifying the Judeo-Christian posture with American nationalism [or, presumably, with the Constitution that is the scriptural record—the decalogue equivalent—of the American incarnation] is to lose the transcendent and absolute nature of the Christian faith. For Christians and Jews, loyalty to God must transcend any earthly loyalties."[11]

One might consider in this context the decision by the chairman of the Israeli Knesset to bar Meir Kahane from taking any part in the activities of that parliamentary body after Kahane had refused to take the oath of allegiance required of members of the Knesset: "I promise to pledge allegiance to the state of Israel and to faithfully fulfill my mission in Parliament." Instead, Kahane committed himself (only) "to the keeping of Your [God's] Torah always and forever." As a spokesman for Kahane explained, "He refused to pledge the oath because we are not willing to say we will support every law of the state, only the laws of the Bible."[12] Presumably, Kahane means to suggest that in any conflict between the law of the state and the law of God (as he interprets it), the latter will always prevail in regard to his own obligations. Even if we do not share the theological presuppositions of Professor Simmons or Rabbi Kahane, we might still acknowledge that deification (or idolatry) of the nation-state (including its Constitution) is not necessarily an advance over deification of a deity. In any case, it is no small matter what one announces as one's "faith" and repository of primary loyalty.

Why would a morally serious person* say the things that we re-

---

* In a (probably futile) effort to avoid a misunderstanding of my argument in this chapter, let me emphasize that I do *not* equate being "morally serious" with adopting any kind of "absolute" grounding of morality, whether in natural law, divine revelation, or any of the other candidates that have contended with one another over the centuries. To be "morally serious" here means that one is concerned with the evaluation of one's actions or intellectual positions in terms of the welfare of others; that one always accepts as relevant and takes into account, when discussing the merits of a particular position deemed to have some consequences within the world one lives in, the likelihood that others will suffer. ("Suffering" can obviously range from the infliction of physical pain to the deprivation of opportunity for access, say, to what one regards as great works of art.) That persons may be unable to offer a "foundational" defense of their views does not mean that these views are not of great import in "constituting" their identity. There are extremely few people who genuinely accept a designation of being thoroughly "amoral" or, more seriously, "nihilistic" in regard to what people, either individually or as collectively organized, can do to one another.

It is distinctly not the purpose of this book to address the questions of metaethical and metaepistemological discourse that have become so pervasive in contem-

quire our justices to say, i.e., that they will happily subordinate their private religious or moral convictions to the demands of the public law? One answer is that there is ultimately no genuine conflict between these ostensibly different obligations, that "the law" is itself substantially similar to the moral visions thought to be contained at least within the so-called Judeo-Christian tradition of the West. Of course, one need not be religious in order to have moral visions, and both the question and the answer would be the same for a committed Kantian or an adherent of any other moral theory.

The issues raised by constitutional interpretation—whether in "identifying" the Constitution in the first place or in giving meaning thereafter to the canonical text(s)—are obviously related to the "fit" between the Constitution and morality. Owen Fiss, for example, denounces the "arid and artificial conception of interpretation" that he labels "textual determinism," which he links with the form of legal positivism that emphasizes "the 'written constitution' and stresses factors like the use of particular words or the intent or beliefs of the framers, *all of which have little or no moral relevance.*"[13] The problems with these modes of interpretation go well beyond the theoretical difficulties in ascertaining the true meaning of the text or the intentions of its authors, which for some are enough to doom them as coherent enterprises.[14] As Fiss argues, even if one assumes the theoretical plausibility of the positivist enterprise, there remains the problem that "[a] too rigid insistence on positivism will inevitably bring into question the ultimate moral authority of the legal text—the justness of the Constitution."[15]

Fiss concedes, for example, that an all-too-comprehensible Constitution might well be read to have protected slavery. But such a Constitution would be unworthy of respect and obedience. When he still viewed the Constitution as "a pro-slavery instrument," Frederick Douglass said of the document, "I cannot bring myself to vote under [it], or swear to support [it]."[16] Indeed, as Fiss points out, the mere ability to raise the possibility that the Constitution is immoral indicates "[a] moment of crisis in the life of a constitution."[17]

For Fiss, the resolution to any such crisis is close at hand. It lies in a judge willing "[t]o read the moral as well as the legal text. The judge

porary philosophy. No philosopher will (or ought to) be satisfied with the obviously informal sketch outlined above. The point of this note is simply to help the reader understand how I am using the word "morality" in the ensuing discussion.

quickly learns to read in a way that avoids crises."[18] Indeed, Fiss accords the judiciary a "[s]pecial competence to interpret a text such as the Constitution, and to render specific and concrete the public morality embodied in that text."[19]

Fiss is certainly not the only person to articulate such views. Thus Stephen Macedo, in the course of defending what he terms "principled activism" against critics from the so-called New Right, argues that "[b]y fusing constitutional interpretation and moral theory, principled activism vindicates the Constitution's authority by establishing its rightness."[20] Such views are obviously enticing because they promise a pleasant resolution to any perceived conflict between law and morality. Little recognition is given to the possibility that life under even the American Constitution may be a tragedy, presenting irresolvable conflicts between the realms of law and morality.

Fittingly enough, this problem posed by American civil religion and its key text—the Constitution—has its analogue in traditional religion. It can variously be described as the problem of theodicy or of nominalism; in both cases, the crucial issue concerns the relationship, if any, between the stipulated sovereignty of God and one's definition of goodness, i.e., that which is worthy of moral respect. The question of theodicy invariably involves judging God by human standards of justice: How could God be good—and thus worthy of loyalty and respect—if God passively tolerates (or even worse, brought into being or commands) evil? To save the goodness of God through a description of *inability* to eradicate evil destroys the attribute of sovereignty allegedly entailed by the very conception of God. One response is to emphasize the unlimited sovereignty of God and to define whatever God brings into being as necessarily good, even if beyond our capacity to understand. Nominalism thus emerged in the late Middle Ages "as a philosophy designed to save God's omnipotence."[21] There are no limits on God's power; the world is radically contingent, capable of being transformed at any moment if the sovereign God so wills it. A necessary result is that "human experience and reason lose their power to glimpse the truth of the world."[22]

This loss of power extends to moral truths as well; there is no independent test of goodness other than God's command. From this perspective, no judgment of God's handiwork is possible. Among other problems with this notion, though, is the paradox that praise of that handiwork as "good" becomes tautological, because there is nothing else that it could be, given that the test of goodness is the handiwork itself. Genuine praise requires an ability to judge by some *other* criterion than itself, but that, obviously, is the problem.

There is a strain of Western thought going back several hundred years, however, that makes quite confident reference to "the reason and nature of things: a principle which will impose laws even on the Deity,"[23] whatever the irony involved in recognizing that a God that *must* be good is by virtue of that requirement not truly sovereign. Adherence to goodness "represent[s] the pinnacle and the limit of God's creative powers."[24]

Not even the most ardent constitutionalist genuinely views the Constitution as the equal of God, but a pale version of the religious dilemma is nonetheless present. What is the relationship, if any, between the Constitution—and the sovereign people ostensibly represented in its terms—and morality? Constitutional faith requires the linkage of law and morality even as most twentieth-century jurisprudence has emphasized their analytic separation. All calls for renewed faith in the rule of law and renewal of the constitutional covenant imply that submission to the Constitution will create not only order but also the conditions of a social order worthy of respect. In order for us to see the logic and desirability of submission to the rule of the Constitution, we must examine much more closely the assumed linkage between it and morality.

"Not Under Man But Under God and the Law": An Outworn Joinder?

When John Adams defined a constitutional republic as "a government of laws, and not of men," he was invoking an understanding of law and social life that is now almost wholly alien to our own. For Adams and most other pre-nineteenth-century adherents of the rule of law, law was inextricably linked with timeless moral norms. This notion can be traced back at least to Aristotle. Even today the front pediment of Langdell Hall at the Harvard Law School features the statement of the medieval jurist Henry de Bracton, "Not Under Man, But Under God and the Law." The essential point, though, is that God and the law are joined together, for law was defined by the medievalists as the product either of natural reason given by God or of immemorial custom itself incarnating natural justice, or as the commands of political leaders ordained by God and therefore given the right to rule.

Adams's notion of the rule of law, at least in the American context, was based on this older conception of law as rooted in a common religious and moral order. "We have no government," said Adams, "armed with power capable of contending with human passions unbridled by morality and religion. Our constitution was made only for a moral and a religious people. It is wholly inadequate for the government of any other."[25] Adams viewed individuals as members of political communities to which they would be willing to subordinate their selfish personal interests in behalf of a "common good." Like many of his contemporaries, he blended, however precariously, belief in individual rights and liberties with the equally strong belief in an overarching community.

Subordination to law was thus subordination only to that part of ourselves willing to recognize primary obligations to the community, a community in turn recognizing obligations to adhere to fixed moral principles. Adams in many ways was more "old-fashioned" than other Founders, but Cass Sunstein has suggested that even the considerably younger and more "modern" James Madison retained a linkage to this older tradition when he spoke, in the 10th Federalist Paper, of "the permanent and aggregate interests of the community" that a well-chosen (and virtuous) leadership could be trusted to recognize and protect.[26]

These ideas have barely, if at all, survived. Indeed, the 10th Federalist Paper is much more often cited for its emphasis on the "propensity of mankind to fall into mutual animosities"[27] that make the envisioning (and achievement) of a genuinely common good impossible. Indeed, the dominant tendency of self-consciously "modernist" intellectuals (in whose group I place myself) is towards an ever-more-radical moral pluralism tending toward relativism (or, at least, "anti-anti-relativism").[28] The most influential accounts of political liberalism all tend to emphasize the required "neutrality" of the state toward the various ways that people choose to live their lives or, as it is sometimes phrased, "express themselves." Devotion to a completely "private" life of consumer satisfaction, for example, is no longer denigrated as against a more "public" life of community service; both are equally legitimate as means of "self-realization," at least from the perspective of the neutrality theorist.[29] As Ian Shapiro puts it, in a valuable analysis of the origins of liberal thought, "The existence of a public sphere was merely to facilitate private interaction" rather than to provide a special forum for the transformation of the "private" person into a "public" citizen devoted to the common weal (and common-wealth).[30]

Whatever rhetoric might be heard about the duty of persons to adhere to the common good, most of us seem to believe that (and certainly act as if) our primary duties are to ourselves and our families alone. Liberty has come to focus evermore on freedom *from* the community or the state rather than the realization of a common vision *through* the community and its institutions. Although the state can intervene to prevent the infliction of harm upon its citizenry, the prohibited "harm" cannot, according to most versions of the "neutrality" argument, include psychic distress at the knowledge that others are living immoral or unworthy lives.

The explanation for these developments does not lie simply (if at all) in the ability of new ideas, such as those of Hobbes, to persuade readers to change their lives. Michael Walzer notes "[t]he extraordinary transformation in social scale which has occurred in the past century and a half," nowhere more so than in the United States, which has brought in its wake "a radically different kind of political community—one in which relations between individual and state are so attenuated as to call into question all the classical and early democratic theories" of politics. As a result of these transformations, "[t]he individual has become a private man, seizing pleasure when he can, alone, or in the narrow confines of his family. The state has become a distant power, never again firmly within the grasp of the citizen."[31]

The eclipse of this older "republican" tradition evoked (and enacted) by Adams does not mean, however, that it has entirely died out. Its call, whether beacon or siren song, continues to be heard by some influential contemporary constitutional theorists. Cass Sunstein, for example, defines as one of his central projects "to help revive aspects of an attractive conception of [republican] governance . . . and to suggest its availability as a foundation from which judges and others might evaluate political processes and outcomes." He recognizes that the "animating principle" of republicanism is "civic virtue"—which includes the ability of people, coming together as citizens in public discussion, "to escape private interests and engage in pursuit of the public good." Republicanism (and Sunstein) denies "that decisions about values are merely matters of taste." Instead, " 'practical reason' can be used to settle social issues."[32]

Another devotee of republicanism is the sociologist Robert Bellah, who helped spark the modern revival of interest in civil religion, of which this book is a part. He writes of a particularly republican kind of civil religion linked with promotion of commitment to the common good and a conception of citizenship focused on its attainment. Because "a republic must attempt to be ethical in a positive sense and to elicit the ethical commitment of its citizens," says Bellah, it must "inevitably push[] toward the symbolization of an ultimate order of existence in which republican values and virtues make sense." Although the symbolization can turn into a kind of worship of the polity by itself, the worst form of nationalism, Bellah more optimistically asserts that "the American case" includes "the worship of a higher reality that upholds the standards the republic attempts to embody."[33]

Michael Perry, like Sunstein a professor of law, has adopted Bellah's arguments in order to justify a particularly "prophetic" role for judges. According to Perry, "[t]he American people still see themselves as a nation standing under transcendent judgment: They understand—even if from time to time some members of the intellectual elite have not—that morality is not arbitrary, that justice cannot be reduced to the sum of the preferences of the collectivity." As a result, they are responsive to "moral leadership" that can promote the "moral evolution" of the polity. Judges can play this vital role of recalling to the public its status "as a people committed to struggle incessantly to see beyond, and then to live beyond, the imperfections of whatever happens at the moment to be the established moral conventions."[34]

To put it mildly, though, many analysts would reject these arguments, whether offered as description or as advice. At a descriptive level, such analysts would agree with Justice Marshall's 1971 statement that "[o]urs is a Nation of enormous heterogeneity in respect of political views, moral codes, and religious persuasions,"[35] making impossible a striving for a "public philosophy" that at bottom rests on the notion of consensus and shared values. Indeed, some of those most likely to support Sunstein and Bellah in their professed goals would also be those most sharply critical of their continuing belief in a genuine American community. Thus Alasdair MacIntyre writes that "[t]he notion of the political community as a common project is alien to the modern individualist world."[36] And many writers note that a defining characteristic of modern liberalism is "fundamental skepticism about basic answers in life," though the lack of a common grounding is viewed as "a positive thing, a basis for the virtue of social pluralism and intellectual diversity."[37]

For Adams and the older generations, law was based on moral principle. Yet, ironically, it was the American Revolution itself, made in the name of the "fundamental law" that allegedly had been breached by the British, that hastened the demise of this older notion. Conjoined with the "higher law" argument was another that emphasized the claims of popular sovereignty—the right of the collective people to take charge of their own destiny. Popular sovereignty as a motif emphasized the energy and the moral authority of will (and willful desire) rather than the constraints of a common moral order to which the will was bound to submit. Thus, Thomas Jefferson believed that it "was the will of the nation which makes the law obligatory." That is, "consent of the governed" shifted from being a consensual recognition of *a priori* truths to being a more *self-validating* procedure stripped from association with the increasingly unconsidered norms of purportedly self-evident morality. In the past, law was legitimate because it was based on moral principles; in the future, law would receive its legitimacy from being the incarnation of the focused energies of the body politic.

The transition of the basis of law from principle to will has the effect of analytically separating law from morality; there is the dissolution of any guarantee that fidelity to law necessarily will mean equal fidelity to principles of moral conduct. Even by 1787, during the Philadelphia Convention, there was at least muffled recognition of this implication of the new emphasis on popular sovereignty. Thus James Wilson of Pennsylvania, second in importance at the convention only to James Madison, noted that the Constitution, which he strongly supported, would nonetheless allow laws that "may be unjust, may be unwise, may be dangerous, may be destructive; and yet not be so unconstitutional as to justify the judges in refusing to give them effect."[38] One important aspect of Wilson's remark, of course, is its assumption in behalf of judicial review, with its attendant authority to invalidate those enactments of the legislature deemed "unconstitutional." But surely as important is Wilson's rejection of any easy identification of the Constitution with justice or wisdom. By definition, the set of "unconstitutional" laws did not overlap perfectly even with "unjust," "dangerous," or "destructive" ones, let alone those which were merely "unwise."

Wilson pointed toward what was to become the dominant view of law for future generations (and certainly the view emphasized today at most major law schools): Law is stripped of any moral anchoring, becoming instead the product of specific political institutions enjoying power under the Constitution. Political institutions thus become the forum for the triumph of the will, expressed as positive law, and it is the duty of the legal official to implement the public will. It should be immediately noted, though, that adoption of what might be termed "robust positivism," where putatively unjust law is privileged over the demands of justice, is not something done lightly. The preferred rhetorical strategy, seen vividly in the discussion by Owen Fiss that began this chapter, is obviously to point to the happy correlation of law and morality rather than emphasize their difference. Still, occasions arise where a choice must be made.

SLAVERY AS A PROBLEM
OF LEGAL INTERPRETATION

The most obvious struggle between law and morality within the American historical context surely involves chattel slavery. It may have been the case that the Declaration of Independence, written four-score-and-seven years before Lincoln's monumental 1863 address, promised to all a birthright of liberty, but the Constitution, written three-score-and-sixteen years before the bloody confrontation at Gettysburg, spoke only haltingly regarding the negation of that promise—chattel slavery. Nowhere does the Constitution use the word, but several of its sections cannot be understood except as responses to America's "peculiar institution."[39] Thus Southern representation was enhanced significantly by counting three-fifths of the total number of slaves within the pool to be "represented" in the House of Representatives.[40] Southern slaveholders were reassured, by Article IV, Section 2, that their runaway slaves would be treated as miscreants to be returned rather than as refugees to be given liberty; Congress was specifically prohibited from outlawing American participation in the international slave trade until 1808; and direct taxes were limited by the same three-fifths clause of the "enumeration" for representation, lest Congress count slaves in their full number for taxation and thus make their ownership more costly.

As William Wiecek points out, these last two provisions, together with the assignment of equal membership in the Senate, are the only parts of the Constitution made exempt from the ordinary process of Article V amendment, so skilled were the slaveowners in gaining entrenchment for their interests. It cannot be a complete surprise, then, that there would be those like William Lloyd Garrison who, far from venerating the Constitution, would declare it a "proslavery compact," a grim realization of the "covenant with death" and "agreement with hell" mentioned by the prophet Isaiah.[41]

To appreciate the tensions caused for jurisprudence (and jurisprudents), one might consider two opinions written by John Marshall, one treating "ordinary" law, the other involving slavery. The first, *Fletcher* v. *Peck*,[42] is an 1810 decision involving the constitutionality of a Georgia statute that would have rescinded the State's sale of land encompassing much of what is now Alabama and Mississippi because of the manifest fraud involved in the decision by an earlier legislature to sell. Marshall, for the Court, held the statute unconstitutional. One ground was its violation of the Contracts Clause of the Constitution, which prohibited any state from passing a law "impairing" a contract; but Marshall went on to suggest that the law might be unconstitutional even in the absence of the textual provision because it violated one of the "general principles which are common to our free institutions."[43]

Indeed, Justice Johnson in concurrence relied entirely "on a general principle, on the reason and nature of things." It was precisely in this context that he delivered his description quoted earlier in this chapter—"a principle which will impose laws even on the Deity."[44]

Neither Marshall or Johnson did so, but both could well have cited a 1798 opinion written by Justice Samuel Chase in *Calder* v. *Bull*, which spoke of "acts which the Federal or State Legislature cannot do, without exceeding their authority. There are certain vital principles in our free Republican governments, which will determine and overrule an apparent and flagrant abuse of legislative power; as to authorize manifest injustice by positive law. . . . An ACT of the Legislature (for I cannot call it a law) contrary to the great first principles of the social compact, cannot be considered a rightful exercise of legislative authority."[45]

The second Marshall opinion[46] does not, technically speaking, involve the Constitution. It concerns the importation of slaves into the United States, which had been prohibited by Congress in 1808. A ship, the Antelope, was apprehended off the coast of Florida by a United States revenue cutter; 280 Africans were on board. United States law of the time provided that persons discovered attempting to import slaves would forfeit their ships and that the slaves would be returned to Africa. What made the case difficult was that the Antelope was in the control of pirates who had seized the Africans from several slave ships. The original Spanish and Portuguese "owners" of the slaves sued to get their "property" back, claiming that *they* had not attempted to circumvent the American law and that they therefore deserved to have their slaves returned to them. Marshall wrote the opinion for a unanimous Court ordering the return of at least some of the slaves to their "owners."[47] He adopts a very different rhetoric from that observed in *Fletcher*.

Marshall begins his discussion by reminding the reader that "this court must not yield to feelings which might seduce it from the path of duty"; it "must obey the mandate of the law."[48] But what might be the seduction that so worries Marshall? The answer lies in the moral claims to be made against slavery and the concomitant temptation to act in accordance with those claims.

Justice Story, one of Marshall's colleagues, had earlier denounced the slave trade as "repugnant to the great principles of Christian duty, the dictates of natural religion, the obligations of good faith and morality, and the eternal maxims of social justice." And he had gone on to say that "it is impossible that [the trade] can be consistent with any system of law that purports to rest on the authority of reason or revelation."[49] Marshall himself notes how "abhorrent this traffic may be to a mind whose original feelings are not blunted by familiarity with the practice." Indeed, it "will scarcely be denied" that slavery "is contrary to the law of nature."[50]

All of this having been said, though, the Court cannot escape recognizing that "[t]he Christian and civilized nations of the world, with whom we have most intercourse, have all been engaged in" the slave trade, and that established international law protects the trade, at least in the absence of domestic prohibition.[51] The United States can surely prevent Americans from engaging in the trade and, of course, can prevent anyone from importing slaves into the United States. But, Marshall held, the United States must recognize the claims of "innocent" foreign owners who were not violating the law of their own countries in attempting to ship slaves to a country that could legally receive them. Similarly, Story, whatever his views about the morality of slavery, upheld the constitutionality of the Fugitive Slave Act of 1793 when it was challenged in *Prigg* v. *Pennsylvania*.[52]

Story was not just another justice on the Supreme Court. Appointed to the Supreme Court at age 32 by James Madison, Story was almost legendary in his erudition and analytic abilities. Among his copious writings was a three-volume treatise, *Commentaries on the Constitution*, that attempted to do for the United States what Blackstone had done a century earlier for English law. H. Jefferson Powell, perhaps the leading contemporary analyst of Story's thought, notes that early suggestions by Story that the federal judiciary could look to rules of natural justice for guidance ultimately fell before a much more positivist analysis of the Constitution's ultimate foundation in popular will. Thus, according to Powell, "[i]f the majority chose to endorse the oppression through constitutional forms, those whose rights were infringed had only 'the ultimate appeal to the good sense, and integrity, and justice of the majority of the people.' "[53] Should the majority not bend before such appeals, that was the end of the matter, at least so far as the legal system was concerned. The amending power allowed the sovereign people to "change the whole structure and powers of the government, and thus legalize *any* present excess of power."[54] There was no analytic bar, therefore, to the Constitution becoming "the instrument of injustice."[55] To be sure, Story can be read as tolerating a right of rebellion against injustice, but this right obviously came from outside the law and was itself a critique of the legal order.[56]

HOLMES, BICKEL, AND
THE RAVAGES OF HETEROGENEITY

The radical difference between the two conceptions of law, and of the Constitution, outlined above—i.e., Constitution as guarantor of justice versus Constitution as instrument of sovereign will—is made most clear in the thought of Oliver Wendell Holmes. Holmes was one of the most influential shapers of modern American legal consciousness, as was his most notable disciple, Felix Frankfurter. Both defined the task of courts in a democracy as giving almost unrestrained enforcement to popular will as measured by legislative prowess.

For Holmes, government was a reflection of power, and nothing more. The "excellence" of a given government was measured by its "correspondence to the actual equilibrium of force in the community—that is, conformity to the wishes of the dominant power."[57] The only moral content of the law lies in the extent to which law reflects the moral notions of the dominant group, but these notions obviously need not be shared by those who are dominated. For Holmes history was basically comic, with a happy end assured, whatever the difficulties and pratfalls its characters might encounter on the way. As he himself admitted to the philosopher Morris R. Cohen, "I do in a sense worship the inevitable."[58] There is here spelled out the subordination of an independent moral sensibility to the brute force of history, which itself becomes moralized.

Holmes regarded the problem of coming to terms with the existence of moral evil in the world as "drool," and he had only contempt for those who took the problem seriously, including judges. He saw the role of the judge as that of the good bureaucrat—the enforcement, without question, of orders given by superiors: "I strongly believe that my agreement or disagreement has nothing to do with the right of the majority to embody their opinions in law. . . . [States] may regulate life in ways which we as legislators might think as injudicious or if you like as tyrannical."[59] Holmes delivered these comments in one of his most famous constitutional dissents, where the majority invoked the Constitution in order to strike down a New York law that would have limited to 60 the number of hours that bakers could be made to work by their employers. As a result, his dissent—which included his memorable phrase, "the Constitution does not enact Mr. Herbert Spencer's *Social Statics*"—became an anthem of sorts for political progressives who identified majoritarian government with political reform. His comments on "tyranny" were basically ignored.

Had some of his admirers read more carefully Holmes's dissent in a 1911 case concerning the enforcement of Alabama's vicious peonage laws, they might have been less ready to offer him such acclaim.[60] Alabama in effect made it a crime for a (black) worker to walk off a job for which he had received an advance payment (as opposed simply to requiring repayment of the advance). The majority struck down the law as a violation of the Thirteenth Amendment, which prohibited slavery and other forms of involuntary servitude. Holmes dissented here as well, thereby vindicating fully his promise in the earlier case that the Constitution need not be read to prevent "tyrannical" laws. One might, in a sense, admire Holmes for his candor and consistency, for there is no attempt to hide the fact that adherence to constitutional norms might produce tyranny instead of liberty or justice. It is at this point, though, that we are required to ask if the legal process (let alone any particular law) deserves our respect. Why should faith in the Constitution be affirmed rather than questioned?

Justice Frankfurter, whom we saw at the very outset of this book articulating his almost "religious" devotion to the Constitution, also provides surprisingly little reason to share his creed. Echoing James Wilson, he says, "Much that should be rejected as illiberal, because repressive and envenoming, may well not be unconstitutional."[61] And he summarizes his vision of the role of courts by stating that "our duty to abstain from confounding policy with constitutionality demands perceptive humility as well as self-restraint in not declaring unconstitutional what, *in a judge's private judgment*, is deemed unwise and even dangerous."[62] This last remark is drawn from a conceptual universe wholly different from that of Bracton or even John Adams, for the possibility of universal recognition of what constitutes common morality and the common good, and therefore law, has been replaced by a sharp split between "private" judgment and public notions. We are in the realm of a world consisting of isolated individuals pursuing merely personal visions. At best, they can co-exist; at worst, they are mutually exclusive and endlessly conflicting.

Law, even as bounded by the Constitution, is a series of outcomes of a bargaining process among atomistic beings, and there is no guarantee that such outcomes will not include "repressive, envenoming," "unwise and even dangerous" laws. The substantive content that underlay Bracton's and Adams's concepts of law has vanished, and the notion of law has been transformed (some would say decayed) into pure proceduralism—the recognition of public will as mediated by the institutions authorized by the Constitution to pass laws. One need not denigrate the importance of procedures, which we might well cherish and defend as necessary to any proper notion of a decent political order, in order to point to dangers attendant on viewing them as sufficient to evoke the generalized reverence Frankfurter claims for them.

Majority rule is simply not the same thing as constitutionalism, as that concept was classically defined. One cannot understand the notion of a constitution, at least prior to twentieth-century thought, without including its role of placing limits on the ability of majorities (or other rulers) to do whatever they wish in regard to minorities who lose out in political struggles. It is not that constitutionalism and majority rule are antithetical, but they coexist in a tense equilibrium, and the reduction of the Constitution to notions of procedure, however "purified," are apt to leave minorities insufficiently protected. Alexis de Tocqueville had noted in his otherwise admiring remarks about lawyers that if they "prize freedom much, they generally value legality still more: they are less afraid of tyranny than of arbitrary power; and, provided the legislature undertakes of itself to deprive men of their independence, they are not dissatisfied."[63]

So long as law is identified with will, even majority will, then any argument for the moral integrity of law must identify what it is about certain wills and their manifestations that makes them worthy of respect. Holmes himself made no effort to engage in such an argument, and Frankfurter spent most of his energies denying that constitutionality and wisdom, or even decency, were necessarily joined together.

The followers of Holmes and Frankfurter hoped that Alexander Bickel would provide a resolution of the tensions within their views. A graduate of the Harvard Law School, a clerk to Frankfurter, and for twenty years one of the leading members of the Yale Law School, Bickel was seen by some as uniquely equipped to construct a coherent vision of the Constitution. He published in 1962 an extraordinarily influential book that offered a moderate defense of the role of the Supreme Court in articulating our "fundamental values," whether or not clearly incribed within the constitutional text itself.[64] By the end of the decade, though, Bickel had clearly become disillusioned with much of the work done by the Warren Court in the name of "fundamental values," and he began a reconsideration of his position. Although his life was tragically cut short, he did write, in *The Morality of Consent*, the outline of his mature argument.[65]

Bickel quotes Holmes's own comment that the Constitution "is made for people of fundamentally differing views."[66] At the same time, though, Bickel also quotes Edmund Burke for the view that social life demands some "uniform rule and scheme of life," which Bickel goes on to describe as "principles, however provisionally and skeptically held."[67] For Bickel these principles are, in some way, provided by history. "We find our visions of good and evil . . . in the experience of the past, in our tradition, in the secular religion of the American republic."[68] The syntax makes it unclear whether the "secular religion" *is* "the American republic" or whether there is some particular strain of thought within our republic that constitutes the one (true?) religion by capturing its essence. It appears that the answer is the latter, especially when Bickel, after noting that "few principles are inscribed sharply in the Constitution itself," goes on to describe "the Supreme Court speaking in the name of the Constitution" as filling, "in part, the need for middle-distance principles that Burke described."[69] Either formulation seems to assume, without strong argument, that there is a relatively unequivocal American tradition that can be identified and adhered to by persons of good will.

If such a consensus be the case, though, one wonders what meaning can be given to the assertion of the existence of "fundamentally differing views." Holmes, too, had suggested the same contradiction when he referred at one point in his *Lochner* dissent to the existence of "fundamental principles as they have been understood by the traditions of our people and our law,"[70] but he characteristically made no effort at all to indicate what these principles might be or how they were to be discovered. There is a shell-game quality about this aspect of Holmes's and Bickel's arguments, for "fundamental differences" turn out not to be so fundamental after all if they are encapsulated within sufficient social uniformity.

But Holmes and Bickel were right the first time. What explains our contemporary uncertainty (some would say "crisis") in regard to the Constitution is the assertion of fundamentally different values within the political realm. (I do not want to suggest that earlier times were a "golden age" featuring greater unity, except insofar as "unity" was purchased through systematically silencing the voices of those victimized by the rule of dominant elites. Today's conversation, whatever its deficiencies, is certainly more open to different—and discordant—voices than earlier ones.) One person's notion of justice is often perceived as manifest tyranny by someone else. As already seen, slavery presents the easiest case historically, though more recent times are replete with examples as well. Latter-day disputes concerning the legitimate role of race in governmental decisionmaking, whether for purposes of segregation or of affirmative action, or the legitimacy of the state's allowing the cessation of the possibility of life, whether by abortion or by euthanasia, also present differences of the greatest magnitude regarding conceptions of justice.

At this point, however, all Bickel can do is to offer a highly conservative injunction: "Our legal order cannot endure too rapid a pace of change in moral conceptions, and its fundamental premise is that its own stability is itself a high moral value, in most circumstances the highest. . . . If the pace is forced, there can be no law."[71] As a legal sociologist, Bickel is almost certainly correct, but his argument fails to establish a reason for those who feel tyrannized by the existing legal order to recognize it as legitimate. Even if they share the regard for stability, which is certainly important, they might well not regard it as of such fundamental importance as to override any contrary values. There are surely cases, as Bickel himself recognizes, in which one might prefer "no law" to the maintenance of an existing iniquitous legal order, even one that professes to be subject to a "constitution," as with South Africa, for example. And even if one endorses Bickel's prescription to go slowly, there would presumably be no moral bar to seizing power if there were no practical bar as well.

There is no doubting Bickel's moral seriousness; his is not the complacent world of Holmes. But one doubts whether Bickel can resolve the problem he sets forth by first asserting a thoroughgoing moral skepticism, and then announcing that "we can as a society and a culture discover some boundaries" to the meaning of the moral realm.[72] Our maintenance as a society might well depend on the social reality of such common boundaries, but this begs recognition of the very social situation that brings forth most political and legal theory—the perception that social life as we know it is being challenged and may even be dissolving into an ever-greater Heraclitean flux.

The family of John Adams itself observed the passage of Massachusetts from a relatively homogenous society to a nineteenth-century conglomeration drawn from a variety of backgrounds. In 1780 Massachusetts was still able to style itself as a commonwealth, and its Constitution, written in large measure by John Adams, explicitly referred to the duty of the state to inculcate a common morality among the citizenry. By the middle of the nineteenth century, this notion of common association lay in ruins in a new America dedicated to the pursuit of private wealth.

Indeed, one reason for the emphasis on reverence for the Constitution, whether articulated by Lincoln or by present-day figures, is the realization that there may be no other basis for uniting a nation of so many disparate groups. The Constitution thus becomes the *only* principle of order, for there is no otherwise shared moral or social vision that might bind together a nation. Louis Hartz once suggested that our political theories are as much indicia of our common yearnings as they are illuminations into the actualities of our lives. The recurrent reiteration by many (especially officialdom) of the need for reverence for a sanctified law is eloquent testimony to their yearning for a national (and moral) community. It is at our peril, though, that we regard it as a reality.

There can never be more than momentary respite from the overarching concern about the ability of constitutional discourse to evoke shared social values or, as some contemporary philosophers might prefer to put it, "ways of life."[73] The Constitution, for better or worse, cannot remain in a transcendent aloofness "above" ordinary life, like modern British royalty; instead, those who speak in its name are viewed all too often as attempting to influence, regulate, or prohibit that ordinary life. The question of constitutional interpretation—and, more particularly, of the relationship between constitutional and moral norms—returns to haunt the social conversation. Those charged with interpreting the Constitution must always ask if that task can be separated from moral analysis. Those who must submit to "the Constitution" can always inquire if they are merely bending before power or are instead acknowledging norms worth respecting.

LEGAL INTEGRITY AND
THE BOUNDARIES OF CONSTITUTIONAL
INTERPRETATION: SLAVERY REVISITED

The world portrayed above is one of a deep moral pluralism (some might say amoralism) that makes a joinder of law and morality not only difficult but, more significantly, perhaps incomprehensible. Yet, as already indicated, the problem with reading morality out of law, or making the two entirely separate forms of analysis, is that one can no longer assume that law is worthy of respect. It might be, of course, but the very point is that the attribute is entirely contingent on the law passing whatever moral tests one subjects it to. Its mere status as law, though, no longer provides a sufficient condition for esteeming it. At the very least, a nonmoralized law is unworthy of faith.

There is yet another problem with this abstract analysis, one exposed most sharply when one descends from abstract discussion of the Constitution in general and instead engages in the *doing* of constitutional analysis, i.e., the putting forth of a constitutional interpretation designed to illuminate a disputed issue. H.L.A. Hart made a distinction many years ago between an "external" and an "internal" perspective of the law.[74] If we were social scientists studying an alien culture, we would obviously be viewing from the "outside," and it seems eminently sensible with such a perspective to use as a concept of law one that distinguishes between law and morals. But as we move to a perspective "inside" our own culture and, in particular, take some responsibility for defining that culture, including its legal element, the separation makes less and less sense. To adopt the same kind of detached perspective that is suitable to analysis of a "foreign" society would (by definition) be to alienate ourselves from our own. When Americans talk about American constitutional law, they are necessarily talking about themselves and, ultimately, what kind of persons they wish to be.

Ronald Dworkin captures this practical phenomenology of law very well in his recent work, *Law's Empire*. He presents a complex theory of legal interpretation whose full analysis is beyond the scope of this book, but its relevance to this chapter is captured in his discussion of what he terms law's "integrity." Among other important aspects of the law is that its practice has a point: "[I]t serves some interest or purpose or enforces some principle—in short, . . . it has some point—that can be stated independently of just describing the rules that make up the practice."[75] The point of American constitutional law in particular is presumably to attain the values summarized in the Preamble and otherwise found within the materials of the American political tradition.

How does one interpret the Constitution or resolve a delicate constitutional controversy? For Dworkin, the legal analyst faced with that task must embed a particular analysis within an overall interpretive narrative that binds the wide range of relevant legal materials into a story capable of gaining our respect. Someone trying to interpret a legal system must "impose *meaning* on the institution—to see it in its best light," and to resolve disputes accordingly.[76] Respect comes because the audience of the narrator recognizes the narrative as drawing on what is best within the range of its cultural possibilities. The Dworkinian narrative makes "a complex claim: that present practice can be organized by and justified in principles sufficiently attractive to provide an honorable future." To declare that something is "the law" is not merely to say that someone with power desires a particular outcome. Instead, "[w]hen a judge declares that a particular principle is instinct in law," he is making "an interpretive proposal: that the principle both fits and justifies some complex part of legal practice, that it provides an attractive way to see, in the structure of that practice, the consistency of principle integrity requires."[77] Dworkin's argument in many ways reduces to one of interpretive charity; i.e., in reading someone, whether friend or foe, one should interpret his or her remarks in a way that maximizes the ability to respect what is being said. There is an affinity between Dworkin's emphasis on the duty of the judge to provide "attractive" narratives and Sotirios Barber's insistence that the Constitution be interpreted "aspirationally," as containing "the best conception of the good society known to us for the time being," even as we recognize that those conceptions might change at some future point.[78]

At one level, it seems impossible to dispute Dworkin and Barber, for why would a constitutional analyst ever prefer a "less attractive" conception of the Constitution to a "more attractive" one? If we wish to respect the Constitution, then surely the most plausible operative rule of interpretation is something like, "Always adopt the interpretation that makes the Constitution most worthy of respect."

We have earlier seen how slavery provides a central interpretive dilemma for those who would moralize the Constitution. Recall, for example, Frederick Douglass's statement describing the Constitution as "a pro-slavery instrument" that he simply could not "swear to support" or, presumably, to respect. However, one can observe in Douglass's own thought the application of the maxim of charitable interpretation as a means of extricating oneself from what would otherwise be a terrible bind.

Douglass underwent a remarkable reversal of belief, as exemplified by a speech delivered in Glasgow, Scotland, on March 26, 1860, where he gave a spirited defense of the Constitution, which he now described as "anti-slavery."[79] Douglass "den[ied] that the Constitution guarantees the right to hold property in man."[80] The national government could therefore abolish slavery upon the election to office of such officials "as will use their powers for the abolition of slavery."[81] The crucial point, of course, is that the use of such power would be entirely congruent with fidelity to the Constitution.

Douglass's interpretive strategy is summarized in several "rules of interpretation" that he offered: 1) "[T]he language of the law must be construed strictly in favour of justice and liberty." 2) "Where a law is susceptible of two meanings, the one making it accomplish an innocent meaning, and the other making it accomplish a wicked purpose, we must in all cases adopt that which makes it accomplish an innocent purpose."[82] He went on to use these rules to establish his antislavery reading of the Constitution.[83]

In regard to the entrenchment of the slave trade until 1808, Douglass said that it is equally important that the Constitution clearly countenanced its abolition, at least after 1808; even more significant, according to Douglass, is the fact that most thinkers in 1787 "looked upon the slave trade as the life of slavery" and therefore presumed that its abolition would lead to "the certain death of slavery." Thus, "American statesmen, in providing for the abolition of the slave trade, thought they were providing for the abolition of slavery."[84] Article V, "if made to refer to the African slave trade at all, makes the Constitution anti-slavery rather than for slavery, for it says to the slave States, the price you will have to pay for coming into the American Union is, that the slave trade, which you would carry on indefinitely out of the Union, shall be put an end to in twenty years if you come into the Union. . . . [T]he intentions of the framers of the Constitution were good, not bad. . . ."[85]

One may or may not be entirely persuaded by Douglass's argument, but it is an excellent example of how the principle of charity operates. One cannot begin to engage in constitutional interpretation without having in mind a model of the point of the entire constitutional enterprise. That point of the American Constitution, if we are indeed to have any "faith" in its goodness, must be to achieve a political order worthy of respect, and there is a very heavy burden of proof on any analyst who would say that the Constitution *must* be interpreted in a way that brings it disrespect.

Identical arguments operate, of course, even if one declares that he or she is going to follow the "original intentions" of the constitutional authors, for everyone agrees that these intentions are never self-declaring; they themselves must be interpreted, and Douglass's "rules" seem more attractive than any competitors. Thus, when Robert Bork argues in behalf of "the proposition that the framers' intentions with respect to freedoms are the sole legitimate premise from which constitutional analysis may proceed,"[86] we are still left with the task of constructing a model "framer" whose stipulated intentions can breathe life into a disputed text. Why would we model a framer whose intentions do not include a commitment to the moral worthiness of the overall enterprise, of which the particular clause being interpreted is itself only a part and against which it must inevitably be analyzed?

This is the point captured so well in Ronald Dworkin's "parable"[87] introducing his well-known distinction between "concepts" and "conceptions." Dworkin speaks of a father telling his children that they should adopt as their guide for the treatment of others the *concept* of "fairness" or "respect." It may be that the father (sincerely) holds a *conception* of "fairness" that allows chattel slavery, but most of us believe that the children would be more faithful to their instructions if they ended up freeing the slaves, after developing a more sensitive understanding of what "fairness" and "respect" require of one, than if they woodenly adhered to the parental conception. According to Dworkin, the father might well be, indeed *should* be, treated as having said that he "meant the family to be guided by the *concept* of fairness, not by any specific *conception* of fairness I might have had in mind."[88]

This principle of interpretation, and the necessary joinder of law and morals that is entailed, seems clearest when one is discussing not the judges, but rather the ordinary officials who have made their promises to be guided by the Constitution. In determining what the Constitution might "require" of them, they must surely resolve to decide any of their own mental disputes in favor of the conception of the Constitution most worthy of respect, where respect is defined in terms of the values enunciated by the Preamble to the Constitution, with its insistence on the blessings of liberty and the promotion of justice. It is obviously irrelevant that a "framer" of the Constitution might have had a different understanding of what specifically was worthy of respect; what one can assume is that he wished to be himself a person worthy of respect. Different historical understandings, under this view, demonstrate the existence of different conceptions of what makes one worthy of respect, but not the repudiation by the earlier individual or culture of the basic norm of respect.

What, then, explains the fact that Dworkin's and Barber's ideas are extremely controversial within the legal community? The answer is that their opponents are fundamentally dubious of the existence of a shared moral reality, even if interpreted, as Dworkin would wish, only as a shared set of conventional narratives that set out the social meanings we ascribe to our lives. Instead, their critics would argue, echoing the motif of the earlier part of this chapter, we live in a radically pluralistic world. It is not only that beauty (or "attractiveness") lies in the eye of the beholder, for Dworkin (though not Barber) in substantial ways would agree, but also that there are simply too many beholders, each with his or her own idiosyncratic sense of beauty. There is thus a disinclination to accept the reality of the "we" or "us" whose existence underlies the modes of interpretation embraced by Dworkin and Barber.

Moreover, people obviously differ in the level of moral demands they are willing to place on themselves, even if in some sense they share a recognition of what morality in the abstract might require. Consider, for example, Max Weber's separation of "all systems of ethics" into "two main groups. There is the 'heroic' ethic, which imposes on men demands of principle to which they are generally not able to do justice, except at the high points of their lives, but which serve as signposts pointing the way for man's endless *striving*." In contrast, there is "the 'ethic of the mean,' which is content to accept man's everyday 'nature' as setting a maximum for the demands which can be made."[89] One might imagine the injunction to "help the needy." Only the "heroic" (or "saintly") take this as far as Mother Teresa has; most of us settle for a "meaner" ethic that can be satisfied at a far less significant level of sacrifice of conventional personal goals.[90] One way of reading Dworkin, Barber, and Perry is as adopting what might be termed a "heroic ethic" of constitutional interpretation, which would force the social order to transcend its ordinary, more "natural" inclinations, including the acceptance of "tolerable" levels of injustice that deviate from the aspirational norms of the Constitution.

One might accept an "heroic ethic" for oneself. Often at question, though, is the legitimacy of imposing this ethic on persons who much prefer an "ethic of the mean." The norms of self-respect under the two ethics can differ enormously. One difficulty with the maxim of respectful interpretation is that it may suggest that the audience for the interpretation is only the interpreter herself, presented as an isolated individual. Many contemporary analysts would argue that the interpretations we construct, even of communications directed to ourselves by name—e.g., love letters—can be understood only as the products of the interpretive communities within which we live and which, among other things, teach us how to read such a complex literary genre as a love letter. But one need not address such issues when discussing constitutional adjudication, for much of the time the interpretations are addressed to the community at large, to be accepted or rejected.

Moreover, the preceding sentence is potentially misleading insofar as it may describe constitutional adjudication as akin to a conversation, with the participants free to come to their own conclusions about the positions put forth. For a principal social reality of law is its coercive force, which comes from the fact that many legal interpretations are imperative rather than interrogative in form. And the persons speaking these imperatives are privileged to call on the police to back up their demands should any listener fail to catch the point. The disruptions that can be generated by an interpretation that takes the form of a legal decision are no more "conversations," at least in a standard sense, than a Maoist revolution is a tea party. Or, at least, they are not conversations from which one can gracefully exit.

As Justice Holmes emphasized, courts, and the law in whose name they profess to speak, ultimately incarnate not reason—or even civility—but the coercive power of the state. The ever-increasing "constitutionalization" of political life, touching on issues ranging from abortion to school busing to prison reform, has not only brought the judiciary into additional prominence as an important agent of governance, but has also generated many losers of legal disputes who are always prepared (and morally entitled) to ask for justifications. These losers—and many more detached onlookers—are often quite ready to believe that the reasons offered are but ill-disguised impositions of alien political values held by undisciplined judges. The need to submit constitutional adjudication to the response of the public audience returns us to the implications of the lack of a sufficiently shared sense of what is "fair" or "worthy of respect" that might allow recourse to the Constitution to resolve disputes rather than simply to redescribe them.

One must concede first that the constitutional text—especially those parts of the text that in fact serve as the source of most constitutional litigation—is genuinely debatable. Even if every disputant adopts Douglass's or any other charitable theory of interpretation, that is still no guarantee of general agreement. It is simply that we will disagree about what is "fair" or "worthy of respect." And a special difficulty is generated if we adopt our principle of charitable interpretation in regard to the acts of the legislators themselves, for then by definition we are led to assume their good faith in making genuine "judgment calls." At this point, the question presented is the legitimacy of a judge's repudiation of the decision in the name of the Constitution.

ROBERT BORK AS CONSTITUTIONAL INTERPRETER

Many of the most bitter controversies about constitutional law involve the relative interpretive authority of "first-order" decisionmakers—especially legislators—and "second-order" reviewers—especially judges. The distinction between first-order and second-order decisionmaking is at the heart of Robert Bork's analysis. Bork, though rejected by the Senate upon being nominated for the Supreme Court by President Reagan, remains one of the most prominent conservative critics of a variety of constitutional decisions (and methods of decisionmaking) identified with the Warren Court. He sees members of that Court as having been far too willing to confuse their preferred moral visions with the demands of the Constitution and to impose the former in the name of the latter.

Bork does not deny the intimate connection between law and morals at the first-order stage. He quotes Richard John Neuhaus in behalf of the proposition that law "is a human enterprise in response to human behavior [which] is stubbornly entangled with beliefs about right and wrong." Law is therefore necessarily a "moral enterprise." But, says Bork, only the initial decisionmaker, whether the constitutional framer or the legislator, is entitled to decide what moral content the law requires. The role of the judge becomes the enforcement of the views of the framers or legislators. "The sole task of the [judge]—and it is a task quite large enough for anyone's wisdom, skill, and virtue— is to translate the framer's or the legislator's morality into a rule to cover unforeseen circumstances. That abstinence from giving his own desires free play, that continuing and self-conscious renunciation of power, that is the morality of the jurist."[91]

The obvious problem, though, is how one conceptualizes the "morality" that is supposed to be translated by the judge. Would Bork seriously argue that those committed to "morality" in the first place (and Bork makes no attempt to define morality or to indicate if it is anything other than a sheer preference or desire[92]) would prefer to be interpreted in a way that would make them the objects of scorn rather than respect? Indeed, it seems difficult to imagine anyone proferring such a rule of interpretation for her own writing.

Now obviously one might be fearful of an over-readiness of reviewers to substitute their "moralities" for one's own, and one might therefore emphasize to them the necessity of following one's "exact instructions," without deviation. But this injunction, however understandable as an effort to preserve one's autonomy as against the reading (and interpreting) audience, ultimately makes little sense. The problem is that what counts as the "exact instruction" can be delineated only in light of some complex theory of the writer, including a constructed image of her moral life. Consider, for example, a mother writing a note to a neighbor who regularly takes care of her son. Little Johnny has begun to return late, and the mother writes as follows:

> It is very important to me that Johnny return home precisely at 5:00 from now on. He simply *cannot* stay at your house even one second beyond 5:00, however much he enjoys it. Therefore, I am ordering you to shoo him out the door no later than 5:00 from now on, and *under no circumstances* are you to violate my order. (And, of course, he can't leave a minute earlier than 4:55, since I don't want him to get home before I arrive at 5:00.)

It turns out that a tornado[93] begins its trip through the town in question, beginning its turn up Johnny's street about 4:55 and continuing to display its might at 5:00. Presumably no one would regard the neighbor as behaving *wrongly*—"immorally"—in keeping Johnny past 5:00. But that is not the interesting question, at least in the context of this chapter. Rather, we must ask, did the neighbor violate her instructions? That is, did the neighbor violate the law—the mother's instructions—in the name of morality, or can we read the neighbor as both morally admirable *and* law-abiding?

To say that the neighbor violated her instructions requires a belief that the mother is in fact not devoted to her son's welfare and places a weight on the rhetorical use of "cannot" and "under no circumstances" that is simply unsustainable. It is implausible (though not logically impossible) to read the note as requiring Johnny's departure in the hypothetical case. Should we wish to invoke the intentions of the mother, we would simply say that we are assuming that she would have intended the outcome had it been brought to her attention. To interpret the instructions "literally" (the better term would be "artlessly" or "thoughtlessly," inasmuch as the very notion of "literal" interpretation makes no sense if it suggests that one can interpret a word or term independent of the context within which it is used) would in fact be exceedingly counterproductive to the interests imputed to the original decisionmaker. At the very least, we would place an enormous burden of proof, which in practice could never be overcome, on anyone who argued that the mother had been disobeyed.

Indeed, for better or worse, something similar to the process outlined in the previous paragraph has become a staple of contemporary constitutional theory. For example, the Contract Clause of the Constitution states that "No State shall . . . pass any . . . Law impairing the Obligation of Contracts."[94] Yet "it is well-settled that the prohibi-

tion against impairing the obligation of contracts is not to be read literally."[95] Indeed, this specific repudiation of literalism goes back to
one of the seminal cases underlying the contemporary welfare state,
Home Building & Loan Association v. *Blaisdell*,[96] where the state of
Minnesota had imposed a so-called "moratorium" on the duty to make
mortgage payments under the terms of existing contracts. Chief Justice Hughes, viewing the legislation as a "reasonable means to safe-
guard the economic structure upon which the good of all depends,"[97]
wrote for a five-justice majority to sustain the Depression-era statute.
Hughes rejected "the perversion of the clause through its use as an
instrument to throttle the capacity of the States to protect their fundamental interests.[98] More ominously, perhaps, the same "literalism"
has been rejected in regard to the First Amendment, which has a
linguistic structure identical to that of the Contract Clause when it
states that "Congress shall make no law . . . abridging the freedom of
speech. . . ." Although there is a heavy presumption against the legitimacy of any such law, the equally important point is that the presumption can be overridden if "compelling" governmental interests
are shown to be present.[99] Although Justice Black insisted that the
First Amendment was indeed an "absolute" preventing all abridg-
ment,[100] there are almost no analysts today who regard as conclusive
the Constitution's suggestion that "no law" could be legitimate if it
abridges speech.[101]

The histories of the Contract Clause and the First Amendment
should lead us to be skeptical of *any* purportedly "literal" mode of
constitutional interpretation, especially when we are most tempted to
cite the text as conclusively determining the answer to a legal issue.
Consider, for example, our present certainty that there is no practical
way to alleviate the patently unfair population imbalance manifested
in the equal Senate representation of Vermont and New York. Why is
there no way? The answer appears to lie in Article V, which concerns
constitutional amendments. It states that "no State, without its Consent, shall be deprived of its equal Suffrage in the Senate." The "obvious" meaning is that Vermont would therefore have to consent to its
own weakening, a truly unlikely event. The "obviousness" may be
deceptive, though. As both Mark Tushnet and Bruce Ackerman have
noted, the impact of this clause was scarcely treated as obvious in the
aftermath of the Civil War, when a number of southern states, which
in theory had never left the Union, were nonetheless deprived of
their representation in the Senate and "readmitted" into the Union

only upon ratification of the Fourteenth Amendment.[102] Dramatic events can put into question the meaning of any piece of allegedly firm text and reveal "latent" ambiguities and complexities that call for self-conscious decisions (as opposed to the unself-conscious decisions that we pretend are not decisions, or "interpretations," at all).

This well-justified retreat from "literalism" does not, however, translate into a license for decisionmakers, whether Congress, judges, or the neighbor in our example above, to do "whatever they think best" in any uncomplicated sense. To return to that example, we might well feel that it would be best for Johnny to stay until 5:30 in order to watch a particular educational television program, but nevertheless submit to the instructions in the belief that 1) reasonable people can differ about Johnny's interest; 2) his parents are given presumptive authority to declare what is in his interest; and 3) texts should be read in a manner compatible with conventional expectations. In this case, those expectations would almost undoubtedly take the form labeled "literal" unless an extraordinary event like the tornado (or the Great Depression of the 1930s) forced us to confront all of the assumptions underlying such an apparently effortless reading.

Judge Bork might suggest that my example is misleading in the following way: What if we concluded that the parent is "in fact" a child abuser, who would therefore be entirely likely to wish her child to be exposed to great risk and trauma? How could we deny that we would be violating *her* wishes if we kept Johnny safe at our home? Now we might in fact be legally privileged to ignore those perverse wishes because of a collective social determination, reflected in positive law, that parental rights, however extensive, are limited. But when we engage in constitutional interpretation, at least according to Judge Bork, there is no "trump" that can be invoked against the actual desires of the legal sovereign. If we determine that the sovereign, whether described as "framers," "the people," or whatever, had manifestly unjust desires (such as the protection of chattel slavery), that does not in the least affect the legal validity of the commands manifesting those desires or justify our describing our refusal to enforce them as anything other than a "violation" of our legal duty.

Judge Bork's argument (or at least the one I am imputing to him) has real force. One might respond that an immoral law simply cannot be treated as legally binding; that is, as traditional Catholic theorists phrased it, an "unjust law" is not "law" at all, for part of the "essence" of genuine law is that it be just. I am not comfortable with that response, for reasons ranging from the inability to define justice to the disutility of using a definition of "law" that would make it impossible to describe the "legal system" of highly unattractive countries like South Africa or Nazi Germany. What I would argue instead is that only rarely are we presented with sufficient evidence to justify interpreting someone else as committed to manifest injustice or even gross stupidity. Most often, the relevant language, both of law and life, speaks in more complicated ways.

Consider, for example, the wedding vow—the "constitution" of the marital community. In particular, we might note its promise by one spouse to the other that "care" will be given "in sickness." Assume that the best medical opinion at the time of the wedding held that the correct treatment for a given illness was bleeding by leeches. That is, had the husband fallen ill the very day after the wedding, the wife would have taken care to summon the doctor to bleed him. Medical opinion obviously changes over time, and I assume that no one, including Judge Bork, would count it a violation of the wedding vow for the spouse at a much later time to reject the now-discredited theory of bleeding in favor of newfangled theories. Some of these theories may have been completely unknown at the time of the wedding; others may have been known but dismissed as crazy. All of that would be irrelevant. One must give the best care *as determined by the thought of the time at which one is seeking care.* If we would recognize as foolish (if not worse) a person bound by the medical understandings of the past, we have cause to wonder if it is any more sensible to feel bound by the specific moral, social, or political understandings of the past.

Bork is clearly correct in suggesting that reviewing judges should be chary of displacing the moral claims of others with their own. That is itself a "disrespectful" act, for it assumes either that the initial decisionmakers are not committed to being moral beings or that, whatever their good intentions, they were simply incapable of grasping the requirements of moral decisionmaking in a way open to the judge. Still, chariness and respect for the autonomy of others do not themselves dictate solutions to problems of constitutional interpretation, as Bork sometimes seems to suggest. We are still faced with the inescapable task of constructing interpretations of those others and deciding, along the way, how drastic their "otherness" is in terms of a shared common culture (or membership in an "interpretive community").

There is some reason to believe that Judge Bork could happily concede the point of the wedding vow example, for it concerns merely the elaboration of a value already manifestly present in the notion of marriage. However, what if a spouse claimed that the "true understanding" of marriage involved the addition of a new value to those covered by the vows? Imagine, for example, that the spouse claimed that the value of "personal growth" was implicit in marriage and that failure by one spouse to tolerate activities conducive to such "growth" constituted a violation of this understanding, even though no such promise was specifically given or written down. Would we accept the response that the absence of such specificity defeated the claim?

It is the introduction of such allegedly new values, such as the right to privacy, that Judge Bork has most vehemently criticized, rather than the sometimes surprising elaboration of values that are undoubtedly part of the written text, such as freedom of speech.[103] Ironically, given his purported devotion to the text and the intentions of its authors, Bork pays astonishingly little attention to those parts of the text that seem to invite the interpreter to engage in the kind of moral reflection suggested by the ethic of respect. The Ninth Amendment, for example, however "forgotten"[104] it may be by many, specifies that "[t]he enumeration in the Constitution, of [only] certain rights, shall not be construed to deny or disparage others retained by the people." Similarly, the Fourteenth Amendment prohibits any state from passing a law "which shall abridge the privileges or immunities of citizens of the United States," and there is good reason to believe that the framers of the Amendment believed that they were referring to certain notions of fundamental rights, some written as in the Bill of Rights, others unwritten, that would be enforced by the judiciary against state deprivation.[105] To be sure, one can well debate how one decides what "retained though unenumerated" rights might be. It is, nonetheless, unfaithful to the description of the framers' own conceptions of their task to assume that they believed that the written text of the Constitution contains an exhaustive listing of rights protected against governmental control.

Though the Amendment is scarcely transparent in meaning, there is overwhelming evidence that it was designed to assure that the protection of specific rights in the first eight amendments of the Bill of Rights would not become a warrant for asserting that they exhausted the set of rights protected against governmental interference. James Madison, in introducing the proposed Bill of Rights to the first Congress, took note of some very powerful objections that had been raised against the notion. "[B]y enumerating particular exceptions to the grant of power, it would disparage those rights which were not placed in that enumeration; and it might follow, by implication, that those rights which were not singled out, were intended to be assigned into the hands of the General Government, and were consequently insecure."[106] The Ninth Amendment would serve to dispel such objections. Bork, like Justice Black before him, reveals a kind of hyperprotestantism by choosing to ignore a piece of text (and the apparent intention of its proponents) that points to the unwritten Constitution that accompanied the written document out of Philadelphia. Instead, he does precisely what Madison feared: He "disparages" unenumerated rights and scoffs at the idea that they are constitutionally protected, albeit unwritten.[107]

Embracing the possibility of unenumerated rights suggested by the texts mentioned above would scarcely provide us with unequivocal solutions to the practical problems that divide the polity. *Nothing* "dictates" unique solutions to constitutional dilemmas. (They would hardly be dilemmas if the culture were committed to a unique solution.) Solutions are always fabricated or improvised in regard to concrete dilemmas; but whatever model of decisionmaking we use, whether as primary decisionmaker or reviewer, will require us to link law and morality together in ways seemingly denied by the most artless reading of legal positivism.

CONCLUSION: AGAINST IDOLATRY

All this having been said, are the endings to all constitutional tales happy ones, and is the Constitution therefore *necessarily* worthy of respect, even from the interpreter who conscientiously follows the rule of charity in interpretation? The answer, alas, is no, unless one adopts the nominalist proposition that the Constitution is itself the *source* of all criteria of respect. In that case, as noted at the outset, the Constitution's "worthiness of respect" is tautological and trivial.

Anything can be interpreted charitably, including *Mein Kampf*, but this does not guarantee that one will in fact find plausible a reading worthy of respect. Indeed, one's anger at the text or practice being interpreted may be all the greater if the interpreter has genuinely "leaned over backward" to give it a "respectful" reading and has nonetheless concluded that the enterprise remains worthy of contempt rather than of respect. (There is obviously also a spectrum of intermediate positions.)

It is no coincidence that so much of this chapter has focused on slavery and its challenge regarding the respect one should give the Constitution. Even one committed to Douglass's reading of the Constitution would find it hard to argue seriously that Congress could have abolished the slave trade prior to 1808. A member of Congress who sought to pass such a law would have been behaving "unconscientiously," at least from the perspective of his oath to be constrained by the Constitution's limitations. Such a law, had it passed, would have been properly invalidated as "unconstitutional." There is no need to keep piling up examples. Suffice it to say that not even Ronald Dworkin insists that the Constitution can *always* be plausibly interpreted in an attractive manner, though he has devoted most of his formidable talent to show that more can be achieved than might first be thought. Still, so long as one rejects a complete identity between the requirements of one's morality and those of the Constitution, it remains ill-advised to give too much respect to the Constitution or to promote automatic respect by others.

Irving Kristol, whom we earlier saw describing the Constitution as one of the central trinity of the American civil religion, argues that "[a] 'covenant' is meaningless unless it is based on [or, as I would prefer to put it, inextricably linked to] moral truths which, if not undisputable in the abstract, are not widely disputed in practice."[108] Anyone who accepts Kristol's condition precedent for our covenantal Constitution's "meaningfulness" can hardly be optimistic about its ability to sustain the polity. Nor, more importantly, can constitutional faith be regarded as anything other than idolatrous if it leads its adherents to suspend their independent evaluation of the tenets of the faith.

One of the central tensions in Western culture, at least since the Enlightenment, concerns the linkage between religious faith and morality. Some persons view the two as synonymous: Either religion is the source of morality or, slightly more modestly, religious faith provides the character structure necessary to recognize what morality requires. Those persons influenced by the Enlightenment, however, are likely to believe that, at best, there is no connection whatever between religious faith and morality or, more ominously, that faith is an enemy of the rationality necessary to perceive what morality requires.

"Constitutional faith" replicates this tension. Some believe that the
Constitution is the source of the civil morality that constitutes us as
an (admirable) nation; others focus more on an ineradicable potential
for tension between constitutional and moral norms. As suggested by
the discussion of Justice Brennan at the outset of this chapter, public
officials—and sometimes the more general citizenry—are often asked
to swear specific fealty to the Constitution or otherwise to manifest
their unequivocal "attachment" to "constitutional values." The problematic character of any such demands is the focus of the next two
chapters.

LOYALTY OATHS:

THE CREEDAL AFFIRMATIONS

OF CONSTITUTIONAL FAITH

INTRODUCTION: THE CONSTITUTION
OF "FAITH COMMUNITIES"

I AM SUGGESTING in this book that important aspects of our constitutional tradition can be illuminated by taking seriously the analogies suggested by treating the Constitution as a central feature of American "civil religion." Previous chapters have examined central problems involved in identifying (or having respect for) the source of doctrinal guidance within a given faith community. These next two chapters deal with a quite different problem, identifying *who* is within the community. One task presented any analyst of religion is to define the members of the relevant religious communities. One thinks immediately of two central determinants of membership. The first is birth, where one is described as "born into" a particular community. The second emphasizes the willingness of a person to "join" the community by engaging in a "confession" of belief in certain propositions shared by members of the "faith community."

An example of a community using the first determinant, historically, has been Judaism. The formal testing of one's faith commitments has not been a major aspect of that faith, though the religious liturgy certainly contains aspects similar to propositional creeds.[1] Many Jews do not in fact attend services, in part because of their inability to affirm these creeds. However, they do not lose their identity as Jews, for the tenets of Judaism define being a Jew essentially as an ontological status rather than the free choice of the individual in question. Membership in the community for most Jews is a function of biology, i.e., being born of a Jewish mother. No Jew is asked to indicate his or her adherence to a list of theological propositions; there is no analogue to the Apostles' Creed within Judaism. In this sense, Judaism is an example of a "descent-based" community,[2] save for what have been, historically, the relatively few converts to Judaism. Conversion to Judaism raises a number of fascinating problems, though even there one finds almost no emphasis on the propositional content of Judaism; far more important is the expressed willingness of the convert to take on the behavioral duties attached to Judaism, the performance of the commandments.[3]

The reference above to the Apostles' Creed points to the creedal (and intentional) nature of the dominant religion within the Western tradition. In many branches of the Christian religious community, membership requires public commitment to a particular creed, a particular church's propositional "understanding of the meaning of Scripture."[4] Many Protestant denominations in particular have registered suspicion of infant baptism and have emphasized "adult baptism" as a means of ensuring that the commitment being symbolized is truly volitional.

OATHS AND THE CONSTITUTION

Whether because of the Protestant background of colonial America or not, the framers of the Constitution took immense care to require oaths of allegiance as part of a sound framework of government. Although the Constitution is often praised for its relative spareness— John Marshall described it as consisting more of "great outlines" and "important objects" than as "an accurate detail of all the subdivisions of which its great powers will admit"[5]—it is striking that the authors of the 1787 document twice saw fit to write in requirements of oath-taking by governmental officials.

Article II requires the president of the United States to take an oath that states: "I solemnly swear (or affirm) that I will faithfully execute the Office of President of the United States, and will to the best of my Ability, preserve, protect and defend the Constitution of the United States." More significant politically is the requirement laid out in Article VI: "The Senators and Representatives before mentioned, and the Members of the several State Legislatures, and all executive and judicial Officers, both of the United States and of the several States, shall be bound by Oath or Affirmation to support this Constitution." This pledge of fealty to the new Constitution by state officials was correctly seen as one of the linchpins for creating a genuine nation, for it requires both recognition of and commitment to the supremacy of the United States Constitution over the suddenly "inferior" state constitutions.

Indeed, the Fourteenth Amendment, the most important formal addition to the Constitution since 1791 (the date of the Bill of Rights), includes, in one of its more obscure sections, a recognition of the importance of oaths. Thus Section 3 denies the right to serve as a political official of either the United States or any State to any person who had "previously taken an oath, as a member of Congress, or as an officer of the United States, or as a member of any State legislature, or as an executive or judicial officer of any State, to support the Constitution of the United States" and thereafter had "engaged in insurrection or rebellion against the same, or given aid or comfort to the enemies thereof." Note well that participation in the rebellion was not itself a disqualifying act; abrogation of the solemn oath was, at least unless "Congress[, by] a vote of two-thirds of each House, remove[d] such disability."

Section 3 is a dramatic example of the importance ascribed to the taking of the oath. Similarly, the formal oath had earlier played a crucial rhetorical role in John Marshall's seminal opinion in *Marbury* v. *Madison*, where he enunciated the rationale for judicial review of congressional statutes. He argued that the very existence of the Constitution presupposes that it "is to be considered, in court, as a paramount law." "Why otherwise," Marshall asked, "does it direct the judges to take an oath to support it?" For judges to enforce unconstitutional laws would be to have them become "knowing instruments, for violating what they swear to support!" Moreover, the First Congress deemed it necessary to supplement the constitutionally mandated oath with a second one, "completely demonstrative of the legislative opinion on this subject." Marshall quoted it, with suitably added emphasis: "I do solemnly swear that . . . I will faithfully and impartially discharge all the duties incumbent on me as ———, according to the best of my abilities and understandings, agreeably to *the constitution*, and laws of the United States." Then followed another question: "Why does a judge swear to discharge his duties agreeably to the constitution of the United States, if that constitution forms no rule for his government? If it is closed upon him, and cannot be inspected by him?" Marshall pronounced such a vision, whereby judges would be forced to enforce laws thought by them to be unconstitutional, as "worse than solemn mockery. To prescribe, or to take this oath, becomes equally a crime."[6]

Oaths are no small matters.[7] We saw in the preceding chapter the implication that the public oath of fidelity to the constitution takes precedence over all other loyalties, including faithfulness to one's "private" religious or moral precepts. Even this brief review should make clear at least two things: First, oaths were deemed important to the very establishment of new political institutions. Although the examples so far have focused on oaths extracted from those who would take positions of leadership, there are ample examples as well of oaths demanded from more ordinary citizens. No less a figure than John Locke had pronounced "[p]romises, covenants, and oaths" to be "the bonds of human society."[8] During the Revolutionary War, as we shall see below, oaths were widely used to identify and then separate patriots from those labeled by historians, perhaps ironically, as "loyalists." Indeed, as governor of Virginia during the war, Thomas Jefferson supported test oaths expressing commitment to the new political order, which a biographer summarizes as "a kind of naturalization oath [that] became the instrument of citizenship."[9]

It can be no surprise that the Philadelphia participants, influenced both by their wartime experience and in some measure by Lockean understandings of politics, found oaths worthy of specific mention in the document they drafted. James Madison wrote in 1792 regarding "charters of government" that, "[a]s trusts" to be executed by public officials, "none can be more sacred, because they are bound on the conscience by the religious sanctions of an oath."[10]

The constitutionally-mandated "test oath" of fidelity to itself suggests that the American community may be quite different from what Karl Barth, analyzing the European context, termed "the civil community," which "has no creed and no gospel."[11] To be sure, this is a creed and a gospel that are not "religious" in the sense of enunciating a "common awareness of [the community's] relationship to God," but a "creed" and a "gospel" the constitutional epic most surely is. Indeed, my first point here is that loyalty oaths serve as the equivalent of more traditional creedal affirmations that announce the speaker as a subscriber to the central tenets of a faith community. It will be the task of this chapter to examine the implications of this point.

Establishing that creedal affirmations are thought to be important does not mean that one has also identified with precision that which the affirmations are said to endorse. The second point raised here is that immediate controversy arose concerning what counted as compliance with the oath. This second point will be addressed in Chapter Four.

THE AMERICAN CREED

How do political communities form and maintain themselves? Perhaps the central answer to that question within the Anglo-American tradition of political theory involves some notion of a social contract, in which the transition from a prepolitical "state of nature" to a polity takes the form of the giving of mutual promises by the individuals who are constituting the new order. This image of voluntary oath-taking (or -giving) at some level captures what we might mean by a government predicated on the "consent" of the governed. After all, how better to test the presence of consent than by seeking evidence of an overt oath manifesting it?

Many of our most fundamental self-conceptions, and political theories, do indeed involve notions of "chosen identities" and "intentional communities." Werner Sollors, who views the tension "between *consent* and [the imposed identities of] *descent*[] as the central drama in American culture," describes "consent relations" as including "those of 'law' or 'marriage,' " and he goes on to note that "consent language stresses our abilities as mature free agents and 'architects of our fates' to choose our spouses, our destinies, and our political systems."[12] Choice in this case allows not only collaboration in common enterprises, but also the dissolution of bonds, whether by divorce, moving from one religion to another (or to no religion at all), or emigrating from one country to the voluntary embrace of another.[13] And Sollors well demonstrates the linkage in American writing between conceptualizations of "private" realms of love and marriage on the one hand, and the public realm of citizenship on the other: The "arranged marriage," by which one's spouse (almost invariably from one's own "ethnic group") is chosen by one's parents, is systematically rejected in favor of the consensual marriage (often to an ethnic "outsider") sparked by romantic attachment. "American allegiance, the very concept of citizenship developed in the revolutionary period, was—like love—based on consent, not on descent, which further blended the rhetoric of America with the language of love and the concept of romantic love with American identity."[14]

This emphasis on one's own ability to determine whether or not to become an American is one of the things that sets the United States apart from many other political cultures. "For most peoples," writes Samuel P. Huntington, "national identity is the product of a long process of historical evolution involving common ancestors, common experiences, common ethnic background, common language, common culture, and usually common language." It is the fate of the United States, however, to be different from "most peoples," for here national identity is based not on shared Proustian remembrances, but rather on the willed affirmation of what Huntington refers to as the "American creed," a set of overt political commitments that includes an emphasis on individual rights, majority rule, and a constitutional order limiting governmental power.[15]

Huntington's argument is very similar to one presented earlier by Whittle Johnson, who distinguished the American and European experiences by virtue of the fact that, in contrast to Europe, "America has placed relatively little emphasis throughout its history on ethnic bonds, state religion, or hierarchic class structure as a basis of cohesion." As a result, what Johnson calls the "positive uniqueness" of the American experience "is found in the centrality of the constitutional tradition." Although many other countries have constitutions, "the difference between the American constitutional tradition and that of, say, Britain or France, is of the utmost importance: in France or Britain constitutional history is an *aspect* of the history of the nation; in America, the history of the nation is a *consequence* of the Constitution." It is at this point that Johnson states what was quoted at the very outset of this book about the meaning of being American: "To be an American means to be a member of the 'covenanting community' in which the commitment to freedom under law, having transcended the 'natural' bonds of race, religion, and class, itself takes on transcendent importance."[16]

Huntington points to the "novelty" of the striving for independence by Americans in that it was not based on any claims of ethnic, linguistic, cultural, or religious differentiation from their British brethren. Instead, the language of assertion involved the "explicit political principles" of the Declaration of Independence, and Americans were defined substantially as those "who adhere to" the "truths" enunciated in the Declaration. Indeed, given the absence of a genuinely shared organic history, it is only this creed which Americans have in common.[17]

Both Huntington and Johnson therefore trace the origins of the United States to a "conscious political act," consisting of "the assertion of certain basic political principles" coupled with "adherence to constitutional agreements based on those principles." One can therefore speak "of a body of political ideas that constitutes 'Americanism' in a sense in which one can never speak of 'Britishism,' 'Frenchism,' 'Germanism,' or Japanesism.' Americanism in this sense is comparable to other ideologies or religions."[18]

Huntington quotes the historian Hans Kohn, who described the United States Constitution as "unlike any other: it represents the lifeblood of the American nation, its supreme symbol and manifestation. It is so intimately welded with the national existence itself that the two have become inseparable."[19] Huntington adds his own gloss by commenting that in the United States, to abrogate the Constitution is to abrogate the nation, for the act would "destroy the basis of community, eliminating the nation and, in effect, returning its members—in accordance with the theory on which that nation was rounded—back to a state of nature."[20] The United States is, from this perspective, a distinct "faith community," with the Constitution as perhaps its central sacred text.[21] And, as Gary Jacobsohn argues, constitutional interpretation becomes especially portentous: What in other countries might be treated as merely legal (or political-legal) analysis here becomes "the articulation, preservation, and perpetuation of the ideals and aspirations that define the national character."[22]

It is this emphasis on creedal orthodoxy that, ironically enough, has made possible the historically remarkable acceptance of immigration by a wide variety of ethnic groups into the United States. Consider the recent comment by Anne Norton: "Lacking that common ethnic history which purportedly bound Americans to one another, the immigrants could establish commonalty with the natives only on principle."[23] The "only" is necessarily double-edged; if it points to the limited nature of the American community, it also captures the move toward universalistic criteria and the almost unique openness to social strangers that are so much a (sometimes disputed) part of American history.

The Constitution sets out oaths of political office. But it is arguable that the most important office within a republic is that of citizen. The First Congress addressed the issue of naturalization—the process of accepting newcomers into the political community. One has the feeling of inevitability in seeing oaths play an important role in that process. A willingness by immigrants to endorse the principles of Americanism became the benchmark of citizenship; residence requirements have always taken second place to affirmation of shared principle. And, of course, the central affirmation demanded of those who would become American nationals was to the Constitution.

The United States, as a nation created almost entirely by immigrants (as signified by our modern assignment of the term "native Americans" to our beleaguered Indian population), has almost uniquely posed throughout its entire history the problem of chosen identity. A "double choosing" is involved: An immigrant's choice to adopt an "American" identity is coupled with that immigrant's need to be chosen by the United States itself as suitable to be a member of the political community. Michael Walzer has written in *Spheres of Justice* both that "the primary good that we distribute to one another is membership in some human community" and that the "distinctiveness of cultures and groups," a value that most of us support, "depends on closure." This means, among other things, that a "sovereign state" must be permitted to "take shape and claim the authority to make its own admissions policy, to control and sometimes restrain the flow of immigrants."[24] And Peter Schuck and Rogers Smith have recently argued that "republican" thinkers, much admired in some circles these days,[25] endorse the right of a political community to "refuse consent to the membership of those who would disrupt their necessary homogeneity."[26] A "community" truly open to all comers is almost a contradiction in terms, although it is clearly possible to endorse such an open-arms policy in behalf of values other than community.[27]

The ability of a community to choose, as well as to be chosen, itself generates profound tensions. The American creed suddenly takes on a potentially exclusionary character, even if its primary historical import has been to accept the inclusion of groups with quite different histories from that of the dominant population. Thus Garry Wills castigates Abraham Lincoln for reducing America to a set of propositional terms—even so noble a proposition that all men are created equal—that must presumably be endorsed by "true" Americans. Wills quotes

Lincoln as saying, "I am exceedingly anxious that this Union, the Constitution, and the liberties of the people shall be perpetuated in accordance with the original idea for which the struggle was made." Wills laconically comments that this assertion is "inoffensive to most Americans—which explains why things like the House Un-American Activities Committee were inoffensive for so long."[28] Indeed, Huntington also notes that one result of American creedalism has been a "pre-occupation with 'un-American' political ideas and behavior."[29]

The problem, as Wills sees it, is that "[i]f there is an American *idea*, then one must subscribe to it in order to be an American." It must be affirmed "on entry to the country" and proclaimed, even by native-born citizens, with sincere devotion. "Unless we know what our fellows *think*, we do not know whether they are American at all, much less whether they are *truly* American."[30] And how does one ascertain thought? One major answer is to exact from persons propositional utterances or promises indicative of their proper mental states. Examples of such exactions in the political realm are pledges of allegiance, loyalty oaths, or, indeed, oaths of office. Their central function is to test the presence of the required commitment to the national covenant, the Constitution, that has become the basis of membership in the national community.

We can now see a bit more clearly the mixed implications of the term "American creed," with its overtones of reference to more orthodox faith communities and their test oaths and affirmations. John Leith notes that within Christianity, "[t]he creed has the negative role of shutting the heretic out and setting the boundaries within which authentic Christian theology and life can take place."[31] And in an essay building on the tradition of social analysis going back at least as far as Emile Durkheim, Robert Post writes, "A community without boundaries is without shape or identity; if pursued with single-minded determination, tolerance is incompatible with the very possibility of a community." Preservation of "community" necessarily implies that "tolerance must at some point or another come to an end. Exactly where that point is depends a great deal on the importance one attaches to the viability of community and to the exercise of freedom of expression as a reflection of individual autonomy."[32] In any case, the limits of tolerance may be marked by oaths that both measure assent to the community's central propositions and put the oath-takers on notice of the boundaries beyond which they go only at peril of communal reproach.

Oaths are mixtures of pure form and substantive content. Their formal nature may remind us of the "contentless" seals formerly used to give legal validity to contracts.[33] Vows additionally signify a desire to be considered a member of a particular community and a willingness to remain within its boundaries. This chapter will focus on the American political community and its exaction of loyalty oaths attesting to a shared commitment to certain beliefs—usually involving the legitimacy of the state, its particular political structure, or its ideological aspirations. However, I will consider as well two other kinds of communities. One, the classical religious faith community, was already mentioned at the beginning of this chapter. The other community has been alluded to much more indirectly: It is the marriage, marked by wedding vows, by which (in our culture at least) two individuals join together in constituting a special kind of common enterprise.

Perhaps the most interesting and important aspect of these oaths is their role as signifiers of a transformed consciousness. The transformation signified is often a purportedly "new" (or, at least, substantially changed) identity on the part of those persons taking the vow. This signifying role is clearest in the wedding vow, but a transformation certainly can be present elsewhere, especially in political naturalization and religious conversion. For instance, the symbolism of religious conversion often includes "birth" or "rebirth"; after all, one is enjoined to "lose one's life in order to save it."[34] Also, it is surely no coincidence that one of the major events of the recently enacted national liturgy involving the restoration of the Statue of Liberty was a nationally televised oath-taking, which transformed recent immigrants into fellow citizens.

POLITICAL LOYALTY OATHS

Loyalty oaths have been part of American history from its (English) origins in the seventeenth century. The Puritan settlers of New England had agreed even before they left old England to prohibit settlement of those "not conformable to their government," and by 1634 local governments measured conformity in part by a citizen's willingness to take an oath of loyalty pledging "by the great and dreadful Name of the Everliving God" to be "true and faithfull" to the government of the commonwealth. This entailed, among other things, a commitment to "yield assistance and support thereunto," not to mention "submitting . . . to the wholesome Laws and Orders made and established by the same." Perhaps most interesting (or ominous) is the promise that the oath-taker "will not plot or practice any evil against [the government], or consent to any that shall do so; but will timely discover and reveal the same to lawfull authority now here established, for the speedy preventing thereof."[35] The very first item printed by the first printing press in the English-speaking colonies was this loyalty oath, in 1639.

The controversy about loyalty oaths, however, is as old as their use. Roger Williams is only the most famous early protestant against the Massachusetts Bay Colony oath; since then, the conflict between the proponents and opponents of oath-taking has never ceased. Part of the reason for the intensity of the debate has to do with the history of the United States as both a revolutionary and an ideological community. Many persons regarded the American Revolution as a distinctively ideological struggle between the friends of "liberty" or "republican virtue" and the corrupt forces of the English court.[36] There was nothing "natural" about the social character equipped to maintain a republican political order; the community had to actively monitor the individuals who comprised the social order and make sure that they did not succumb to decidedly unvirtuous temptations.

For obvious reasons, monitoring was especially important during the Revolution itself, when the fate of the fledgling country depended on the transformation of patriotic loyalties from England to the newly declared United States of America. [T]hroughout history," as H. W. R. Wade has written, "oaths have been used to secure revolutionary changes, such as the Reformation in the time of Henry VIII and the Revolution in the time of William III."[37] George Washington himself wrote in December 1775, "[I]t is high time a test act was prepared and every man called upon to declare himself; that we may distinguish friends from foes." He also advised each of the new states to "fix upon some oath or affirmation of allegiance, to be tendered to all the inhabitants without exception, and to outlaw those that refuse it."[38] The "father of our country" thus helped to spawn its first loyalty oaths, as both the Continental Congress and the states followed his advice. Harold Hyman, the ranking American historian of loyalty oaths, has pointed out that Washington was notably insistent on enforcing the congressionally mandated loyalty oath.[39]

I do not necessarily intend this as criticism of Washington (or of loyalty oaths). As already suggested, an altogether plausible implication of "consent of the governed" is the manifestation of actual consent through a loyalty oath. It would have been paradoxical indeed had a revolution based in part on consent proved indifferent to how that central attribute of a legitimate government would be ascertained.[40] And, to put it mildly, it has not proved easy for liberal theorists to derive more satisfactory theories of political obligation. Many candidates, including the Lockean chestnut of "tacit consent," are significantly less respectful of individual autonomy than is overt oath-taking.

Loyalty oaths have returned to the forefront of American political consciousness whenever the United States has been (or has been perceived as being) at war. Thus the great clash of 1861-65 provoked both the Union and the Confederacy to guarantee the loyalty of their citizens by requiring oaths.[41] In the modern period, the "Cold War" has generated demand for proofs of loyalty, and American politics of the late 1940s through the early 1960s featured regular struggles about the propriety of loyalty oaths.[42] Those who regard themselves as "liberal" in their political views, however, have criticized loyalty oaths. Many would argue that a liberal state has no business inquiring into the political views held by its members. As members of the polity, our obligation is not to affirm or otherwise hold certain beliefs, but rather only to behave in conformity with legal requirements.

A distinguishing feature of the modern period of our history is the frequency with which the struggles over loyalty oaths have taken legal form and led to pronouncements of the Supreme Court concerning their constitutionality. One of the great testaments in behalf of what I defined above as the "liberal" notion of a behaviorally oriented state can be found in *West Virginia State Board of Education* v. *Barnette*,[43] a case decided during World War II. A child who was a member of the Jehovah's Witnesses was punished for refusing to enact a peculiarly American form of the loyalty oath—the pledge of allegiance to the American flag at the beginning of the public school day, as required by state law. The Supreme Court reversed the child's suspension from the public school, with Justice Jackson writing one of the most quoted sentences in all constitutional law: "If there is any fixed star in our constitutional constellation, it is that no official, high or petty, can prescribe what shall be orthodox, in politics, nationalism, religion, or other matters of opinion or force citizens to confess by word or deed their faith therein. . . ."[44] Justice Frankfurter dissented, saying that the state could legitimately try to inculcate patriotism through a compulsory pledge of allegiance. *Barnette*'s "fixed star" is almost invariably cited whenever the state tries to require its employees to take loyalty oaths indicating their commitment to certain beliefs, including, for example, the impropriety of overthrowing the American government by force or violence. After a somewhat checkered pattern of case law, the Court has proved quite hostile to most loyalty oaths.[45]

The current doctrine of American constitutional law can be seen in the Supreme Court's review , in *Cole* v. *Richardson*, of the dismissal of a research sociologist by the Boston State Hospital because she refused to take the following oath required of all state employees:

> I do solemnly swear (or affirm) that I will uphold and defend the Constitution of the United States of America and the Constitution of the Commonwealth of Massachusetts and that I will oppose the overthrow of the government of the United States or of this Commonwealth by force, violence or by any illegal or unconstitutional method.[46]

Although Chief Justice Burger, writing for the majority, upheld the oath, he went out of his way to affirm several earlier decisions, extremely controversial less than a decade before, striking down a variety of oaths. Thus he stated that the state cannot condition employment "on an oath that one has not engaged, or will not engage" in such speech as "criticizing institutions of government; discussing political doctrine that approves the overthrow of certain forms of government; and supporting candidates for political office." Nor may employment be conditioned on oaths "denying past, or abjuring future, [constitutionally protected] associational activities" such as "membership in organizations having illegal purposes unless one [1] knows of the purpose and [2] shares a specific intent to promote the illegal purpose."[47]

Cole represents what might be termed a "minimalist" position in regard to the demands that the state can ask of its employees. And, of course, our state and federal governments have not required a general loyalty oath from the citizenry as such; it is primarily those seeking government employment (including membership in the armed forces) or joining licensed occupations like the bar who are forced to swear even the minimal oath.[48] Whatever the ideological emphasis on consent in the American polity, our allocation of citizenship has a heavily descent-oriented aspect derived from the Fourteenth Amendment, which makes birth within the territory of the United States a sufficient condition for citizenship and whatever benefits that status brings. It is not, for example, a prerequisite for voting that one swear even a *Cole* oath.

The United States *does*, however, look into propositional beliefs and requires a loyalty oath of nonemployees in at least one important instance—when a person wishes to join our polity. As a predicate condition for becoming a naturalized citizen, applicants must show themselves "attached to the principles of the Constitution of the United States and well disposed to the good order and happiness of the United States."[49] As David Weissbrodt writes, "The purpose behind this requirement is the admission to citizenship of only those persons who are in general accord with the basic principles of the community." Courts have identified these principles as including "belief in representative democracy, a commitment to the ideals embodied in the Bill of Rights, and a willingness to accept the basic social premise that change only be effected in an orderly manner."[50] Among other disqualifications for citizenship is voluntary adult membership in the Communist Party or any other totalitarian group, as well as the advocacy, irrespective of membership in any particular organization, of the overthrow of the United States government by unconstitutional means.[51]

One aspect of satisfying these predicate conditions is an oath-taking, as set out in the United States Immigration and Nationality Act. The Act requires a five-fold oath that must be taken "in open court" by the citizen-to-be:

(1) to support the Constitution of the United States;
(2) to renounce and abjure absolutely and entirely all allegiance and fidelity to any foreign prince, potentate, state, or sovereignty of whom or which the petitioner was before a subject or citizen;
(3) to support and defend the Constitution and the laws of the United States against all enemies, foreign and domestic;
(4) to bear true faith and allegiance to the same; and
(5)(A) to bear arms on behalf of the United States when required by the law, or
 (B) to perform noncombatant service in the Armed Forces of the United States when required by the law, or

(C) to perform work of national importance under civilian direction when required by the law.[52]

Whatever one might think of this particular set of commitments, what is most striking is that *only* naturalized citizens must make them in order to establish their status as citizens and to receive the benefits of that status. Kent Greenawalt, who recognizes the distinctive character of the naturalization oath, goes on to defend it by emphasizing that the grant of citizenship is a privilege rather than a right. "A country has no moral obligation to admit most permanent residents to citizenship." It is thus acceptable that the government choose "to extend citizenship only to those who agree to comply with its laws," even though no such promise is extracted from birthright citizens.[53] Given the modern view that the State can only minimally distinguish between citizens and resident aliens (or other "persons") in allocating burdens or benefits,[54] the principal benefit conferred only on citizens is the right to vote and thus choose those who govern. This distinction between citizens and noncitizens, it should be emphasized, is contingent rather than logically necessary. As Gerald Rosberg has pointed out, a number of states allowed resident aliens to vote throughout the nineteenth century.[55]

As a person born in the United States, however, I received *my* citizenship—and suffrage—"for free," as it were, without any requirement of an affirmative manifestation of community membership on my part other than formal registration to vote. I have taken several loyalty oaths, one when I became a member of the California Bar, others when I accepted employment at various universities, and yet another when I applied for a passport. Many other native-born citizens of the United States have also been forced to take such oaths, but more significant is the presence in our polity of literally millions of compatriots who have never had to swear fealty to the United States or its Constitution.

Thus the obvious question: Why is a naturalized citizen required to take an oath in order to vote while I am not? One can simply argue that this question is misleading: Naturalized citizens do not take an oath "in order to vote," but rather in order to become citizens, which renders them eligible to vote. And one might go on to point out that the Fourteenth Amendment assigns citizenship to every person "born . . . in the United States," so that an oath for native-borns is wholly superfluous.

The question, though, concerns the extent to which we ought to collapse the status of "citizen" into that of "voter." We certainly know that in fact citizenship does *not* entail a right to vote. The most important historical example in this country is certainly women, whose citizenship did not protect them from denial of the franchise until the ratification of the Nineteenth Amendment in 1920. And today we deny the right to vote to such citizens as children, convicted felons, and some of the mentally retarded. So even a textual explanation of why I become a *citizen* without having to subscribe to an oath cannot explain why I am entitled to participate in community decisionmaking by voting even if I am unwilling to make a public commitment to minimally shared values.

One might argue, of course, that merely by being born and raised in the United States, I absorb the central values of American culture in a way that people born and raised elsewhere do not. There is obviously some measure of truth to this, but there is just as easily a significant measure of exaggeration. At any rate, this is an empirical rather than a theoretical proposition. One might devise techniques for measuring "Americanness"—and its structural partners "non-Americanness" or even "un-Americanness"—and see what the actual results are when placed against a sample population.

The United States has always been more notably pluralistic than any other major world community. And the United States is becoming ever more genuinely pluralistic as immigration patterns shift from their traditional emphasis on Europe to Asia and Latin America.[56] "Americans" speak different languages and worship different gods. Hackneyed references to the "Judeo-Christian" tradition will not prove attractive to growing Islamic communities in Detroit or Brooklyn; opportunistic reference to the monotheistic "Judeo-Christian-Islamic" tradition will prove no more attractive to some of the religious communities with roots in the Far East. Even among native-born citizens, examples of pluralism abound. Among other things, parents can send their children to private schools imbuing values significantly antagonistic to those of the public schools. Certainly one can debate the extent of a genuine common political or cultural identity within the United States.

Might one rationally require that a loyalty oath identical to that asked of our new citizens be asked even of native-born persons, at least if they wish to participate in community decisionmaking through voting? Why should persons who refuse to adhere to central community tenets even conceive (or be allowed by others to conceive) of themselves as members of the community? If readers are offended by this suggestion, then they should ask themselves why it is legitimate to impose such a requirement on naturalized citizens. Why do we not open membership in the American polity to all persons simply on a first-come, first-accepted basis, save for any further exclusionary standards that would have to be rigorously "content-neutral" in regard to political beliefs?[57] This would allow the United States to exclude the sick or the indigent, but not the Communist or, for that matter, the South Afrikkaner refugee whose greatest delight would be the establishment of apartheid in North America. No longer could newspaper stories be written about immigration officials interrogating applicants for citizenship on their knowledge of, or commitment to, principles of "Americanism."[58] Why do we assign the right to vote on the basis of mere descent?

Genuinely to answer such a question involves coming to a decision about the nature of the community that is being entered. After all, one might conceptualize politics as simply the forum in which participants try to maximize their personal satisfactions, which are significantly "prepolitical" in their formation. From this perspective, no "transformation" occurs in the process of becoming a citizen. The polity is simply a convenience that makes it more likely that essentially disconnected individuals will be able to achieve their desires. This basically liberal conception of politics is devoid of any real notion of "community," and it is this, among other things, that has called forth communitarian critiques.

It is at this point that I want to juxtapose the most public of all communities—the polity—with what is usually regarded as the most private—the marriage. This contrast between the "public" and the "private" is itself problematic. As we have seen both in Chapter Two and earlier in this chapter, the republican notion of political membership involves the development of a socialized "self-understanding" that is significantly different from that of the isolated individual. Nor can one understand marriage as entirely private; the social form of marriage is profoundly public, whether one refers to the simple fact that a married couple is usually surrounded by an onlooking community of witnesses or to the legal regulation of marriage by the state. The central event of the standard wedding ceremony is, of course, the formal exchange of vows; indeed, the taking of such vows "constitutes" the marriage as a legal entity. Finally, it is hard to remove an aura of the sacred from marriage, even within secular culture. It is truly noted that many persons participate in the ceremonies of their churches or synagogues only upon their marriages or their deaths, and even thoroughly secular weddings usually are accompanied by a heightened consciousness appropriate to expressions of ultimate concerns. Can analysis of weddings help us to understand polities?

THE INTENTIONAL COMMUNITY OF MARRIAGE

Marriage provides an especially tricky problem in regard to the debate now taking place concerning liberal social and political theory. The liberal image of politics, with its theoretical emphasis on disconnected persons sharing only an abstract autonomy—and ability to make a binding promise, should they wish to—has not gone uncriticized. In particular, there is an increasing interest by many writers in varieties of "communitarianism," whose underlying notions involve critiques of the individualist premises behind classical liberalism. Much of the contemporary interest in community, as in the work of Michael Sandel, for example, focuses on notions of "encumbered" selves whose task it is, at least in part, to come to recognize—to discover—the communities within which they are already embedded.[59]

Perhaps the central symbol of such "encumbrance" is the family. One does not *choose* to be a member of one's family; one *is* a member, with whatever implications follow from that fact. Werner Sollors has recently emphasized that "descent" plays a crucial role in providing one's identity. "Descent relations are those defined by anthropologists as relations of 'substance' (by blood of nature)." In turn, the language of descent "emphasizes our positions as heirs, our hereditary qualities, liabilities, and entitlements." One implication of a focus on descent, on the preestablished nature of one's identity, is that institutions that operate by descent principles, such as families, do not often ask for overt promises manifesting a willingness to accept membership in the institution. For better or worse, membership has been thrust upon one by birth.[60] Indeed, to ask one's children to make overt profession of their devotion is a recipe for disaster, as unforgettably demonstrated by King Lear.

Sollors quotes the famous comment by Horace Kallen, a major early-twentieth-century theorist (and defender) of cultural pluralism: "Men can change their clothes, their politics, their wives, their religions, their philosophies, to a greater or lesser extent: they cannot change their grandfathers."[61] One sees these views reflected in one author's contemporary description of her ambivalence when observing the intense bond between her husband and their infant daughter: "I am sometimes sad at being displaced. Their tie is blood, and mine with Leon is based only on volition. Ours can be broken; theirs cannot."[62]

Yet the "family"—presented as a paradigm case of "descent" relationship—is obviously infused with its binary opposite of "consent" in at least one crucial aspect—the formation of a new family setting through the spousal bond. Recall that for Sollors the paradigm instance of a consent relationship was the marriage. And recall as well the metaphor invoked by Frances Wright about true Americans being those who "wed the principles of America's Declaration to their hearts and render the duties of American citizens practically in their lives." Marital imagery could not be effectively evoked if marriage were not a continuing social institution. That it surely is, but the constitution of marriage is nonetheless highly problematic, in ways that throw light on the meaning of the constitutional loyalty oath.

Even among intellectual circles thoroughly imbued with the skeptical ethos of late-twentieth-century modernism, one finds people getting married. Indeed, a particularly interesting phenomenon is the decision to "get married" that is made by irreligious couples who have lived together for some years. This may mean only that they make an appearance in front of a justice of the peace; often, though, oaths are ceremonially taken in front of friends and family. What do such couples believe they are doing? One answer, the obviousness of which should not mask its significance, is that they are announcing a transformation of status, from "single" (atomism) to "married."

At least within the major traditions of the West, the public taking of vows has long been a part of entering into marriage.[63] During the medieval and early-modern periods, the "betrothal" was more significant than the actual "wedding," and an agreement was the key to a successful betrothal. Although the church through this period was (successfully) attempting to play an increasingly significant role in the ceremonies of marriage, "the church's own courts recognized that, in the absence of church rites, the various forms of betrothal—spousals, handfasts, trothplights, contracts, represented a valid marriage." The required proof for a valid marriage was "that vows had been made voluntarily, in the present tense, or when in the future tense were followed by intercourse."[64]

"The seriousness of a commitment," notes an historian, "was measured by the degree of publicity that attended it. Promises made in private were regarded as having little worth as compared with those before witnesses." The vows spoken in the sixteenth century are recognizably similar to those probably taken by the married readers of this book. Thus John Brotherton in 1560 pledged to Alice Ince that "Here I take the, Alice Ince, to my wief, before all other women, so God me helpe. . . ." By the seventeenth century, one reads of a wedding in which the man and woman involved were commanded to confirm their intention "to have and to hold for better for worse, till death us do part."[65]

Obviously the vows that announce (or are a performative utterance establishing) one's "marriage" announce as well an *already* transformed consciousness, whereby one has accepted the potential of self-*re*definition in terms of this new two-person community. It would indeed be odd if this act were performed in "private," because almost by definition one is eager to affirm to the world this transformation of self.

An additional aspect of marriage vows is that they announce an unequivocal priority of commitment to the new spouse.[66] To "foresake all others" may or may not include sexual fidelity. However, it almost certainly must include the renunciation of overriding emotional loyalties to any other person besides one's spouse, at least so long as competing loyalties are not legitimated by being entirely descent-based, as would be the case, for example, with loyalties to one's parents or children. What presumably cannot be tolerated is the prospect of multiple *consent*-based loyalties.

In the case of both marriage and politics, the oaths are in obvious tension with social realities: Emigration and expatriation are real options for many, and divorce rates testify to the reality of similar options for the married. Some have even suggested that latter-day wedding vows take these new realities into account, though no one, I think, has suggested a plausible set of oaths. Does one pledge, for example, to love, honor, and protect "so long as nobody better comes along," or "so long as you fulfill my needs"?[67]

Moreover, in regard to wedding vows, one rarely reads an argument, often asserted with regard to political loyalty oaths, that it is fruitless to ask for overt promises because of their manifest ineffectiveness—or worse. Thus, Donald Herzog has written, "loyalty oaths generate not loyalty, but hypocrisy, resentment, and even secret illegal behavior . . . , even as pushing for religious conformity in early modern Europe multiplied religious opposition."[68] Presumably, anyone who intends to be loyal will be so without a specific promise, and those who are in fact disloyal will further demonstrate their perfidy by cheerfully lying about it and making promises that they have no intention of carrying out. Yet similar arguments could surely be made in regard to wedding vows. They undoubtedly generate measures of "hypocrisy [and] resentment," and they no doubt contribute in their own way to encouraging the "secret illegal behavior" of adultery. Nonetheless, as a social order we have tacitly agreed to accept these consequences because of the presumably greater goods generated by the availability of the wedding ceremony and the public exchange of vows.

The emphasis on vows indicates the extent to which marriage is similar to any other voluntary contract. But there is a distinguished tradition that criticizes this comparison in favor of other conceptualizations. Consider, for example, David Hartman's description of marriage as creating a "close and intimate" relation that, while not "abolish[ing] the individuality of either partner," nonetheless generates a "commitment to respond to the feelings and needs of the other . . . so strong that the other becomes a part of one's own self-definition." Although each partner remains "autonomous, . . . it is an autonomy in which the relationship framework is fundamental to one's self-understanding." Hartman uses the metaphor of marriage to try to evoke the covenantal relationship between persons and God, the central topic of his book, *The Living Covenant*; he counts on the ability of the reader to recognize a marital "fusion of relationship self-understanding and autonomy. The love of the covenantal community for God is such that its members do not act with an isolated consciousness. Their self-definition includes their relationship to God."[69]

Hartman captures with great beauty the difference between a genuinely deep relationship—including a covenantal one—and a mere contractual agreement. The latter is presumably often the product merely of self-interested reasoning; each party collaborates only because of an individual decision that egoistic interests will be better served by agreeing than by rejecting an offer. There is no notion at all that "an isolated consciousness" is overcome merely because two parties agree to a joint endeavor. Hartman is working within a distinguished tradition; it was Hegel, after all, who defined as "shameful" a marriage that "is degraded to the level of a contract for reciprocal use." The point, Hegel says, is to "transcend the standpoint of contract" as the marriage partners grasp their relationship in terms of "love, trust, and the common sharing of their entire existence."[70]

Classical American law views a contract as generating surprisingly little *obligation* to adhere to the agreement if one of the parties comes to a decision that a breach would be "efficient."[71] Someone who keeps a contract even where simply paying damages would have been cheaper is regarded with some perplexity, perhaps even ultimately labeled "irrational." The marriage relationship defined by Hartman and Hegel is obviously something different. If the other truly becomes part of one's own self-definition, then the language of egoistic individualism is no longer descriptively adequate. In harming the other (or not being concerned with achieving the good of the other), one is also in a significant sense harming oneself (or expressing insufficient concern about one's own well-being).

So we return to the existence (and meaning) of marriage in our modern world. Our ability to adopt ironic postures toward protestations of undying future love or commitment is a testament to our modernity. But our willingness to continue exchanging such vows—and to be moved at the wedding ceremonies we are privileged to attend— is a testament as well to our recognition of the possibility (and worth) of a transformed (and socialized) consciousness. The question this raises, within the context of the present chapter, is whether this acceptance of marriage vows is in some sense "generalizable" to politics. One might, after all, sanctify the wedding vow precisely because it speaks to a privileged realm of one's *private* life, whereas a political loyalty oath might be perceived more as the incursion of a threatening, external *public* order.

An "Intimate" Polity?

Perhaps the central question is whether one can imagine referring to one's fellow citizens in the same terms that Hartman evokes in relation both to one's spouse and to God. Should an invitation to enter a political community be similar to beseeching a newcomer to forgo an "isolated consciousness" and replace it with "a relationship that is close and intimate," whether the comparison is to a family or a covenantal faith community? Does one want to offer the polity as a candidate for a "relationship framework . . . fundamental to one's self-understanding"? Surely one of the powerful visions pervading much contemporary social thought is that of political community. Yet inevitable tensions exist between the notion of liberal freedom, with its historic emphasis on individuated, if not indeed "isolated,"[72] consciousness, and the claims of community. Among the traditional concerns of the "republican" tradition of community is the inculcation of a civil consciousness within the citizenry, so that commitment to the common good will prevail over merely selfish desire. Adopting a more explicitly Rousseauean vocabulary, one could talk of the process whereby "men" (and "women") become transformed into citizens.[73] It is not at all coincidental that Rousseau is also associated with the notion of "civil religion," whereby the state inculcates its authority in part through adopting techniques borrowed from sectarian religion.

It is clear that a single oath cannot transform an unwilling private person into a publicly committed citizen, any more than a genuine marriage is achieved simply by saying the words of the vows. For a republican sensibility, far more would be required by way of socialization. Yet, it seems hard to deny that ceremonial loyalty oaths could themselves play a part in generating the kind of social milieu that republicanism envisions. Emile Durkheim refers to the "collective sentiments and collective ideas which constitute [a society's] unity and personality." What he calls the "moral restoration" of a social order "can only be obtained through meetings, assemblies and congregations, where individuals, drawing close to one another, reaffirm together their common feelings." Indeed, Durkheim specifically compares Christians or Jews celebrating key events in their respective religions with "a meeting of citizens commemorating the institution of a new charter of morality or some great event of national life."[74] As we shall see in the concluding chapter of this book, one way of conceptualizing the Bicentennial is not only as a commemoration of a past event, but also as a call for renewed individual commitment to the maintenance (and perhaps restoration) of its presumed vision.

Of course, the transformation from personhood into citizenship is not at all inevitable. Indeed, it is this lack of inevitability that leads to the necessary focus of "republican" theorists on creating the conditions for the transformation of consciousness, whether these conditions lie in a particular relationship to the land (Jefferson) or the role of the state in generating, through proper education, what Benjamin

Rush called "republican machines." The absence of such conditions leads to the equal absence of genuine citizenship. Michael Walzer has suggested that most contemporary "citizens" of a country like the United States are more accurately described as psychological resident aliens than genuinely active participants (the *sine qua non* of most theories of citizenship) in the society.[75] One need not even condemn this passivity, but social and political theory must take account of such realities. More particularly, one must ask if a country consisting primarily of resident aliens can sustain itself as a community with ideals worth professing.

Liberalism more obviously contains the scaffolding to support a loyalty oath, given its emphasis on *consent* as the basis of political obligation. That notion, of course, has always proved theoretically recalcitrant. Active consent as an operative principle seems to doom the state to practical impotence; among other problems, no one who had not given such consent would be obligated to obey the laws of the state. Those persons within the political community clearly accord it great legitimacy—after all, they made an affirmative decision to enter it; but the state is usually interested in imposing notions of obligation upon everyone, not only the active consenters. Thus is derived the Lockean solution of "tacit" consent, though this ultimately removes what is most attractive about active consent. One might have maximum obligation, but only at the cost of minimizing the strength of a legitimacy based on the (active) consent of the governed.[76]

One way to handle the problem of consent—and to remain faithful to one of the best aspects of the liberal heritage—is through a loyalty oath. That presumably is one of the reasons for the requirement that new citizens take such an oath. Native-born citizens (like myself) are presumably viewed as manifesting tacit consent, but no such assumptions are made about naturalized citizens, even if they have lived in the United States for many years as resident aliens. Moreover, naturalized Americans, at least, cannot be radical "protestants" in defining what "Americanism" means to them, as those of us who are native-born "Americans" presumably can. *We* are free to regard the Constitution as an abomination and even support its violent replacement by a more agreeable substitute; naturalized citizens, however, are formally bound to swear that their new self-definition of being "American" will include *at least* the propositions laid out in their oath, and these propositions refer not simply to something that might be called generalized "national" loyalty, but also to the specific creedal affirmations laid out in the Constitution.[77]

THE SPECTRE OF
MULTIPLE COMMUNITY MEMBERSHIPS

Thus far this chapter has examined three notions of self-definition, and of actual and potential oaths announcing those definitions. I want to conclude by focusing upon perhaps the most important problem generated by the imposition of loyalty oaths—the requirement of exclusivity of attachment, whether to one polity, one spouse, or one God.[78] All of these oaths are attempts to fend off the feared development of dual loyalty, which, like *imperium in imperio* in eighteenth-century thought, is seen as close to a logical absurdity.

Dual loyalty as an issue cuts straight to the heart of both theory and practice. Consider Michael Walzer's comment that "a pluralist, at bottom, is a man with more than one commitment, who may at any time have to choose among his different obligations."[79] However much we may choose pluralism as the preferred path for ourselves, there is inevitably something disquieting about recognizing the same pluralistic openness in our fellows, for it may be their presumed obligations to ourselves that they choose to reject. Thus one can perceive loyalty oaths as a hedge against Walzerian contingency. Institutions and individuals, whether the state, one's spouse, or God, are, in sociologist Lewis Coser's term, "greedy,"[80] always seeking ways of making themselves the true center of attentions. Ideally, from their perspectives, the kind of pluralism described—indeed celebrated—by Walzer becomes impossible. Few devotees of pluralism in the abstract are willing to genuinely embrace the divided loyalty of a spouse, for example, and those who take the nation-state with the utmost seriousness often prove just as uncomprehending of the legitimacy of multiple attachments.

Recall that the new citizen is asked to "renounce and abjure absolutely and entirely all allegiance and fidelity to any foreign prince, potentate, state, or sovereignty of whom or which the petitioner was before a subject or citizen." We demand that naturalized citizens give priority to the new polity, although the notion of hyphenated citizenship recognizes the continuation of at least sentimental ties to the old culture as well. Such "abjuration" oaths are not universal, however.

James Kettner, in his magisterial study of theories of American citizenship, writes of state naturalization policy following the Revolution that, "[a]lthough applications for citizenship were expected to swear or affirm publicly their allegiance to the new states," only "[o]ccasionally [were] they required to disavow explicitly all foreign attachments."[81] The Constitution made naturalization a matter of national, rather than state, concern.[82]

The Naturalization Act of 1790, the first passed by Congress, required an affirmative oath of allegiance but did not demand renunciation of previous commitments.[83] The renunciation requirement arrived only in 1795, with the passage of a more comprehensive naturalization act. Some of the pressures for revision resulted from the dislocations in Europe touched off by the French Revolution and the consequent warfare on the continent. The United States, committed to splendid neutrality 3000 miles away, proved attractive to "disenchanted Englishmen, aristocratic Englishmen, German Pietists fleeing forced military service, French planters escaping from West Indian uprisings led by Toussaint l'Ouverture, and Irishmen in flight from British repression."[84] This in-migration of a "large number of refugees with passionate political beliefs"[85] led to heightened concern about the prerequisites for becoming a member of the American community. The amended act required not only explicit abjuration, but also renunciation of any title of nobility borne by the newcomer.[86] Both the abjuration and the renunciation have been a part of American law ever since.

Yet to this day not all countries require abjuration from their new citizens. The most important example in the contemporary world is almost certainly Israel. The ability to become an Israeli citizen without renouncing prior loyalties is precisely what allows retention of United States citizenship (and passports), as loss of that citizenship requires explicit renunciation rather than the mere act of becoming a citizen of another country. To this extent, then, American law tolerates dual nationality so long as the second political marriage follows, rather than precedes, the acquisition of United States citizenship.

One does not have to be religious in order to be skeptical of the workability of bigamy. Similar doubts can arise concerning the implications of dual nationality. If conflicts surface, it is hard to believe that the United States does not expect a resolution in favor of itself where basic issues of loyalty are concerned. Consider, for example, the fate of Tomoya Kawakita, a dual national of both Japan and the United

States who had lived in Japan during World War II and engaged in serious mistreatment of American prisoners of war. He was prosecuted and convicted of treason, a crime that can be committed *only* by a citizen; indeed, he received a death sentence. The Supreme Court, through Justice Douglas, upheld the conviction.[87]

Kawakita had been born in the United States in 1921; he therefore had birthright citizenship. He went to Japan in 1939, travelling on a U.S. passport. "To obtain it he took the customary oath of allegiance." Staying in Japan, Kawakita, after registering with the American consulate as an American citizen, entered Meiji University. "In April, 1941, he renewed his United States passport, once more taking the oath of allegiance to the United States."[88] Remaining in Japan throughout World War II, he accepted employment as an interpreter with a Japanese corporation that used American prisoners of war as factory workers. It was his conduct toward these workers that constituted the treasonable acts for which he was convicted.

Kawakita returned to the United States, on an American passport, in 1946. "He stated under oath that he was a United States citizen and had not done various acts amounting to expatriation."[89] It was only after his return, when he was recognized by a former prisoner of war, that he was arrested, tried, and ultimately convicted. His lawyers argued at trial that he had renounced his American citizenship and thus had no duty of allegiance to the United States.

The courts found no evidence that Kawakita had actively renounced his citizenship. However, the Supreme Court referred to "an administrative ruling of the State Department that a person with a dual citizenship who lives abroad in the other country claiming him as a national owes an allegiance to it which is paramount to the allegiance he owes the United States." This recognition of "paramount" status did not, however, prevent the Court from upholding the conviction—and the death sentence. It pointed out that Kawakita could have taken himself out of the reach of the treason laws by renouncing his citizenship in the United States. But having retained his citizenship, he also retained at least "a minimum of allegiance which he owes to the United States while he resides in the enemy country. . . . An American citizen owes allegiance to the United States wherever he may reside."[90]

I presume that Israeli citizens, however much they may hold on to United States, Canadian, or other passports, are in fact expected unequivocally to prefer the interests of Israel over those of the other country. A truly complete dual citizenship, which would have to mean equally genuine dual loyalty (or else what do we mean by "citizenship"?),[91] is no more an operative part of American ideology than is social (or legal) tolerance of bigamy. Yet current constitutional doctrine requires legal tolerance of dual citizenship,[92] even if not, at least not yet, of bigamous marriage.

But an equal promise of priority is included in the wedding vow. Not surprisingly, this conflict between the public and the private, the family and the state, itself generates exquisite problems in the law. For example, most states grant testimonial privileges against the forced (or perhaps even voluntary) testimony by one spouse against another, and all states protect confidential statements from even voluntary disclosure before a court.[93]

A classic tension in republican political theory, in fact, is that between the claims of chaste public life and those of the more sensual private realm. This is revealed by a telling piece of Americana, the debate at the time of the Revolutionary War over the official seal for the new country. John Adams suggested that the seal show Hercules, staring resolutely ahead at a mountain labeled "Virtue" while being enticed by a half-clothed woman labeled "Sloth," who would, according to Adams, be "wantonly reclining on the ground, displaying the charms both of her eloquence and person," luring travellers toward "her flowery paths of pleasure."[94] Those engaged in a specifically *republican* Revolution, with the Constitution to become its ultimate expression shortly more than a decade later, were obsessed with preserving a civil consciousness—republican virtue—that would itself maintain a constitutional republic. Maintenance of such virtue would require the stern subordination of the sensual and, in a deep sense, even of the family insofar as accepting its sovereignty permits the direction of energies (and loyalties) *away* from the life of the polity.

In his book detailing the relationship between art and the French Revolution, Jean Starobinski has a full chapter on "The Oath," which includes a marvelously illuminating analysis of a mid-1780s painting by the French artist Jacques-Louis David, "Oath of the Horatii."[95] As the three Horatii brothers pledge their lives to the fatherland, David depicts their father as gazing directly at the arms he is entrusting to them rather than at his sons, for he "holds victory dearer than the lives of his children. The sons," says Starobinski, "belong henceforward more to their oath than to themselves. The heroic impulse involves the leaving behind of tangible attachments and natural bonds for the sake of an idea." There is a group of women off to the right of the painting expressing "the helpless force of grief." Starobinski contrasts the "dramatic demonstration [of] firm masculinity, by which a man forgets himself in order to perform a mortal duty," to a more "sensitive femininity, which cannot face up to death and lets itself be overwhelmed by horror."

Within less than a decade, David would be moving from a depiction of classical oath-taking into a delineation of the 1789 Tennis Court Oath where the hitherto limited-in-power deputies of the Third Estate transformed themselves into a National Assembly and swore to give France a constitution. Indeed, Starobinski specifically notes that among the the "many oaths" central to the politics of 1789 was George Washington's April 30 presidential "oath of allegiance to the American Constitution."[96] And Garry Wills, in his own illuminating analysis of the iconography surrounding Washington, analyzes as well many of the same paintings as Starobinski while emphasizing that "[p]rivate emotion had always to wait on public duty while Washington was in office."[97]

It is not only the family, or the lure of sensual pleasure, that threatens necessary commitment to the polity. As already suggested in the previous chapter, religion itself also makes obvious claims of sovereignty as against other social institutions. The Protestant theologian Stanley Hauerwas has recently criticized an overemphasis on the formal freedom of religion in American thought by arguing that this freedom has in significant measure been purchased by a diminution of the willingness of believers to present "the Gospel as truth" and the concomitant weakening of "a Church that has a people capable of saying 'no to the state' " or, indeed, "capable of challenging the state."[98] This is obviously not a vision of religion that neatly divides the world into the nonantagonistic realms of God and Caesar or, even better (from the perspective of Caesar), exhibits a willingness to use religion as an undergirding of the legitimacy of the state.

It is the possibility of a potentially radical, antistatist religion that draws the fire of a conservative philosopher, Nicholas Capaldi, who apparently supports the toleration by the state of religious "subcultures" only if they do not challenge the legitimacy of the tolerating state. "There is nothing wrong," Capaldi says, "in helping to subsidize religious schools in general, especially given that such schools have produced model citizens. What is not acceptable is tolerating religious groups who refuse to recognize the moral and political sovereignty of the secular community by, for example, refusing to salute the flag."[99] There is obviously a fundamental gulf between the views of Hauerwas and Capaldi, a gulf expressed, among other ways, in the language of sovereignty and creedal affirmation. A staple of political theory following the development of the notion of political sovereignty by Bodin is that there cannot be two sovereigns within a polity. By definition sovereignty is an exclusive status. Yet the major Western religions all celebrate a God as an alternative sovereign to the claims of the State, however much the claims are dissipated by doctrines like the Talmudic injunction to follow the local law or by Christian doctrines about God and Caesar. Dissipation does not mean elimination, as revealed by the theology of Hauerwas or the behavior of the Jehovah's Witness children seemingly condemned by Capaldi.

All political states, then, face the problem of multiple loyalties of their citizenry; this is the price of a pluralist culture. Sometimes the competing loyalty is to other political entities; on other occasions, though, the competitors are other institutions within the society, whether family or religious community. Generally speaking, we do not treat these competitors equally. Thus we presumably find understandable—and endorse—the demand made by the United States that its new citizens repudiate their previous primary loyalties to other countries. Yet I am quite sure that most of us would condemn as totalitarian an explicit requirement by the United States (or any other country) that one affirm primary loyalty to *it* over the competing loyalties of family and religion. I believe that there is more of a problem here than the traditional learning allows.

CONCLUSION

Over 2500 years ago, the prophet Amos asked, "Will two walk together, / Except they have agreed?"[100] The particular context of his writing suggests that the "two" being discussed are God and the people of Israel. But the question haunts even a secular consciousness concerned with constructing social orders among human beings. To what extent can strangers walk together in everyday life unless they can count on one another to have agreed on a minimal common way of life or common morality, to have entered into what might portentously be called a common covenant based on those understandings? It is, after all, such understandings, whether or not predicated on myths of social contract or covenant, that help to define that elusive thing called "community."[101]

Concerns about loyalty can arise only in a pluralistic world of multiple communities. The handling of conflicts engendered by pluralism of communal attachment, especially when those communities are "intentional" in form, raises profound problems in both theory and practice, especially for those societies, like the United States, that classify themselves as "liberal." An essential question of our internal politics is what, if anything, constitutes the "common ground" of our social and political life. Is it sufficiently solid to allow us to walk together, or is it so divided by rifts and threatened by sinkholes as to make any journey precarious?

Robert Booth Fowler, reviewing Anthony Lukas's prize-winning study of three Boston families, *Common Ground*,[102] notes the profound paradox contained within the title. The ultimate commonality seems to be only uneasily (indeed, angrily and sometimes violently) shared territorial space; otherwise, according to Fowler, Lukas "reflects modern liberalism's fundamental skepticism about basic answers in life." The lack of a common ground of "basic philosophical or religious answers," however, is viewed as "a positive thing, a basis for the virtue of social pluralism and intellectual diversity." What, Fowler then asks, "is the 'common ground' this book is [ostensibly] about?" Beyond Lukas's own profoundly liberal ability to delineate with respect the radically discordant worlds of his subjects, "*Common Ground* finds and can offer us no common ground. It reflects modern liberalism at bay."[103]

No one can seriously doubt that genuinely stable common grounds are constructed out of years of everyday practices, just as a "marriage" is ultimately achieved in the relationship between the spouses. Yet, the achievement of marriage usually includes a constitutive oath, and it is not fanciful to believe that memory of the oath sometimes will encourage perseverance in the marriage at inevitable times of strain. Similarly, so do political entities recurrently turn to the loyalty oath as a means of achieving community by creating ties and bonds capable of withstanding the temptations posed by competitors. Starobinski has described "[t]he act of taking the oath [as] a physical moment of tension founding the future in the exaltation of a moment."[104] Perhaps we find it hard to recognize a political loyalty oath (or even the contemporary marriage vow) within his heightened language, though I continue to find it interesting that we adhere to the forms that come down from the ancient and indeed mythical past.

One of the central questions facing anyone contemplating the meaning of membership within the American political community is the extent to which that membership is indeed contingent on achieving the "wedding" of each citizen to one another through the bonding commitment to shared values as expressed in the central sacred text of our civil religion, the Constitution. It would be no surprise if many readers felt intense disquiet at the implication of the analogy between law and religion that is the foundation of this book. My intention is not so much to resolve this disquiet (for I feel it as well) as to delineate some of the problems presented if we try to develop a genuinely coherent approach to oaths, including those testing political loyalty. Much of the contemporary discussion is based on "local" controversies posed by particular oaths in particular times. It may be, of course, that only such particularities are worth discussing, but that conclusion in itself would have significant implications for how we approach moral and political issues, including those generated by the notion of community.

There is one other assumption that lies behind this chapter—that loyalty oaths matter because they have real content. That is, one is affirming something both comprehensible and significant when one agrees to be bound by the Constitution. Whether or not the values putatively contained within the Constitution are "eternal,"[105] there is the assumption that they are at least relatively stable and provide a vantage point by which one can assess the oathtakers' fidelity to their promises. This assumption itself needs to be more closely examined, and that is the task of the next chapter.

CHAPTER FOUR

CONSTITUTIONAL "ATTACH-
MENT": IDENTIFYING THE CON-
TENT OF ONE'S COMMITMENT

INTRODUCTION:
THE CONTESTED CONSTITUTION

 EVERYONE MIGHT, in the abstract, profess admiration for, even commitment to, the Constitution of the United States. That does not, however, begin to answer a crucial question: What precisely "is" the Constitution to which we are referring? More to the point, can we confidently ascertain when someone is violating the commitment to be bound by its requirements? (The "someone" could be either ourselves, conscientiously trying to comply with our own oath, or another person whom we suspect of breach of constitutional faith.) As the previous chapter noted, professions of constitutional loyalty were an important part of the document drafted in Philadelphia. The framers presumably believed that abstract declarations of loyalty to the Constitution would help to still at least some of the vigorous disputation they saw as threatening the survival of the young country.

We also saw in the previous chapter how Marshall relied on the oath to justify judicial review in *Marbury*. Many analysts have remarked that Marshall's argument proves too much. As Judge Gibson, one of the ablest of Marshall's critics, pointed out in an 1825 opinion harshly critical of judicial review,

> The oath to support the constitution is not peculiar to the judges, but is taken indiscriminately by every officer of the government and *is designed rather as a test of the political principles of the*

man, than to bind the officer[, including the judge,] in the discharge of his duty: otherwise, it were difficult to determine, what operation it is to have in the case of a recorder of deeds, for instance, who, in the execution of his office has nothing to do with the constitution.[1]

The implication of the judicial oath extends only to the judges' "official duty." Gibson argues that the terms of the oath "may be satisfied by restraining it to official duty in the exercise of the *ordinary* judicial powers. Thus, the Constitution may furnish a rule of construction, where a particular interpretation of a law would conflict with some constitutional principle; and such interpretation, where it may, is always to be avoided. "But," says Gibson, in an interesting reversal of Marshall's rhetoric, "the oath was more probably designed to secure the powers of each of the different branches from being usurped by any of the rest; for instance, to prevent the house of representatives from erecting itself into a court of judicature, or the supreme court from attempting to control the legislature. . . ." There is no duty incumbent upon the judge, therefore, "to stray from the path of his ordinary business, to search for violations of duty in the business of others. . . ."[2]

What of the argument that judges violate the oath "when they give effect to an unconstitutional law?" Gibson responds that, so long as the "law has been passed according to the forms established in the constitution[, t]he fallacy of the question is, in supposing that the judiciary adopts the acts of the legislature as its own. . . ." However, he argues, "the enactment of a law and interpretation of it are not concurrent acts, and as the judiciary is not required to concur in the enactment, neither is it in the breach of the constitution which may be the consequence of the enactment; the fault is imputable to the legislature, and on it the responsibility exclusively rests."[3]

Even Gibson, however, seems to acknowledge that the Constitution has some genuine meaning, even if the judiciary should resist the temptation to believe that compliance with the oath requires imposing *its* meaning upon a legislature. A conscientious legislator, for example, might well have an independent duty to measure suggested legislation against his or her thought-out conception of the Constitution and, albeit reluctantly, reject those bills which do not pass muster. Such a belief in conscientiousness, wherever found, rests on several assumptions, not the least being that the Constitution can be sufficiently "decoded" to provide firm guidance to the political officials who have solemnly agreed to obey it.

Practically speaking, though, few treat the Constitution as having an easily knowable, fixed identity. Perhaps the best proof of this point is that we do not in fact sanction political officials for many acts that are deemed by the judiciary to be "unconstitutional." Thus, when President Truman ordered the seizure of the steel mills during the Korean War, almost no one seriously suggested that he be impeached upon the determination, by a split Supreme Court, that the order was unconstitutional.[4] We tend to recognize that decisions about constitutional meaning are "judgment calls," and that good-faith differences are possible. To the extent that our operative political culture has, rightly or wrongly, granted a special status to courts in deciding between such differences, the key issue is transformed into the willingness of an official to obey the court. "Honest" mistakes, where "mistake" is basically defined as an inability to predict how a court would decide, are easily forgiven inasmuch as we all recognize the complexity of constitutional analysis and the "indeterminacy" of its application to the difficult problems facing political officials.[5]

Indeed, the Constitution can be said to be a model instance of what the philosopher W. B. Gallie has labeled an "essentially contested concept." As explained by William E. Connolly, an "essentially contested concept" arises "[w]hen the disagreement does not simply reflect different readings of evidence within a fully shared system of concepts." Instead, it is the meaning of the concept itself that quickly emerges as the focus of disagreement. More particularly, such contests occur when

1) the concept (in this case the Constitution and its adjectival form "constitutional") involves *appraisal* "in that the state of affairs it describes [i.e., to be constitutional] is a valued achievement";

2) the practices attendant to the concept (behaving constitutionally) are "*internally complex*" inasmuch as their "characterization involves reference to several dimensions"; and

3) the ostensibly "agreed and contested rules of application [constitutional interpretation] are relatively *open*, enabling parties to interpret even those shared rules differently as new and unforseen situations arise."[6]

When these conditions are joined, there will be "endless disputes about their proper uses on the part of their users."[7]

"Endless disput[ation]" itself generates multiple connotations, ranging from the comparative quiet of the seminar room to the much more ominous sounds of the battlefield. At the very least, Gallie's notion is useful in reminding us how unlikely it is that presumed agreement on the importance of abstract words will in fact still the disputes that required negotiation in the first place. The dream that the contest can be ended itself reflects a search for self-interpreting language and contact with an unmediated "reality" beyond the vagaries of perspective and interpretation.

We see such a dream reflected in a reading found in a Jewish prayer book: "And peace for all men will come to the world when all men pledge their supreme loyalty to the Holy One, the King of Kings. Then will the world be at one with itself."[8] This loyalty would presumably be manifested by universally common behavior in accordance with a universally understood language of divine desire (or command). What the dream does not, indeed probably cannot, recognize is that professions of even "supreme loyalty" to any one (or One) or to any text, whether the Scriptures or the Constitution, do not resolve disputes, but rather set the stage for them, even if they will now be conducted in a somewhat different language. And, ironically, the very fact that the disputants believe that they are joined by allegiance to a given concept may make the disputes more bitter than those between recognized antagonists. Betrayal of ostensibly shared visions almost always generates greater animosity than the opposition of forthrightly identified opponents.

What, then, constitutes "the Constitution" that is the subject of this book (and, more importantly, the object of our professed public veneration)? The previous chapter concerned the merits of loyalty oaths in general. It left unexamined an assumption of the debate about requiring such oaths—that they have some genuine content. Presumably one is being asked to make some knowable affirmation, and it is that asking which is so controversial. Here, however, the focus shifts to an examination of that assumption: What exactly is one affirming when pledging loyalty to the Constitution or announcing one's "constitutional faith"? Is it possible that the national covenant is without content, or at least is unspecifiable? This chapter includes an intensive examination of one particular case requiring what might be termed a "meta-analysis" of the Constitution. The subject matter of the case involves the meaning of the "attachment" to the Constitution required in order to become a naturalized citizen of the United States.

Schneiderman v. United States:
THE SETTING

William Schneiderman became a naturalized citizen of the United States in 1927. At the time, he was an active member of the Workers (Communist) Party of America and the Young Workers (Communist) League of America. Nonetheless, he claimed, when applying for citizenship, that he had "behaved as a person attached to the principles of the Constitution of the United States," a statutory prerequisite for becoming a citizen. Twelve years later, in 1939, the United States attempted to cancel Schneiderman's certificate of citizenship, on the grounds that it had been illegally procured. His Communist activity had, according to the government, manifested behavior inconsistent with his profession of attachment.

A federal district court in California ruled in favor of the government and therefore stripped Schneiderman of his citizenship; this decision was upheld by the court of Appeals for the Ninth Circuit. Schneiderman appealed to the Supreme Court, which heard the case in December 1942. Between 1939 and 1942, of course, relationships between the United States and the Soviet Union had undergone radical transformation, though the Court in the first paragraph of its decision insisted that "our relations with Russia . . . are immaterial to a decision of this case."[9]

The majority, writing through Justice Murphy, emphasized as the crucial circumstance of the case a procedural point: the government was attempting to set aside an award of citizenship "years after it was granted."[10] The majority conceded that its decision might have been different had the case involved someone who was engaging only in an initial application for citizenship rather than someone who had at one time been adjudged worthy of membership in the political community. Because of the circumstances, however, the majority placed a very high burden of proof on the government to demonstrate its assertion of Schneiderman's unworthiness; citizenship *could* be taken away, but only with "the clearest sort of justification and proof."[11] The dissenters took issue with this proffered distinction and the attendant placement of a strong burden upon the government, but that is not important to the concerns of this chapter. What *is* important is the remarkable debate that ensued between the majority and the dissenters concerning what counted as manifested attachment to the Constitution. There is no case quite like *Schneiderman* in the corpus of American constitutional law, for here the Court is necessarily pushed toward a level of analysis that calls into question the very identity of the Constitution that it is ostensibly interpreting. Indeed, J. Woodford Howard, the distinguished biographer of Justice Murphy, describes *Schneiderman* as "one of the decade's most ideologically divisive cases,"[12] as members of the Court, fueled by "unusual emotionalism,"[13] struggled with the difficult issues presented.

GOOD WORKS OR INNER FAITH AS INDICIA OF ATTACHMENT

Does "attachment" refer simply to manifested behavior or instead to an internal state of mind and mental dispositions? "On its face," said Justice Murphy, "the statutory criterion is not attachment to the Constitution, but *behavior* for a period of five years as a man attached to its principles. . . . Since the normal connotation of behavior is conduct," the majority finds "something to be said for the proposition" that the statute "created a purely objective qualification, limiting inquiry to an applicant's previous conduct."[14] It was therefore altogether relevant that Schneiderman's conduct before 1927 had "been law abiding in all respects."[15] Indeed, Justice Murphy points out in a footnote that Congress had later changed the requirement from one of behavior to a demonstration of an applicant's "good moral character, attached to the principles of the Constitution." Quoting an important representative's comment that the new Act involved substantive changes "with a view to preventing persons who have no real attachment to the United States from enjoying the high privilege of American nationality," Justice Murphy added that "[t]his remark suggests that the change from 'behaved as a man attached' to 'has been and still is a person attached' was a change in meaning."[16]

The relationship between observed behavior and inference of internal state of mind is, of course, complex. Justice Murphy seems to affirm that behavior congruent with legal command is evidence of a proper disposition, i.e. attachment to the law. By persons' works shall you know them, either because works are in fact the best evidence of inner commitment or because one cannot in fact delve beneath the surface of behavior into the "minds" of the persons being assessed.

Moreover, as pointed out in the consideration in the last chapter of the West Virginia flag-salute case, *West Virginia Board of Education* v. *Barnette*, there is a distinct part of our constitutional tradition that relies on behavior alone as the province of the (liberal) state. Indeed, *Barnette* was decided the same year as *Schneiderman*, and Justice Jackson wrote an opinion that is almost certainly the high-water mark of what I have termed liberal behaviorism—the emphasis on action alone to the exclusion of legitimate interest in the thought of the citizenry. His emphasis on our system's commitment to a "fixed star" of nonorthodoxy in politics was fresh in the minds of every member of the Court.

But "behaviorism" is scarcely an uncontroversial proposition, whether one is talking psychology or politics. What counts as a human action—that is, as the "behavior" that one is assessing—can present great difficulties. Indeed, the very description of the action, many contemporary theorists argue, requires an interpretation that includes the aims and purposes of the actor, so that it is simply mistaken to believe that "behavioral" description even makes sense when referring to human beings (as opposed, for example, to rocks). Consider how one would differentiate the "behavior" of a surgeon and a peculiarly skillful mutilator. A focus on externally observable hand movements of the knife would scarcely be adequate.[17]

From this perspective, "obedience to law" as a category of analysis must include some reference to the self-understanding of the being assessed. That is, did the conduct in question result from a genuine commitment to the law, so that one is truly "obeying" it or the community that the law is said to signify, or was the conduct entirely opportunistic and derived from a completely different moral universe than that of shared membership and commitment? Chief Justice Stone in conference had indicated that Schneiderman's nonviolation of law "ha[d] nothing to do with it." For him the crucial point was that Schneiderman was presumably one of "[t]hose who go in for force and violence" as a theoretical possibility.[18]

Consider, for example, Georg Lukács's description of "the total, communist fearlessness with regard to the state and the law": "[T]he law and its calculable consequences are of no greater (if also of no smaller) importance than any other external fact of life with which it is necessary to reckon when deciding upon any definite course of action." What is the proper attitude of fearless Communists trying to decide whether to obey the law? They should not regard the risk of disobedience "any differently than the risk of missing a train connection when on an important journey."[19] One might well throughout a lifetime always arrive at the station well before the scheduled departure of the train, but this would scarcely necessarily be described as "attachment" to the principles underlying the schedule. After all, a visitor from a foreign country known to be imbued with alien ideas— even a Communist (assuming he or she can get a visa)—may well be as "law-abiding" as a Daughter of the American Revolution, so long as we concentrate only on observed behavior. Most antiapartheid visitors to South Africa "obey" the laws of that hateful regime for sound prudential reasons; none would allow an imputation of "attachment" to follow from legally correct behavior. Schneiderman's own behavior could therefore have been entirely instrumental, or it could have bespoken "attachment" (though, or course, it might be extraordinarily difficult to tell the difference).

Nor are we at the end of our difficulties when we analyze what counts as genuine obedience to law (or "attachment" to the Constitution), for we are sometimes willing to honor certain individuals, deemed to have been properly motivated, even if their behavior appears to violate the law. What makes someone a "good American" (and it is profoundly important that this term is a rhetorically affirmative staple of our political rhetoric) is that his or her behavior is merely the visible sign of a more internal saving grace—justification by membership in an American faith community that legitimizes departures from the "letter of the law" that "killeth" in favor of the spirit that imbues the law with meaning and "life."[20] Indeed, in what becomes a central paradox in American constitutionalism, it is the presence of such grace that serves to legitimize works that might otherwise be interpreted as illegal and unconstitutional. Not only is "law-abiding" behavior not a *sufficient* condition to establish one as a "good American"; it may not even be a *necessary* condition.

Nowhere is this paradox more fully evident than in the very "founding" of the United States, whether one focuses on the Revolution itself or on the convention in Philadelphia that drafted the Constitution twelve years later. Lincoln, one of the most profound students of the American Revolution in our history, was fully aware of the special status of the founder of a republic. It was his destiny to re-enact that role and therefore to decide what in fact was the message that successor generations should draw from the example of the Founders. No question is more central to the American experience—or to the American civil religion.

Recall David Tracy's assertion that "Christianity considers the scriptures not the revelation itself but the original witness to the revelation." For the Christian community, therefore, "[i]t is the revelatory event and not the witnessing texts that must play the role in Christian self-understanding."[21] "A living covenant," to quote the title of David Hartman's important book in Jewish theology, constantly tries to give meaning to central events—in the case of Judaism, the Exodus from Egypt and whatever occurred at Mt. Sinai—rather than reduce the events to the discrete set of texts associated with them. According to Hartman, one relates to these events in significant part by taking responsibility for acting as God's partner in ongoing creation, an endless process of becoming rather than a submission to a frozen or ossified past.

Can one draw on this distinction between event and text in considering the civil theology of the Constitution? I believe so. The Constitution is intimately connected with the "Founding Fathers" in a variety of complicated ways. Some look to the intentions of these Founders in order to find out what the Constitutional text "means." At the same time, this approach tends to "deify" the Founders (the capitalization is deliberate and telling) and to suggest that their "revelation" to future generations consisted of the constitutional text alone. But the Founders were also highly political actors incarnating a complex vision of what it means to be a responsible statesman. At their best, they stand as symbols—and as models to be emulated—of aroused citizens willing to take risks in behalf of the admirable values outlined in the Preamble to the Constitution. To become Founders, though, they had, like the original Abraham, to be willing to smash idols and to reject traditional understandings. Genuinely to honor them may generate interesting tensions in regard to the specific text that they wrote in Philadelphia. To join in bearing witness to *their* constitutional faith—including their idol-smashing—may take us, just as it took Lincoln, in unexpected directions.

Consider, after all, the circumstances of the Philadelphia Convention itself. The United States was then operating under the Articles of Confederation, ratified in 1781. There was, however, little "veneration" of what was, in effect, our first national constitution. Many of the proponents of the Convention were convinced that there were serious problems with the Articles, and Congress agreed, at least to the extent of authorizing a convention for "the sole and express purpose of revising the Articles of Confederation."[22] Many commentators both at the time and thereafter have viewed Philadelphia as a "runaway" convention precisely because "revision" turned into renunciation and, indeed, "obliteration."* Thus Bruce Ackerman notes that "the Convention was perfectly aware that it had taken a step that many thoughtful citizens would find illegal."[23] Richard Kay expresses the matter even more strongly: "The foundation of American legality was itself the product of a blatant and conscious illegality."[24]

Indeed, those present-day theorists who view fidelity to either the alleged "plain meaning" of the Constitution or the intentions of the Founders as the central norm of constitutional faith are presented with the particular difficulty of explaining the undisputed deviation of the convention from Article XIII of the Articles, which required that any modification be by unanimous consent of the thirteen legislatures of the states then comprising the Union. Ackerman is undoubtedly correct when he states that the assertion in Article VII of the Philadelphia text "that nine state 'Conventions' could adequately ratify on behalf of the People was plainly an extra-legal assertion of democratic authority."[25]

The Founders were scarcely unaware of such charges, and several met them head-on. Thus Edmund Randolph, the Virginia governor who later became attorney general under President Washington, stated, "There are great seasons when persons with limited powers are justified in exceeding them, and a person would be contemptible not to risk it."[26] Even Randolph's colleague, James Madison, who defended the propriety of the convention, was reduced to arguing, in the Federalist no. 40, that the Philadelphia delegates "must have borne in mind, that as the plan to be framed and proposed, was to be

---

* "Obliteration" is intended as a reference to Nietzsche's comment in *The Genealogy of Morals* (trans. W. Kaufmann [New York: Vintage Books, 1967]) that "whatever exists . . . is again and again reinterpreted to new ends, taken over, transformed, and redirected by some power superior to it; all events in the organic world are a subduing, a *becoming master*." To become a "master" requires "a fresh interpretation, an adaptation through which any previous 'meaning' and 'purpose' are necessarily obscured or even obliterated" (p. 77; emphasis in original). It is no easy task to integrate a Nietzschean understanding of genealogies of interpretation within the standard rhetoric of constitutionalism, with the latter's emphasis on stability and presumed constraint of potentially "masterful" leaders.

submitted *to the people themselves* . . . its approbation [would blot] out all antecedent errors and irregularities."[27] It cannot be emphasized enough, though, that the "approbation" in question would extend not only to the "plan," but also to the people involved. Indeed, as Randolph implicitly suggested, the meaning of popular approval would be to turn those who had gone well beyond their limited assignment of power into heroes—the Founders whom we would venerate in equal measure with the text they presented. And, as he explicitly stated, many of those who opposed the convention and its product would be treated with "contempt" precisely because they did not share the visionary politics that ultimately legitimized Philadelphia.

John Locke, a major contributor to American constitutional theory, had himself emphasized the necessity to leave a measure of prerogative power in the ruler established by the social contract. The political ruler is licensed, under certain conditions, to act "against the direct Letter of the Law" provided only that the motivation is protection of the public good.[28] Thomas Jefferson could well have cited Locke when he justified the Louisiana Purchase even as he acknowledged that it exceeded the powers delegated to the president by the Constitution:

> A strict observance of the written law is doubtless *one* of the duties of a good citizen [including those citizens who become President] but it is not the *highest*. The laws of necessity, or self-preservation, of saving our country when in danger, are of higher obligation. To lose our country by a scrupulous adherence to written law, would be to lose the law itself, with life, liberty, property and all those who are enjoying them with us; thus absurdly sacrificing the end to the means.[29]

Locke was deficient in providing a mechanism by which the people could judge the exercise of prerogative power; indeed, he declared that "[b]etween the Executive Power in being, with such a Prerogative, and legislative that depends upon his will for their convening, there can be no *Judge on Earth*." Nor do the people have any "other remedy in this, as in all other cases when they have no Judge on Earth, but to *appeal to Heaven*," which in Locke's terminology is suggestive of revolution.[30] The American tradition is more complex.

The overall Philadelphia event provides a useful context in which to consider Abraham Lincoln's defense of his extremely controversial—and many would say unconstitutional—policy of military arrest and suspension of habeas corpus during the Civil War. Article I, Section 9 of the Constitution is most plausibly read as an assignment to Congress alone of the power to suspend habeas corpus. Presidential power is set out in Article II, which makes no mention of any power unilaterally to suspend habeas corpus. Said Lincoln:

> The constitution contemplates the question as likely to occur decision, but it does not expressly declare who is to decide it. By necessary implication, when Rebellion or Invasion comes, the decision is to be made, from time to time; and I think the man whom, for the time, the people have, under the constitution, made the commander-in chief, of their Army and Navy, is the man who holds the power, and bears the responsibility of making it. If he uses the power justly, the same people will probably justify him; he abuses it, he is in their hands, to be dealt with by all the modes they have reserved to themselves in the constitution.[31]

Note the crucial importance of the words "justly" and "justify" in the argument. To use power "justly" may require going beyond the limited power one has been assigned, as was arguably, and according to the central American narrative certainly, the case in Philadelphia. The sovereign people then "justify" the conduct by conferring their "approbation"—their "saving grace," so to speak—upon what might otherwise be deemed illegitimate conduct. That approval is not at all inevitable, obviously; the people can also confer damnation, as arguably happened with Richard Nixon, whose search for justification took a Lincolnian form, but without the Lincolnian conclusion.* Yet it is necessary to ask whether Nixon's offense was his disobedience to law, or his patent failure to persuade the public that his violations of law

---

* See the interview of Nixon by David Frost:

"Mr. Frost: 'So what in a sense you're saying is that there are certain situations . . . where the President can decide that it's in the best interests of the nation or something, and do something illegal.'

"Mr. Nixon: 'Well, when the President does it, that means that it is not illegal. . . . If the President, for example, approves something, approves an action because of the national security, or . . . because of a threat to internal peace and order, of significant magnitude, then the President's decision in that instance is one that enables those who carry it out to carry it out without violating a law. Otherwise they're in an impossible position.' "

("Transcript of Frost-Nixon Interview," *The New York Times*, May 20, 1977, p. A16, col. 5).

were truly required to protect "national security." Would his illegalities have seemed so important had we been persuaded that he, like Lincoln, was simply sacrificing the equivalent of one law for the sake of the national good? The point is that what counts as political sagacity and statecraft is the product of a complex dialectical encounter between leader and populace rather than any kind of "adherence" to constitutional text or, for that matter, set of pre-existing "intentions."

If one views Philadelphia as generating only a text, then the dialectical tension between fidelity to text and fidelity to the model of action bequeathed by the Founders makes no sense. The fact that it is perfectly sensible, though, suggests that "Philadelphia" is most certainly, and profoundly, an event in addition to a text, and that subsequent American history is shaped as much by deciding what it means to bear witness to the event as by any alleged explication of the text independent from that event. And, of course, "Philadelphia" itself gains meaning only from being placed within a narrative structure, itself of civil religious dimension, that tells a story of America that can ultimately generate approbation rather than contempt.

The discussion above has concerned great, albeit extremely controversial, acts of state. What about ordinary legal disobedience? Does *that* indicate a nonattachment to the principles of the Constitution? Some such theory may in fact underlie the removal of the franchise from convicted felons, who are viewed as having violated a condition precedent in regard to participation in the body politic. Whether or not we require a loyalty oath promising commitment to constitutional principles, as discussed in the preceding chapter, we might nonetheless expect at least fidelity to law from those who demand a role in making political decisions.

Indeed, the Supreme Court on one occasion quoted several decisions holding that violation of the Eighteenth Amendment establishing prohibition of alcohol manifested nonattachment. In *Costello* v. *United States* the Court upheld the denaturalization of Frank Costello, a longtime participant in organized crime, on the ground that he had lied when he listed his occupation as "realtor" in his naturalization application some 35 years earlier.[32] The Court went on, however, to engage in a wide-ranging discussion of the ability of a bootlegger, Costello's putative occupation at the time, to become a citizen. "In 1925 a known bootlegger would probably not have been admitted to citizenship."[33] One ground, of course, is that such conduct would negate the requirement that one demonstrate a "good moral character," as stated by the naturalization law.[34] But several courts linked violation of prohibition to attachment. According to the Court of Appeals for the District of Columbia, for example, "Any person who violates the provisions of the Prohibition Act violates the principles of the Constitution of the United States, and cannot be held to be attached to the principles of the Constitution of the United States."[35] This linkage between infidelity to law and nonattachment was upheld by another judge even as he recognized that "there are many citizens who are not attached in thought or deed to the principle embodied in the Constitution by the Eighteenth Amendment" and that "opposition to that principle with a view to removing it from the Constitution is quite generally thought to be part of good citizenship."[36] The *Schneiderman* Court could avoid confronting these previous cases because of the emphasis on Schneiderman's scrupulous fidelity to law, at least in its own behavioral account.

Justice Murphy, unsurprisingly, did not ruminate on these difficult questions in the philosophy of action and assessment of political activity. Instead, speaking for the majority, he simply placed upon the government "the heavy burden" or proving Schneiderman's "lack of attachment by 'clear, unequivocal, and convincing' evidence which does not leave the issue in doubt."[37] To meet its burden, the government made two claims. The first described Schneiderman's projected changes in the structure of American governance as so "sweeping . . . that he simply could not be attached to it." The second claim was independent of the substance of the changes desired by Schneiderman, for here the allegation was that "he believed in and advocated the overthrow of force and violence of the Government, Constitution and laws of the United States."[38]

A PROPOSITIONAL CONSTITUTION?

The government never denied that a person could consistently be attached to the Constitution even while believing "that the laws and the Constitution should be amended in some or many respects." It did, however, argue that "an alien must believe in and sincerely adhere to the 'general political philosophy' of the Constitution."[39] One might paraphrase Lincoln at this point by emphasizing the "propositions" to which America (and the Constitution) is dedicated and which members of the faith community can be expected to affirm. The Justice Department offered the following specifications of what might be termed constitutional propositionalism:

> The test is . . . whether [the applicant] substitutes revolution for evolution, destruction for construction, whether he believes in an ordered society, a government of laws, under which the powers of government are granted by the people but under a grant which itself preserves to the individual and to minorities certain rights or freedoms which even the majority may not take away; whether, in sum, the events which began at least no further back than the Declaration of Independence, followed by the Revolutionary War and the adoption of the Constitution, establish principles with respect to government, the individual, the minority and the majority, by which ordered liberty is replaced by disorganized liberty.[40]

The majority refused to accept as dispositive evidence the statements of "certain alleged Party principles and statements by Party Leaders which are said to be fundamentally at variance with the principles of the Constitution." Instead, it emphasized "that under our traditions beliefs are personal and not a matter of mere association, and that men in adhering to a political party or other organization notoriously do not subscribe unqualifiedly to all of its platforms or asserted principles."[41] Still, the majority did take cognizance of some of the principles of the Communist Party revealed in its 1927 platform. It emphasized, however, as if to highlight the infinite regress invited by the case, that "there is, unfortunately, no absolutely accurate test of what a political party's principles are." Writings purporting to state such principles, even when issued by a party itself, may be "over-exaggerated polemics" or "opportunistic devices as much honored in the breach as in the observance."[42]

The Court gave particular attention to calls by the Party for the abolition of private property without compensation, the establishment of a proletarian dictatorship with political rights to be denied to persons who were not proletarian and/or members of the Party, and the creation of an international union of soviet republics. Justice Murphy denied that these goals necessarily imply nonattachment to the principles of the Constitution. "The constitutional fathers, fresh from a revolution, did not forge a political strait-jacket for the generations to come."[43] The majority emphasized the presence within the original Constitution itself of Article V, which "contains procedural provisions for constitutional change by amendment without any present limitation whatsoever except that no State may be deprived of equal representation in the Senate without its consent." Article V, coupled with the reality of "the many important and far-reaching changes made in the Constitution since 1787," according to the majority, "refute the idea that attachment to any particular provision or provisions is essential, or that one who advocates radical changes is necessarily not attached to the Constitution."[44] Justice Murphy immediately goes on to quote Justice Holmes in identifying the one "principle of the Constitution that more imperatively calls for attachment than any other"— "the principle of free thought" guaranteed by the First Amendment, whose realm of toleration extends to "the thought that we hate."[45]

To put it mildly, Justice Murphy and his colleagues in the majority take a far more latitudinarian approach in defining (and implicitly assessing) radical political views than did United States District Judge Paschal, who in 1891, while refusing to naturalize one Richard Sauer, an admitted "socialist," described "the principles of socialism [as] directly at war with and antagonistic to the principles of the constitution of the United States." Indeed, they were not only "impracticable and dangerous in the extreme," but, more significantly, "un-American" as well. "[T]hose who apply for the privilege, honor, and distinction of becoming American citizens should be free from doctrines which are not only subversive of constitutional government and our free institutions, but of organized society itself."[46] Judge Paschal was not typical, according to historian William Preston, but he was not unique either, especially after the 1901 assassination of William McKinley by a professed anarchist. A comprehensive naturalization statute passed in 1906 required an applicant for citizenship to affirm that he or she was "not a disbeliever in or opposed to organized government or a member of or affiliated with any organization or body or persons teaching disbelief in or opposed to organized government."[47] It was this Act which added the behavior requirement that, ironically, served as a central basis of Murphy's pro-Schneiderman argument.

As Preston points out, this Act was used with special force against anyone associated with the I.W.W., which was perceived as being sympathetic to anarchism, although no less than J. Edgar Hoover

wrote that "the allegation that this organization is anarchistic can neither be sustained in point of law nor fact [sic]."[48] However, for many
judges, encouraged by the Naturalization Service, membership and
even activity sympathetic to the "Wobblies" constituted grounds for
disqualification from becoming a citizen. Indeed, persons associated
with the organization, even through marriage to a member, were disqualified from serving as witnesses testifying to the "attachment" of
other applicants for citizenship, and the applicants inept enough to
ask such persons to serve as their endorsers were themselves denied
citizenship.[49]

Justice Murphy, to his immense credit, was far more sensitive to
civil liberties and the protection of dissenters. He sharply rejected
any presumption that naturalization is available "only to those whose
political views coincide with those considered best by the founders in
1787 or by the majority in this country today."[50] Indeed, Schneiderman's lawyer, the defeated 1940 Republican presidential candidate
Wendell Willkie, had argued, as described by the Court, that the absence of limitations in Article V means that "a person can be attached
to the Constitution no matter how extensive the changes are that he
desires, so long as he seeks to achieve his ends within the framework
of Article V." The Court, however, specifically declined to adopt this
"extreme position" given the failure of the government to meet its
burden of proof under its own, less generous test.[51]

The court below had stated that the views of the Communist Party
"are not those of our Constitution."[52] Justice Murphy and the Supreme Court majority in effect disagreed. Although noting that the
Fifth Amendment prohibits the taking of private property without
compensation, the Court noted that "throughout our history many
sincere people whose attachment to the general constitutional scheme
cannot be doubted have, for various and even divergent reasons,
urged differing degrees of government ownership and control of natural resources, basic means of production, and banks and the media
exchange, either with or without compensation." And the Court goes
on immediately to point out that "something once regarded as a species of private property was abolished without compensating the owners when the institution of slavery was forbidden." Justice Murphy
then asks if "the author of the Emancipation Proclamation and the
supporters of the Thirteenth Amendment were not attached to the
Constituion?"[53]

ABRAHAM LINCOLN
AND THE TWO CONSTITUTIONS

Justice Murphy's question is presumably meant to be "rhetorical," i.e., admitting of only one answer and thus designed to clinch a particular argumentative point. If *any* person stands as a symbol of constitutional attachment, the reader is supposed to feel, it is Father Abraham, the staunch defender of the Union (and the Constitution) against the Southern secessionists. George Will has labeled Lincoln the "greatest statesman in the history of democracy";[54] indeed, have we not built a monument to Lincoln that itself has become a central place of pilgrimage for adherents to the American faith? However, as we have already seen, just as the framers of 1787 present exquisite difficulties of interpretation in terms of their own fidelity to law, so does Lincoln—and here we are speaking not only of brushing aside congressional limitations, but of choosing to join in what remains the bloodiest conflict in American history.[55]

The conflict of 1861, among other things, divides our constitutional history, and some historians refer to the "first" and "second" Constitutions. The first Constitution—that of 1787—was predicated, among other things, on federalism and recognition of slavery; the second Constitution, on an enhanced national government and individual liberty. The difficulty is that some of Lincoln's activities, including emancipation, preceded the Article V adoption of amendments to the first Constitution, so that the character of his own "attachment" is more relevant—and debatable—than recognized by Justice Murphy. What was intended to be rhetorical must instead become a genuine question to be grappled with.

No less a constitutional interpreter (and professed opponent of slavery) than Justice Joseph Story argued, writing of the Fugitive Slave Clause of Article IV, that that clause had to be interpreted in light of the supposition that the framers saw it as "indispensable to the security of this species of property in all the slave-holding states; and indeed, was so vital to the preservation of their domestic interests and institutions, that it cannot be doubted, that it constituted a *fundamental article, without the adoption of which the Union could not have been formed.*"[56] But the entire formation of the Union is embedded within a context of perceived constitutional protection for the South's "peculiar institution." Gene Nichol is thus altogether accurate when he speaks of "the *two* primary constitutive phases of our history: the founding of the republic and the final forging of the nation through the Civil War."[57] It is the gap between those phases that presents the challenge to the constitutional theorist.

There can be little doubt that the so-called Civil War Amendments—the Thirteenth, Fourteenth, and Fifteenth Amendments—partake of at least a limited constitutional revolution. As Owen Fiss and Charles Krauthammer have written, "[T]hese ammendments represent a second starting point, a basic change in the postulates of our constitutional system."[58] If one believes this, then it is not at all frivolous to view Lincoln as incompletely "attached" to the *first* starting point, that is, the Constitution of 1787. Garrisonian abolitionism quite frankly indicated *its* "nonattachment" by condemning the Constitution as a covenant with death and burning it while calling for Northern secession from the Union. Lincoln was surely no Garrisonian; his approach was to construct a narrative of the American republic that privileged one plot—the "dedicat[ion] to the proposition that all men are created equal"—while placing well into the background an all-too-plausible counterplot—a strengthening of the national government in order to protect the ability of the states to maintain their own favored notions of politics, including those dependent on the retention of chattel slavery. We have already seen in Chapter Two how probably the greatest problem in all American constitutional theory is resolving the tension—one that, after all, led to 600,000 deaths between 1861 and 1865—between these two plots.

Indeed, Lincoln's own placing of the birth of the nation four-score-and-seven years before 1863 itself announces that the genuine scriptural text of the new Israel is the Declaration of Independence, with the Constitution being a merely instrumental means of attaining the scriptural vision. The true definition of the "more perfect Union" that is the object of the Constitution is provided not by compliance with what occurs beneath the Preamble, but rather by achievement of the earlier vision of 1776. The priority given to the Declaration is seen most vividly in an evocative metaphor used by Lincoln in a discussion of the importance of the principle of "Liberty to all":

> The expression of that principle in our Declaration of Independence . . . was the word "*fitly spoken*" which has proved an "apple of gold" to us. The *Union* and the *Constitution* are the *picture* of *silver*, subsequently framed around it. The picture was made,

not to *conceal* or *destroy* the apple; but to *adorn*, and *preserve* it. The *picture* was made *for* the apple—*not* the apple for the picture. So let us act, that neither *picture*, [n]or *apple* shall ever be blurred, bruised or broken.[59]

To be sure, both should remain unbroken, *if possible*. But if the Constitution and the Declaration are in conflict, the latter prevails. As Anne Norton has written in a recent reconsideration of Lincoln, "[T]he preservation of the Union absolved him of the imputation of infidelity to the Founders."[60] Although he "had made a steadfast adherence to the law the first principle of his public pronouncements" (as we have earlier seen, he defined "reverence for the law" as the central tenet of the "political religion" of the nation), one of the most important aspects of his presidency was what Norton terms an "actual indifference to legal niceties in matters of State." [61] Such indifference, according to Norton, manifested itself in such behavior as the suspension of habeas corpus mentioned earlier, the censorship of newspapers, and the Emancipation Proclamation itself.

Like the Constitution itself, Lincoln seems to occupy an "essentially contested" status within American political thought. Surely one reason that he is the most written-about figure in American history is that he incarnates so completely the tensions facing the leader who is attempting to live up to his national responsibilities while being faithful to his solemn oath to act within the confines of the Constitution. Few of us seem happy to join in honoring him if he in fact behaved "unconstitutionally." It seems easier at times to reinterpret the Constitution to be congruent with Lincoln's actions. What such reinterpretation does, however, is to raise the possibility that we may have, to paraphrase Che Guevera, "one, two, three, many Constitutions," so that we must decide *which* Constitution garnered Lincoln's attachment and which, in turn, deserves our own.

Lincoln's own career, like *Schneiderman*, forces us to confront absolutely basic questions about the nature of the American Constitution; to reach consensus about Lincoln would require reaching consensus about the Constitution itself, and it is the argument of this book that the search for any such consensus is chimerical. One can do no better in regard to the difficulties presented by any attempt to assess Lincoln's meaning for constitutionalism than to quote the strong praise of Lincoln delivered by the nineteenth-century diarist George Templeton Strong. Conceding that "[o]f course, subordination of government to the Constitution and to law is good—very good—among the best things," he went on immediately to observe that "it's not the only good thing. To save the country is also good." It was "an object of some public importance" to keep "Jeff Davis from chasing Lincoln out of Washington in 1861," an object that served "to justify a little unconstitutionality." Indeed, Strong raises the possibility that "[r]espect for written law and constitutions may be excessive and no less deadly than hypertrophy of the heart." A nation or a church that becomes "finally crystallized into permanent, definite form and . . . incapable of developing new organs or agencies to meet new conditions is *dead*[; it] will begin to decompose whenever time brings the new conditions." The coming of the war in 1861 "brought us a batch of new conditions, and Abraham Lincoln met them wisely and well. He saved the country." Should "learned counsel prove by word-splitting that he saved it unconstitutionally, I shall honor his memory even more reverently than I do now."[62]

COMMUNISM AND CONSTITUTIONALISM

Justice Murphy's own rhetoric can also be put within the context of "essential contestedness" insofar as he resolutely seems to reject any necessary content to the Constitution, however much his allusion to Lincoln may rest on a different notion of constitutional essence. In any case, writing for the *Schneiderman* majority, he continues his remarkable march through the program of the Communist Party and indication of its potential congruence with constitutional attachment. Thus support of the dictatorship of the proletariat is "constitutionalized," as it were, by noting the "fluid" nature of the concept and the "meager indications of the form the 'dictatorship' would take in this country." In particular, Justice Murphy states that its adoption need not necessarily bring "the end of the representative government or the federal system."[63] It is true that the Party criticized checks and balances, the Senate's legislative role, and "the involved procedure for amending the Constitution"; all were characterized "as devices designed to frustrate the will of the majority." Justice Murphy also took note of the 1928 platform of the Party, even though it occurred after Schneiderman's naturalization. There the Party "endorsed the outright abolition of the Senate, the Supreme Court, and the presidential veto power, as well as "replacement of congressional districts with 'councils of workers' in which legislative and executive power would be united."[64]

The majority admitted that all of these indeed would be "significant changes" in the American government; however, "whatever our personal views, as judges we cannot say that a person who advocates their adoption through peaceful and constitutional means is not in fact attached to the Constitution." Justice Murphy notes that unicameralism has been adopted by one of the American states (Nebraska) and thus presumably does not violate the "Republican form of government" sanctified by Article IV of the Constitution; moreover, criticism of the role of the Supreme Court has been endemic in our politics, and Theodore Roosevelt, with his call for popular recall of judicial decisions, is cited as only one critic "whose sincerity and attachment to the Constitution is beyond question" who would have radically transformed the Court's role in our constitutional system.[65]

Turning from structure to substantive rights, the majority states, "If any provisions of the Constitution can be singled out as requiring unqualified attachment, they are the guaranties of the Bill of Rights and especially that of freedom of thought contained in the First Amendment." However, the Court specifically declined to reach the question of Schneiderman's possible repudiation of those principles by supporting the denial of political and civil rights to nonproletarians or non-Party members, "for on the basis of the record before us it has not been clearly shown that such denial was a principle of the organizations" within which Scheiderman was active. "Since it is doubtful that this was a principle of those organizations, it is certainly much more speculative whether this was part of petitioner's philosophy."[66] Thus Lenin is cited both in behalf of suppressing class enemies and for the possibility of achieving revolution while maintaining certain liberties for the bourgeoisie.

The Court is similarly equivocal on the commitment of the Communist Party to violence. It notes that some judges had found the Party to be so committed, while others had not. "This Court has never passed [as of 1943] upon the question . . . , and it is unnecessary for us to do so now." [67] It specifically declined to say "that a reasonable man could not possibly have found, as the district court did, that the Communist Party in 1927 actively urged the overthrow of the Government by force and violence."[68] Still, it argued that "[a] tenable conclusion" is that the Party, at least as of Schneiderman's naturalization in 1927, "desired to achieve its purpose by peaceful and democratic means," and that discussions of force were only "theoretical" or referred either to "a method of preventing an attempted forcible counter-overthrow once the Party had obtained control in a peaceful manner" or "a method of last resort to enforce the majority will" if the presumptive majoritarian wish for a Communist takeover were blocked by "peculiar circumstances" that left "constitutional or peaceful channels . . . no longer open."[69]

Adopting a strong version of the "clear and present danger test," the majority distinguished between "agitation and exhortation calling for present violent action" and "mere doctrinal justification" of violence "under hypothetical conditions at some indefinite future time . . . leaving opportunity for general discussion and the calm processes of thought and reason."[70] Justice Murphy concludes this discussion by adopting a charitable principle of interpretation reminiscent of Frederick Douglass's presented in Chapter 2: "[W]e do not decide what interpretation of the Party's attitude toward force and violence is the most probable . . . or that petitioner's testimony is acceptable at face value. We hold only that where two interpretations of an organization's program are possible, the one reprehensible and a bar to naturalization and the other permissible, a court in a denaturalization proceeding" should adopt the latter "in the absence of overt acts" manifesting the more reprehensible view.[71] The Court therefore settled for an equivalent of a Scotch verdict: without endorsing Schneiderman affirmatively, it used the high standard of proof it required in order to conclude that the "Government has not proved that petitioner's beliefs on the subject of force and violence were such that he was not attached to the Constitution in 1927."[72]

THE DISSENTERS SPEAK

As already indicated, the Court was bitterly divided. Indeed, Felix Frankfurter had sent Murphy a note, following circulation of a draft opinion, suggesting that the headnote to the opinion read:

> The American Constitution ain't got no principles. The Communist Party don't stand for nuthin'. The Soopreme Court don't mean nuthin'. Nuthin' means nuthin', and ter Hell with the U.S.A. so long as a guy is attached to the principles of the U.S.S.R.[73]

One assumes that Frankfurter was enthusiastic in joining the strong dissent written by Chief Justice Stone (joined as well by Justice Roberts). Stone had earlier proved himself a vigorous defender of the "belief-rights" of individuals, particularly in his eloquent dissent from Frankfurter's opinion upholding a compulsory flag salute (itself overruled by *Barnette*).[74] His well-demonstrated commitment to individual rights thus lent special force to his dissent in *Schneiderman*.

"[W]hat could be more important in the selection of citizens of the United States," Stone asks, "than that the prospective citizen be attached to the principles of the Constitution?"[75] The dissenters therefore vigorously criticized the majority for placing this "most fundamental requirement for citizenship"[76] in a peculiar procedural limbo. The government was effectively constrained from challenging after the fact a possibly deceptive (and therefore illegal) naturalization, though it would presumably have been possible to block the naturalization had the challenge been made before its consummation. Instead, the dissenters would have upheld the withdrawal of naturalization so long as the courts below could have reasonably found Schneiderman not to have been attached to the Constitution at the time of his application for citizenship. The government should not be under any special burden of proof, as required by the majority decision.

Turning to the substance of the dispute, Chief Justice Stone noted that the majority "do[es] not deny that there are principles of the Constitution," and he went on to offer his own list:

> [A]mong them are at least the principle of constitutional protection of civil rights and of life, liberty and property, the principle of representative government, and the principle that constitutional laws are not to be broken down by planned disobedience. I assume also that all the principles of the Constitution are hostile to dictatorship and minority rule; and that it is a principle of our Constitution that change in the organization of our government is to be effected by the orderly procedures ordained by the Constitution and not by force or fraud.[77]

The dissenters then turned to an examination of Schneiderman's career within the Communist Party in order to test the plausibility of his "attachment" to the Constitution. Ironically enough, the theme developed in this part of Stone's dissent is Schneiderman's "unqualified loyalty" and "his complete devotion to Communist Party principles," as proved by the fact that "he had formally pledged his allegiance" to them[78] via the functional equivalent of an oath pledging attachment to those principles. Thus the dissenters quoted from the application card in effect when Schneiderman joined the Workers Party (which later became the Communist Party) in 1924: "The undersigned declares his adherence to the principles and tactics of the Workers Party of America as expressed in its program and constitution [!] and agrees to submit to the discipline of the party and to engage actively in its work."[79]

Chief Justice Stone then discussed the ideas of the Communist Party, as derived from an examination of key Party documents. He quoted from Stalin's *Theory and Practice of Leninism* and *A B C of Communism* (written by Bukharin and Preobraschensky before their expulsion from the Party) in order to show the commitment of the Party to violent revolution and its unremitting hostility to any freedom for the bourgeoisie, including respect for private property. "A man can be known by the ideas he spreads," said the dissenters, "as well as by the company he keeps."[80] They accused the majority of arguing that "the trier of fact must not examine petitioner's gospel to find out what kind of man he was."[81] According to Stone, this position implies that "it is impossible to infer that a man is attached to the principles of a religious movement from the fact that he conducts prayer meetings, or, to take a more sinister example, that it could not be inferred that a man" who had, for more than five years, "diligently circulated the doctrines of *Mein Kampf*" is "a Nazi and consequently not attached to constitutional principles."[82] There is, to be sure, no inevitability about such linkages; a person could "be attached to principles diametrically opposed to those, to the dissemination of which he has given his life's best efforts." It is surely "a normal and sensible inference," however, to believe that the efforts are the best evidence of the principles to which the person is truly attached.

The dissenters differed most dramatically from the majority in emphasizing the role of force and violence in Communist Party ideology. "[R]evolution by force of arms was a universal principle [of the Communist Party] and consequently one which embraced the United States."[83] Regarding the Article V argument, the dissenters replied that "the Constitution provides for its own amendment by an orderly procedure but not through the breakdown of our governmental system by lawless conduct and by force."[84] The dissenters did not stop here, but considered as well "the political system which [Schneiderman's] Party proposed to establish and toward which his own efforts in promoting the Communist cause were directed."[85] That system would lead to the abandonment of "existing constitutional principles" as "the freedoms guaranteed by the Bill of Rights were to be ended."[86] The dissenters thus could easily conclude that the record demonstrated "a basis for finding in the Party teachings, during the period in question, an unqualified hostility to the most fundamental and universally recognized principles of the Constitution."[87]

NAZIISM AND "ATTACHMENT": *Schneiderman* SAVES BAUMGARTNER

Although I have emphasized above the substantive aspects of *Schneiderman*, its immediate import was procedural—a holding that denaturalization must be supported by " 'clear, unequivocal, and convincing' evidence which does not leave 'the issue in doubt.' . . ."[88] Ironically, the first subsequent beneficiary of the *Schneiderman* standard was a Nazi sympathizer. In *Baumgartner* v. *United States*,[89] the Court rejected a denaturalization petition brought against a native of Germany who, after becoming a citizen in 1932 at the age of 37, had actively indicated his esteem and support for the policies of the Nazi regime in Germany. One of the items of evidence, for example, was Baumgartner's diary, which included an entry approving former German nationals who had not "been Americanized, that is ruined."[90] In another entry, after he mentioned listening to one of Hitler's speeches, "wonderful as usual," he went on to condemn "the insane actions of the Government in Washington which have the character of wild, unbridled despotism."[91]

Writing for the Court, Justice Frankfurter described "[a]llegiance to this Government and its laws" as a "compendious phrase" ultimately referring to "nothing less than the bonds that tie Americans together in devotion to common fealty." He fully recognized that determining its meaning "presents difficult and doubtful problems even for judges presumably well-trained in the meaning of our country's institutions and their demands from its citizens."[92] The reason was simple: Naturalized citizens have all the freedoms of native-born citizens, and one of those rights of American citizenship is "to criticize public men and measures—and that means not only informed and responsible criticism but the freedom to speak foolishly and without moderation." Frankfurter emphasized that "the expression of views which may collide with cherished American ideals does not necessarily prove want of devotion to the Nation."[93]

Moreover, the Court deemed illegitimate the use of postnaturalization statements to prove state of mind in 1932, even though Baumgartner had testified that his views had basically remained the same. "Whatever German political leanings Baumgartner had in 1932, they were to Hitler and Hitlerism, certainly not to the Weimar Republic," which was still the legal government of Germany prior to Hitler's taking power in January of 1933.[94] It thus concluded "that the evidence to Baumgartner's attitude after 1932 affords insufficient proof that in 1932 he had knowing reservations in forswearing his allegiance to the Weimar Republic and embracing allegiance to this country. . . ."[95] Communist and Nazi alike therefore seemed to be able to pass the "attachment" standard, at least in regard to postnaturalization proceedings, where the *Schneiderman* standard operated.

It is tempting to view *Schneiderman* and *Baumgartner* as proto–First Amendment cases and, more particularly, to place them within the context of the anti-Communist cases arising in the late 1940s that would lead to a series of dreadful antilibertarian decisions by a frightened Supreme Court. Within that context I find it impossible not to applaud Justice Murphy's opinion and the subsequent vindication of the Nazi-sympathizer Baumgartner. Still, that is not the only context within which to read the cases, and I confess to finding both of these cases much harder than *Dennis* v. *United States*,[96] where the Court upheld the jailing of the top leaders of the Communist Party. The difference arises from the fact that the earlier cases deal at a formal level not with what kind of speech or conduct can be punished, but rather with what we deem ourselves to be as an American community purportedly organized around a common attachment to constitutional principles. *Schneiderman* tends to remove any real "bite" from a decision to affirm one's attachment. The Constitution ends up seeming trivialized by the end of the opinion, even as the cause of civil liberties has probably been vindicated.

One may be tempted to believe that this discussion is merely "academic," safely confined to past events, but I think that is not the case. Imagine, for example, that Afrikaaners begin a process of mass emigration from South Africa to the United States. To be sure, not all Afrikaaners support the viciously racist and repressive policies of the Nationalist Party, but most do. It is hard to believe that any commit-

ted supporter of the current regime could be "attached to the principles of the United States Constitution" if they are interpreted as including a strong commitment to racial equality and one person, one
vote. Should an Afrikaaner immigrant applying for United States citizenship be closely examined on his or her political views, and then
be excluded if these views prove to oppose the post-*Brown* reading of
the Constitution as at the very least preventing state-mandated racial
separation? To say "yes" obviously rejects the Holmesian tolerance for
thought that we hate. A negative answer, though, in effect repeals the
"attachment" statute and brings to the surface the "meaninglessness"
that threatens any serious constitutional faith.

Constitutional Essence
and Constitutional Amendment

There is one final ramification of "attachment" that is worthy of discussion. One of the issues in the debates examined above concerns
the postulation of what I have termed constitutional "essence," a fixed
hierarchy of values (or its logical equivalent, a fixed *telos* toward
which we are to move) that allows us to differentiate between what
might be viewed as the "temporal," or even "trivial," Constitution—
for example, the requirement that a senator be at least 30 years old—
and the "timeless" and "essential" Constitution—for example, the
protection of the right to speak against the policy of the government
of the day. The Constitution does not offer a self-referential ranking
of its own provisions. And one discovers, when reading the debates
of 1787-88, that clauses that are today regarded as extraordinarily limited in import were at the time viewed as absolutely central. Thus a
number of the "anti-Federalists" worked hard to portray assigning
Congress the power to regulate the place and manner of federal elections in Article I as a potential invitation to tyrannical control. (After
all, a malign Congress might set Philadelphia as the sole venue in
which Pennsylvanians could vote, to the obvious detriment of the
farmers.) Still, it is safe to say that *any* notion of constitutional interpretation must generate hierarchies of values, for too many controversies concern clear conflicts among constitutional values.

A somewhat exotic branch of this search for the essential Constitution involves the possibility of giving a limited construction to Article
V, the amending clause that was central to Schneiderman's argument.

A strictly positivist view of the Constitution, for example, would give the populace the right to negate *any* value presumably encompassed by the present document, simply by repealing the current text and replacing it by its opposite. (The only plausible exception for a strict positivist is the guarantee of equal representation in the Senate, which seemingly requires unanimous consent for modification.) Thus proponents of slavery could reconstitutionalize that practice by repealing the Thirteenth Amendment and specifically authorizing the ownership of one human being by another. Proponents of cruel and unusual forms of punishment—say the drawing and quartering of drug dealers—could achieve that end merely by repealing the Eighth Amendment and specifically authorizing their favorite exquisite tortures.[97] And so on.

Such amendments are, one hopes, only theoretical, but the very contemplation of them has caused Walter Murphy to suggest the possibility of "unconstitutional constitutional amendments."[98] Murphy, an expert in comparative constitutional law, has been influenced at least in part by his reading of Indian, West German, and Irish constitutional doctrine. In particular he cites the text of the West German constitution as forbidding "amendments affecting, *inter alia*, human dignity, and, more generally, allow[ing] only changes in any article that 'amend or supplement the text thereof.'" Some amendments, says Murphy, "would materially change, not 'amend or supplement' the Basic Law," and would therefore be unconstitutional.[99]

The main body of Murphy's argument contends that the Constitution is essentially oriented around the value of protecting human dignity. This constitutionalism is an important limit to the value of majority rule precisely because it incarnates a value hierarchically superior to majority rule. For Murphy this understanding of the Constitution entails that "the American people have surrendered their authority, *under that system*, to abridge dignity by any procedure whatsoever," including the procedure seemingly authorized by Article V.[100] Murphy cites as possible support from American constitutional law the statement by Justice Davis in his opinion for the Court in Ex parte *Milligan*[101] that certain protections of the Bill of Rights are "established by irrepealable law," suggesting that an amendment abolishing trial by jury and replacing it with trial before military tribunals would be invalid. As Murphy says, one might regard Davis's comment "as no more than a rhetorical flourish," but he cautions that "it does contain a kernel of what constitutionalism would label truth."[102] He does not deny, of course, that, "[a]s a matter of sheer power, the people can give themselves a new constitutional order with attendant adoption of a new document" repudiating old values and embracing new political ideals. "The current constitutional document, however, makes no provision for destroying the old polity and creating a new one. Thus, its terms cannot supply legitimate procedures for such a sweeping change."[103]

The interpretive framework articulated by Murphy is quite similar to that taken by the late Henry Hart in regard to the much-discussed conundrum of the power of Congress to deprive the Supreme Court of jurisdiction to hear appeals from lower courts, particularly the state courts. The Constitution assigns the Supreme Court original jurisdiction over only a relatively few matters: "Cases affecting Ambassadors, other public Ministers and Consuls, and those in which a State shall be a Party." The text then goes on to assign the Court appellate jurisdiction over all other cases properly within the federal judicial power, "with such Exceptions, and under such Regulations as the Congress shall make."[104] The question then becomes the propriety of Congress "excepting" *all* cases from the appellate jurisdiction of the Supreme Court, leaving it only with the basically trivial docket generated by the original jurisdiction.

At least one Supreme Court decision, written by Chief Justice Waite, holds that the appellate power of the Supreme Court "is confined within such limits as Congress sees fit to prescribe. . . . What those powers shall be, and to what extent they shall be exercised, are, and always have been, proper subjects of legislative control." Thus, "whole classes of cases [may] be kept out of the jurisdiction altogether."[105] Henry Hart, however, wrote that Congress's power was in fact limited: It could indeed eliminate *some* jurisdiction from the Supreme Court, but it could not pass legislation that would negate the "essential role of the Supreme Court in the constitutional plan."[106] Using language very similar to that adopted by Murphy many years later, Hart, while conceding the "indeterminacy" of his standard, nonetheless asked the presumably nonrhetorical question, "But whatever the difficulties of the test, they are less, are they not, than the difficulties of reading the Constitution as authorizing its own destruction?"

CONCLUSION: ESSENTIALISM AND FAITH COMMUNITIES

One of the vital differences between "constitutional faith" and more traditional religious faith is precisely the explicitly authorized amendment process in the former. Most major Western religions have resisted theories of "continuing revelation" that might in effect legitimize strong "amendment" of divine commandment by persons claiming direct communication from God.[107] A defender of papal infallibility, for example, emphasizes that it "is not an active gift to proclaim new truths but a divine assistance given to recognize and proclaim the deposit of revelation."[108] And Judaism is insistent that the age of prophetic revelation closed with Moses. The "prophetic tradition" within Judaism refers only to those who eloquently reminded the people of Israel about their deviations from divine law and the likely consequences of that deviation.

Still, even if we recognize the rhetorical theme of continuity with "the deposit of revelation," it is nonetheless obvious that change occurs. Justification is found in existing materials rather than in claims of new revelation, but change (or what Marshall in *McCulloch* v. *Maryland* termed "adaptation") occurs regardless. Significantly, such adaptation is almost always justified by reference to its *non*-deviation from the genuine foundation or true essence of the faith community and, indeed, the utility of any changes to preserving what is most central to the faith community. It may be especially illuminating to realize that Talmudic Judaism, used by its detractors as the very model of spiritless legalism, not only features remarkable feats of exegesis that defy most readers' initial expectations but, more importantly, explicitly adopts as a category of analysis "circumventing" or even "uprooting" the Torah when necessary in order to protect the most fundamental values of the Jewish community.[109]

One writer has described this rabbinic authority as including the creative ability "to reshape [the Torah]—to determine its official meaning, and to set aside even its explicit rules as the interpreters see fit."[110] Interestingly enough, in light of our earlier discussion of Lincoln and other Founders, what legitimizes rabbinic creativity seems to be a matter more of character than of following any specific rules of interpretation. If a creative act "is carried out by one whose intention is to establish his own systemic primacy over that even of the Torah," Joel Roth writes, the act is illegitimate. "If, however, the action is motivated by a real concern for the preservation of the primacy of the Torah itself within the halakhic [legal] system, and if the situation is such that this preservation can be accomplished best through the abrogation of one of its dictates," the action is legal. "In other words," Roth concludes, "the assurance that rabbinic legislation abrogating the Torah is secondary, not primary, is dependent upon the personal virtues required of the authorities of the system."[111]

The crisis in a faith system occurs when there is no longer agreement on what counts as a "center," "essence," or "foundation" that must be preserved at the necessary cost of sacrificing more peripheral values. Instead, a now-fractured community must confront the problem of pluralism. Consider in this context the views of the great Jewish historian of mysticism, Gershom Scholem, one of whose aims was to overcome a view within existing Jewish historiography that the kabbalistic mystics were in some sense "un-Jewish." Scholem saw such views as essentialistic; in their place, he presented a much more "existential" notion: "Judaism" is constituted by whatever people who call themselves "Jews" happen to do. Because Judaism cannot "be regarded as a closed historical phenomenon whose development and essence came into focus by a finite sequence of historical, philosophical, doctrinal, or dogmatic judgments and statements," the historian of (or participant within) Judaism must confront the possibility that, as "a living entity, having transformed itself at various stages in its history and having made real choices," including the "discarding" of once central aspects of community, it will in the future discard what now appears to be central.[112] According to Scholem, though, it would be no less Jewish for having been transformed: Whatever the Aristotelian notion of noncontradiction, both A and not-A can be equally true descriptions of "Jewish theology" if embraced by persons who designate themselves (and are recognized by significant elements of the relevant community) as Jews. What prevents "Jews for Jesus" from being "authentically Jewish" is not the rejection of some essential aspect of Judaism (that the Messiah has not yet arrived), but rather the failure to gain significant support from persons recognized as Jews by other Jews. But who knows what the future will bring?

The underlying problem of this chapter in effect is whether a historian bold enough to try to write a history of American constitutionalism would be entitled to leave out of that history any given body of thought of persons designating themselves as American constitutionalists. The only certainty I wish to suggest in this chapter is that rallying around a text—or even signing an oath of loyalty to it—is as likely to set the stage for disputation as to end it. And no case better illustrates this point than *Schneiderman* v. *United States*, which seems to view as "attached" to the Constitution a person who no doubt viewed the ordinary constitutional argument as an ideological cover for class oppression and wished to replace what most of us would identify as the constitutional system with something radically different.

The point of this chapter has been to ask what we can learn from *Schneiderman* as a case. In the next chapter, though, we turn to a very different inquiry, which might be introduced as, "What do we have to learn from Schneiderman as a person." For example, what if Schneiderman applied to teach at a law school and were otherwise suitable in terms of formal credentials? Would we wish to exclude him from imparting to the young his own peculiar version of constitutional faith? I turn now to a consideration of how we might answer this question.

THE LAW SCHOOL,
THE FAITH COMMUNITY, AND
THE PROFESSING OF LAW

THE LAST CHAPTER concluded with the image of William Schneiderman applying for a job as a professor of constitutional law. When asked how he would teach the subject, he replies that he would, like most constitutional law professors, focus on decided cases of the United States Supreme Court and attempt to predict future decisions on the basis of these cases. Asked what attitude he would convey about the materials, he gives a complex answer: First, he would emphasize both the extent to which decisions are in fact choices and that the choices made by the Court are systematically in the interests of the ruling class; second, he would convey what we learned in the previous chapter is the attitude of a "fearless communist" as defined by Georg Lukács, in which knowledge about the law does not in the least entail any veneration for what one knows.

Imagine another scene: An atheistic William Schneiderman applies to teach in a divinity school. He notes a longtime interest in theology and would enjoy teaching it. Asked how he would teach it, he replies that he would, like most professors, assign primary texts and try to analyze the arguments contained within them. Asked what attitude he would convey about the materials, he gives a complex answer: First, he would note that theological arguments are choices and that the choices made by varying theologians have profound political implications. The most officially prominent theologians of any given era tend to ratify existing class arrangements, even as other, less-approved theologians (like contemporary liberation theologians in Latin

– 155 –

America) support the interests of the oppressed. Second, he would make no effort to deny his own atheism and thus implicitly to encourage his students to adopt a similar view about the hollowness at the core of God-centered theology.

Does our reaction to these two hypothetical job applications differ? The reference to the divinity school is intended to evoke the fact that almost all faith communities concern themselves with the problem of reproducing themselves in successor generations. Extremely important to this reproduction in most communities is the training of a group of leaders to whom education, whether of children or adults, can be entrusted. Religious education is explicitly designed to socialize new generations into the community and to maintain the socialization of those who have already entered, and it is clearly a part of our standard practices that those who educate are presumed to share the faith that they are teaching.

The community defined by "constitutional faith" is no more natural than that defined by adherence to traditional religious norms. We saw in Chapter Three how loyalty oaths can be viewed as a part of a socialization process aimed at producing a specific kind of civic consciousness. But such oaths are obviously far less important than formal schooling, which includes within its definition matters ranging from structured curricular presentation of inspiring tales of the Founders and the Constitution they wrote to the compulsory pledge of allegiance that continues to be a part of most school programs, even though *Barnette* authorizes those with scruples of conscience to refuse to participate in the ceremony. Although the ideology of public schooling may include emphasis on creating autonomous adults, it should be clear that we are also concerned to channel this "autonomy" within acceptable boundaries. If there is anything that the work of contemporary analysts of culture like Clifford Geertz has taught us, it is that *all* aspects of social life are pervaded by decidedly non-neutral assumptions whose acceptance by a member of the culture define what is "possible" for that person.[1] What culture does is to mold an almost infinitely plastic person into someone who is recognizably a part of his or her community, what Michael Sandel has termed an "encumbered self." One cannot genuinely imagine an alternative to such molding, even though from our own cultural vantage point we are often critical of certain cultures and the specific limitations they impose on their members. In any event, a child in the American public schools is no more encouraged to make fundamental critiques of the American political structure and its presuppositions than is one who attends a specifically religious school encouraged to consider the merits of atheism.[2]

Although "school" may evoke association with "children," it is obviously not restricted to the very young. Law school may be aimed at a far more adult clientele; yet the mixed and (many would say) contradictory tasks of both generating autonomous adults and preparing them to reproduce the central institutions of the culture are no less present. Previous chapters have traced some of the implications of treating law as a quasi-religious system. In this chapter I want to develop another aspect of the religious analogy through a self-conscious examination of the tensions generated when one "professes" law, particularly in the institutional role of a "professor of law." Only such an examination will allow us to decide whether an otherwise qualified William Schneiderman should be hired to profess constitutional law.

"Nihilism" and the Professing of Law

Several years ago, Paul Carrington, then dean of the Duke Law School, triggered an illuminating debate when he expressed his dismay at the presence in the legal academy of what he termed "legal nihilists." Indeed, he went so far as to suggest that these "nihilists" have an ethical duty to choose a career other than teaching law.[3] "Nihilism" is used by Carrington as a shorthand reference to the views articulated by academics identified with Critical Legal Studies, who draw from some of the more radical aspects of Americal legal realism and its skepticism about both the ability of a legal system to generate specific answers to disputes and, just as importantly, the justice (or goodness) of any answer given by judges and other officials.[4] Although Carrington's invitation to exit from the legal academy is extreme, his opposition to CLS represents a widespread sentiment. Owen Fiss of the Yale Law School, who has publicly rejected the assertion that "nihilists" are unfit to teach law, has nonetheless attacked CLS for an unrelenting "negativism" about law that ultimately "den[ies] the distinctive claim of law as a form of rationality." To accept its analysis would, he says, "mean the death of the law, as we have known it throughout history, and as we have come to admire it."[5]

Carrington's own prose is strikingly evocative of religious discourse. He is, let there be no doubt about it, writing about faith and belief.

To be a professor of law, for Carrington, requires belief in the law. "One cannot believe in the worth of one's professional skill and judgment unless one also has some minimal belief in the idea of law and the institutions that enforce it. . . ."[6] Indeed, he quite self-consciously adopts a religious metaphor: "For those university law teachers able to keep the faith of the *secular religion*, let there be no shame in the romantic innocence with which they approach the ultimate issue of their profession."[7] "Nihilists," however, are alleged to have none of this innocence or the requisite faith to be a commendable professor of law.

Carrington cannot be dismissed as a naive cheerleader for law. He confesses to his own dark nights of the soul, in which the "dread in disbelief"[8] makes its appearance. "[T]here have been days, sometimes many of them in a row, when I have asked myself if perhaps I am or was not too cynical about law to be able to teach it."[9] What overcomes such despair is not cold reason. Instead he evokes a notion similar to the phenomenon of a leap of (legal) faith engendered by devotion to, maybe even love of, one's community. "The law . . . is a mere hope that people who apply the lash of power will seek to obey the law's command. Let us not be modest: it is an act of considerable courage to maintain belief in such a hope."[10] This faith commitment comes "not because reason requires it, but because our commitment to our discipline serves the needs of the public to whom, and for whom, we are responsible."[11] Part of the reason for Carrington's dismay at the presence of faithless professors in law schools is the alleged harm done to those aspiring professionals we call students. "Nihilists" are accused of trying to imbue a view that law is at best irrelevant, that is "doesn't matter," in regulating human affairs, or at worst is a vicious evil, a mystifying rhetoric by which rulers dominate those in their thrall. If this is believed, students might well wonder why they should become lawyers. Even more, they might wonder whether they can live up to the "solemn duty . . . to encourage respect for the law and for the courts and the judges thereof,"[12] a duty whose implications were the underpinning of the the discussion in Chapter Two on the relationship between law and morality.

Some of Carrington's critics have accused him of being insufficiently sensitive to academic freedom, with its injunction to tolerate thinkers regardless of their conclusions. In response, he emphasizes the particular role of the professional school. Such schools are committed not to abstract inquiry, to be supported "though the heavens fall," but rather to the training of persons who will carry on the particular professional vocation. "When . . . the university accepted responsibility for training professionals, it also accepted a duty to constrain teaching that knowingly dispirits students or disables them from doing the work for which they are trained."[13]

In responding to Robert Gordon's critique of this view of a law school, Carrington adopts even more explicit religious metaphors. He first tells Gordon that "[t]he obligation to contribute to professional development can conflict with the duty to profess truth if the truth which one is obliged to profess is a refutation of the premises on which the service of the profession is based."[14] He then offers as a relevant analogy an atheist who wishes to teach in a divinity school. Carrington regards atheism as "an eminently legitimate intellectual position," and "any university worthy of the name" should grant haven to the atheist. However, "a professor of divinity for whom atheism is the primary message to profess ought to recognize that he has a conflict of interest, of sorts; he should put in for a transfer to some other department, perhaps the religion department. This seems fairly obvious to me. . . ."[15] Carrington concludes an exchange with Owen Fiss by suggesting that a person preaching legal nihilism is "insulting the faith of those who trusted [the professor] to express their [faith in the law]."[16]

Some of Carrington's critics have pointed out that he is notably unclear in defining the nihilism that he is so quick to denounce.[17] It is not clear, for example, if he is angry at those who deny the efficacy of legal rules because of omnipresent indeterminacy in their interpretation, a view that I have defended elsewhere, or at those who state that law quite clearly safeguards only the interests of the powerful and does not in fact serve to discipline their power. I do not in fact share his optimism that the language of legal "command" will necessarily serve to restrain "the lash of power," rather than simply to justify that power. Still, it is not necessary to analyze Carrington's specific notion of nihilism in order to take his language seriously and use it as the basis for reflections about the vocation of the law professor.

Though this book presents me primarily as a writer about law, it is certainly relevant that "writer" is not an adequate description of my occupational role. I am a professor of law, attached to a specific institution, the University of Texas Law School. But what does it mean to take on the role of a professor of law? How, for example, would one explain the vocation of professing law to those unfamiliar with the notion? One might, of course, advise them to turn to a dictionary in order to find out what a professor is or does. If we turn to the greatest of all English-language dictionaries, the *Oxford English Dictionary*, we discover that immediate problems emerge, and in these problems we see as well some of the sources of the arguments that are the focus of this chapter.

According to the *OED*, all meanings of the word "profess" before the year 1500 involve religion, such as taking the vows of a religious order.[18] When one professes, for example, one is said "[t]o affirm or declare one's faith in or allegiance to; to acknowledge or formally recognize as an object of faith or belief (a religion, principle, rule of action; God, Christ, a saint, etc.)." "Profession" in turn refers not only to what is professed, i.e., "[t]he declaration, promise, or vow made by one entering a religious order," but also to particular orders of professed persons. However, we discover in our dictionary alternative meanings that also have, from our perspective, a long lineage, albeit only to the mid-sixteenth century. By 1577 one reads of someone who "professed husbandry," in the sense of laying a "claim to have knowledge of or skill in (some art of science); to declare oneself expert or proficient in." Also available was the meaning, "[t]o teach (some subject) as a professor." Not surprisingly, all of these various meanings emerge in defining a "professor." One of the early meanings of "professor" is "professed member of a religious order." Just as early, though, is the meaning, "a public teacher or instructor of the highest rank in a specific faculty." Here the "profession" is defined in terms of "a professed knowledge of some department of learning or science" that is applied "to the affairs of others."

The swirl of meanings surrounding the very word that I use to describe myself helps to provide an understanding of the modern controversy involving the professing of law. Let us look more closely at Carrington's comment about the atheist, for example. As suggested at the beginning of this chapter, many organized religious faiths establish seminaries or divinity schools in order to train ministers who will convey the accepted truths of the religion to the lay members of the denomination. In addition, scholars at the better divinity schools might engage in the elaboration of theological propositions associated with the faith, though almost never in a way that leaves the faith shattered at the end of the elaboration.

As we saw earlier, in Chapter Three, it is vitally important that

Christian denominations in particular are usually organized creedally, so that a presupposition of membership within the community is public commitment to its particular creed. As John Leith notes, creeds can never genuinely be learned simply from books. "They must be learned in the midst of the community of worshiping and believing people who share in a common life of which the creed is a common affirmation."[19] In addition, "[t]he creed has the negative role of shutting the heretic out and setting the boundaries within which authentic Christian theology and life can take place."[20]

Surely we cannot seriously object when a seminary devoted to the maintenance of a community of faith limits its membership to those who profess its creed.[21] Consider for example the approach of the Commission on Theological Education of the United Methodist Church. Though it emphasizes the desirability of "freedom of academic inquiry" and the "uninhibited opportunity to address openly and seriously theological issues," it nevertheless recognizes the right of a seminary to "reserve for itself the right to require allegiance to principles and doctrinal or confessional affirmations which are integral or indispensable parts of its institutional life."[22]

A recent controversy within the Catholic Church concerned the status of Catholic University professor Charles E. Curran, who had publicly expressed reservations about Church doctrine concerning birth control and other sexually related activities. Joseph Cardinal Ratzinger, prefect of the Sacred Congregation for the Doctrine of the Faith, in 1985 wrote Father Curran requesting that he "reconsider and retract these positions which violate the conditions necessary for a professor to be called a Catholic theologian." Cardinal Ratzinger pointed to "the inherent contradition . . . that one who is to teach in the name of the Church in fact denies her teaching," and he went on to suggest that Father Curran might lose his freedom to continue as a member of the theology department.[23] This suggestion became reality in August 1986, when Cardinal Ratzinger, in an action apparently approved by Pope John Paul II, revoked Father Curran's authority to teach theology at Catholic University.[24]

An atheist might well wish to teach before a seminary audience in order to dislodge its faith. The Methodist Conference, for all of its embrace of "free inquiry,"[25] presumably rules out any possibility of the appointment of an athiest. Whatever one's views about Cardinal Ratzinger, it is hard to imagine, that a Catholic school is behaving badly in refusing appointments to, or suggesting the exit of, those who would teach that it is the whore of Babylon or, indeed, that there is not the slightest evidence of the existence of God. Likewise, no one can genuinely expect an Orthdox Jewish yeshiva to be hospitable to a teacher who denies that the unique God created the world. Yet, as Carrington rightly points out, most of us *would* be prepared to criticize a department of religion, devoted to a very different task than propagation of the faith, if it refused a haven to an athiest.

The point is that for Carrington, law schools function as the divinity schools of our secular religion. Recall once more Lincoln's call on the citizenry to adhere to the "political religion of the nation," or Chief Justice Burger's Mosaic call to teach the precepts of the Constitution to the young. Does socializing the young, including fledgling lawyers, into the central tenet of the faith—defined by Lincoln as "reverence for the law"—allow toleration within the schoolhouse of the "civil atheist"?

The tension between religious, including civil-religious, and secular definitions of a university's purposes is a recurrent one in American educational history. The shift from religiously dominated to secular universities is a key movement in American higher education.[26] Within a secular structure, one can indeed be "interested in" religion without in the least sharing the creedal commitments of any religion at all. After all, one can be interested in understanding Plato's political thought even if one shares Karl Popper's view that Plato was a dangerous totalitarian who must be denounced.

Only a fool would deny the importance that religious consciousness has played in our history. Nor could an anthropologist interested in grasping the culture of a Sudanese or Javanese tribe ignore religion simply because she found animism, for example, to be an intellectually preposterous way of looking at the world. Similarly, only a fool would deny the importance that legal consciousness has played in the history of the self-descriptions that constitute our culture. "Law talk" can no more be ignored than can "religious talk," even if one finds each equally implausible. One can obviously try to understand all sorts of views with which one disagrees. No commitment is necessary at all save a commitment to articulating one's notion of what is true. I shall presently return to some of the complications contained within this last sentence.

Detached Professionalism
and Obligations to Students

"If we have understood the archeological and textual record correctly," Jonathan Smith has written, "man has had his entire history in which to imagine deities and modes of interaction with them. But man, more precisely western man, has had only the last few centuries in which to imagine religion." Smith is referring to what he calls the "act of second order, reflective imagination which must be the central preoccupation of any student of religion." To be a "student of religion" quite often correlates with *not* being a believer in the deities one is studying or, obviously, in the "real" possibility of interacting with them. Instead, one becomes "interested," for a variety of reasons, in the social phenomena that the academician calls "religion," a term that Smith calls "solely the creation of the scholar's study," which is "created for the scholar's analytic purposes by his imaginative acts of comparison and generalization."[27] The world of the believer, represented in the divinity school, and that of the scholar, represented in the department of religion, are fundamentally different.

Paul Carrington is clearly troubled by analogizing the work of the law school to the detached analyses one might expect from a "department of law." It is not that such analyses are not important, but Carrington seems to be saying that law professors have an additional task. That task is to profess our faith in the meaningfulness and desirability of the rule of law—and in the institutions allegedly incarnating such rule—as a way of encouraging the socialization of the young into it and thus maintaining its civil magisterium into the future.

David Engel, a professor of law and anthropology, suggests that it is peculiar to assume that the legal scholar (or professor?) "owes his/her subject (i.e., existing legal institutional arrangements or legal actors) a special obligation of helpfulness of a very particular sort: to aid or shore up the people and organizations [he or she is] trying to understand." Thus he asks, "Does a marine biologist have an obligation to be helpful to algae?"[28] Or, for that matter, does the detached student of, say, an animistic tribal religion have a duty to help the tribe maintain its (what to us may be its quite) bizarre culture? But that task, to join in common enterprise with the "object" of one's study, so that in some real sense it loses its status as an objective "other" and instead becomes incorporated in the student herself, is not at all "peculiar" within the world of the divinity school. There "apologetics," a richly nuanced term in itself, has always played a central role.

Carrington's critics would sharply reject the divinity-school model. For at least some of them, Engel's question is truly "rhetorical," submitting of only one answer. Law schools should indeed become ever more like departments of religion or marine biology. One need not be helpful to the algae, any more than, say, the delineator of Aztec sacrifice must commend to her students that practice or regret the demise of institutions structured in terms of that practice. Indeed, Arthur Green, president of the Reconstructionist Rabbinical College, makes this point in a remarkable article on the sometimes tortured relationship between academic "Jewish studies" and the tenets of "Jewish faith."[29]

Noting that Jewish studies have become increasingly accepted within the secular academy, Green writes that there is a "cost of this acceptance" that is only now becoming apparent. "To say it succinctly, Jewish scholarship can no longer serve as the handmaiden of Jewish apologetics. The university scholar, unlike his seminary colleague, cannot teach that Judaism is the unique repository of truth, that it is "better," either morally or theologically, than other faiths, or even comfortably preach the values of its continued existence." It may be, of course, that "the very fact of teaching Judaism, including Hebrew sources, to new generations of students does make for Jewish continuity. But the content of the professors' message can hardly dare to allow itself to be the same as that of the rabbis. Here the content of objective research has caught up with itself, and its implications can no longer be ignored."[30]

Owen Fiss, however severe a critic of "nihilists," makes a similar point in regard to the presence of law schools within the regular university. "Law professors are not paid to train lawyers, but to study the law and to teach their students what they happen to discover."[31] If what they discover is that the legal system is bankrupt, they should in fact be free to teach that, however much that differs from Fiss's own strongly argued views.

One can study something called law without having faith in its curative properties. The easiest way to establish this point is by studying "the law" of an alien society, say South Africa or the Soviet Union. We would have little trouble embracing a colleague who said 1) that these countries in fact have legal systems, and 2) that they are terrible and iniquitous legal systems that should be not only deconstructed but also, in large measure, destroyed. (Indeed, I am not aware that a scholar of Soviet law has ever been denied an appointment in a major law school because of insufficient attachment to the Soviet legal system.) We would also accept a person who argued that one of the fundamental deficiencies in German legal thought of the early twentieth century was the unthinking respect it gave to formal legality, so that German jurists were all too willing to fill in the contentless norms of formal legality with substantive commands of almost literally incredible evil.[32] Again we return to the theme of the second chapter, the ubiquitous possibility of a gap between law and morality and the consequent necessity to remember that identifying something as a "legal" system in no way serves to register one's "respect" for it.

The debate, however, obviously concerns what we who profess law should be teaching fledgling professionals about *our own* legal order and the roles they will be assuming within that order. I put it this way because I find unacceptable Fiss's somewhat blithe rejection of defining the social meaning of professing law as including the training of lawyers. Whether I like to admit it or not, my primary occupation, for which I am well paid, is teaching the young who wish to embark on a life very different from mine, i.e., the actual practice of law. Their lives are not *completely* different, however, for one status we will share in common is that of citizen. As a law professor, I am a teacher of those whose conceptions of citizenship might be especially important, given the centrality of the legal profession in our public discourse and life. My professing law is, I hope, one manifestation of my active citizenship within our polity.

If law really does serve as the basis of our civil religion, then there is something ominous in the picture of a legal professoriate identical in its detachment to those of regular academic departments. Such detachment bespeaks what might be termed an "external" perspective, by which academics gaze from the outside on the objects of their study. It may be almost beside the point that their own creed is an otherwise admirable commitment to abstract truth. An astronomer is presumably just as "interested" in an exploding nova as in a live star. One can develop a similar temperament in regard to social life, as exmplified most terribly by Nazi doctors performing "experiments" designed to answer questions involving the capacity of human beings to bear particular kinds of pain. Those are not uninteresting questions, and one can presumably generate "truthful" answers. But trying to answer them requires an alienation from other humans—a denial of basic human community—that terrifies. Among those of us who study the so-called "human sciences," including our own lives as members of political communities, the detachment of the "natural scientist" may be something we distinctly do *not* wish to emulate.

Some of Paul Carrington's allies, particularly those who dislike Critical Legal Studies, view him as defending a detached professionalism against those who are putatively "politicizing" the academy. But Carrington may be read just as easily as a critic of law professors who are *too* detached from—who do not identify sufficiently with—the social order of which they are (or ought to be) a part. If they were not detached, he seems to suggest, they would not be so insensitive to the potentially terrible consequences of the demoralization generated by the views they profess. Better, less-detached citizens would try to prevent such demoralization.

I think it important that at least some of the adherents to Critical Legal Studies resist any attempt to portray them as noninvolved citizens. Consider, in this context, a response by Jay Feinman to an earlier version of this chapter. He implicitly rejected *in toto* any analogy between his approach to teaching law and that of the presumably detached member of a department of religion. Instead, for himself, he embraced the role of the "prophet" attacking the congealed "dogma" of "mainstream legalism."[33] Such professors "do not focus on weaknesses as detached critics, but as involved members of an ongoing moral and political community," and the ultimate "goal is an ancient one—to achieve a righteous way of living."[34]

Michael Walzer, in a recent book on social criticism, has noted that the prophet—in that case, Amos—is the most actively involved of citizens, calling his listeners to account by speaking in a common language appealing to a shared social narrative that gives life its meaning. "Prophecy aims to arouse remembrance, recognition, indignation, repentance." The practice implies "a previously accepted and commonly understood morality."[35] Indeed, for Walzer, all deep "[c]onversation is parasitic on commonality." Without an acknowledgment of shared narratives that unite the speakers, talk is "thin," and there is "little room for nuance or subtlety."[36] In the thicker world of the prophet, "[w]rongdoing and rightdoing are alike social experiences, and the prophet and his listeners are involved in these experiences in accordance with the principle of solidarity."[37]

One can reduce Carrington's argument to the proposition that it is the task of law professors to engender hope in their students that significant, even "fundamental," political and social change is in fact possible, and that they can contribute to it by use of their specifically legal talents. Professors could not engender any such hope if they believed that law simply did not matter. If I am correct in my analysis of Carrington, then it seems unlikely that he would join Charles Fried, who professed law at Harvard before taking his current position as solicitor general of the United States, in assuring students that *whatever* they do as lawyers will be morally admirable. Fried began a famous article by asking, presumably nonrhetorically, if a "good lawyer" is necessarily a "good person."[38] Although the answer might be negative in a fundamentally unjust legal order, Fried assured his readers that, in the United States at least, a lawyer can always, without exception, take a measure of moral pride in his or her activities defending the legal rights of a client, whether slumlord or saint. His critics have read him as supporting a monumental complacency by the legal profession concerning the moral implications of its activities.

But doesn't rejection of Fried's complacent reassurance require the professing law professor at least on occasion to take issue, perhaps even castigate, the moral pretensions of the existing legal structure? Does it not become wholly legitimate to point out that one can be a "good lawyer" but nonetheless a dreadful citizen, at least where citizenship implies commitment to achieving that polity most worthy of respect, and to suggest as well that "citizenship" trumps "lawyer" as a source of desirable identity?

Anglo-American lawyers in particular have emphasized the lawyer's duty of zealous advocacy in behalf of the individual client. One of the most famous of all statements of this position is Lord Brougham's speech to the House of Lords defending the necessity of "separating even the duties of a patriot from those of an advocate, and casting them, if need be, to the wind." The advocate "must go on reckless of the consequences, if his fate it should unhappily be to involve his country in confusion for his client's protection."[39] John Mortimer, the distinguished English barrister-playwright, has given his own twist for anyone interested in analogies between religious and legal behaviors. Describing the task of the advocate as the art of being "most convincing when he is unconvinced," Mortimer finds a commonality between the advocate and the religious mystic: "[H]e can only operate successfully when he is able to suspend his disbelief."[40] Should one be happy with this model of detached advocacy or admire the client-centered lawyer who argues for changes that would make us a less free or less just society? I find it hard to answer affirmatively.

In his critique of liberalism, Michael Sandel has recently reminded us that we live not as disembodied intelligences behind a veil of ignorance or as wholly atomized selves; instead, we are radically encumbered selves who are defined by our commitments to the traditions, groups, and nations that give us our identities.[41] We are constituted by our loyalties, some of them "chosen," some of them "affirmed" in conscious recognition of that which we already are. We thus return full circle to the concerns that dominated Chapter Three: What loyalties should law professors be expected to have? To what extent should the law professor be viewed, first and foremost, as a *citizen* of our particular political order, with the loyalties to maintenance of a republican form of government that citizenship may well entail? Is it at all relevant that I have taken a particular oath quite similar to that of the president and chief justice, i.e., to support, protect, and defend the Constitution of the United States? Finally, what, if anything, constitutes one's creed as a law professor?

I obviously cannot answer for the academy in general. But I can try to clarify what *I* am doing in professing law. Just as authors are often asked, "Why write?" so it is legitimate to ask, "Why teach?" One honest answer to that question is that teaching is the only profession that pays me for what I would love to do anyway, i.e., read interesting cases, articles, and books and then talk about them. Honest though that may be, it is also, I hope, too glib. I would like to think that my teaching law has more than a simply hedonistic meaning.

I do indeed believe that law, especially constitutional law, matters. I also believe that conceptions of lawyering matter. Whether this is an effect of my teaching both constitutional law and professional responsibility or the cause of my choosing to teach those subjects, I do not know. It is obviously relevant, though, that I do not teach law in the abstract, but teach these particular branches of law.

Constitutional law provides a public vocabulary absolutely essential to understanding the nature of political discourse within our society. Beyond this obvious rhetorical importance, it seems impossible to deny that at least some decisions made in the name of the Constitution, whether by judges, presidents, or private citizens, have important consequences for the lives of others. Yet I also deeply believe that law can "matter" negatively just as easily as it can be a source of human betterment. I know of no one who argues that to be a lawyer

– 168 –

is automatically to be either absolutely irrelevant or an all-too-rele-
vant scoundrel. *That* position would demoralize not only students; it
would also be profoundly demoralizing to anyone engaged in teaching
law, for it would truly suggest that what I am doing is at best pointless
and at worst the preparation of students for lives of evil. What I, and
many others, do deny, however, is that becoming a lawyer—or
"thinking like a lawyer"—in any sense makes one *automatically*
praiseworthy.

I quite frankly want to emphasize in my classroom the extent to
which "respectable" legal thinking can in fact be used to defend terrible outcomes. Just as importantly, I want to warn against the development of a "professional" detachment that separates what lawyers
sometimes do from the social consequences of their actions. It is not
without reason that lawyers have been the object of scorn for over two
millenia. It was, after all, Jesus who said, as reported in Luke 11:46:
"Woe unto you also, ye lawyers! for ye lade men with burdens griev-
ous to be borne, and ye yourselves touch not the burdens with one of
your fingers." One must understand why he described lawyers in that
way and why the description can still be relevant.

An important part of my professing law (or should the correct term
be professing antilaw?) is to try to prevent the deification of positive
law at the cost of recognition of one's membership in the broader human community. As Chapter Two revealed, I am an unabashed positivist in one important sense: there is no necessary connection between law and morality, and I have little doubt which is the more
important of those two terms.

A major part of my constitutional law course therefore involves how
legal rhetoric, written by some of the "greatest" judges in our tradition, was used to support, protect, and defend the legal legitimacy of
chattel slavery. Racism gained much of its legitimacy over the years
from American lawyers and judges asserting the autonomy of legal
concepts. Consider once more John Marshall's language in *The Antelope*,[42] a case dealing with slaves as property, and recall his emphasis
that "this court [and presumably lawyers learning from the court how
to think like lawyers] must not yield to feelings which might seduce
it from the path of duty [but instead it] must obey the mandate of the
law."[43] Marshall presented himself as "a jurist[, who] must search for
[the] legal solution" to a question like chattel slavery. Though recognizing that slavery was "contrary to the law of nature," he was prohibited from behaving as "a moralist."[44] One wonders whether portraying

Marshall in *The Antelope* as an edifying model for contemporary students is any less dispiriting than anything said by the nihilists of whom Carrington disapproves.[45]

Am I able to profess faith in the law, in Carrington's sense? I honestly do not know, because he is much too unclear about what he really wishes to assert. What I can say is that being a lawyer gives me access to certain forums, including classrooms and, when I engage in litigation, courts. Within the classroom, I try to point out the implications of various positions taken in terms of the kinds of societies— and individual lives—they seem to suggest. In conducting litigation, I am especially aware of modes of argument that are useful in gaining what I consider meritorious results, such as protection of civil liberties that I consider necessary to maintain a republican form of government.

I will admit that my definition of a meritorious result is ultimately external, based on moral or political views rather than on a belief generated from within the legal community itself that compliance with the law is a good in itself. There are some laws that I believe ought *not* be complied with, where the admirable thing to do is to break the law. I thus reject the position taken in the Code of Professional Responsibility that "[a] lawyer should never encourage or aid his client to commit criminal acts or counsel his client on how to violate the law and avoid punishment therefor."[46] To argue the contrary is to deify the law, which I am unwilling to do. Therefore, not only am I unwilling to socialize my students in unstinting respect for law, I am also insistent on making them aware that disobedience to the commands of the law may on occasion be required of someone committed to self-respect and the respect of other morally admirable people.

PROFESSION, PRAGMATISM, AND TRUTH

Do I believe that my statements in class are "true," in the sense that they reflect either the one best understanding of the Constitution or a true moral theory that exists out there in the world to be grasped and recognized by our intellection? The answer is no, which raises a separate problem that also deserves some analysis.

Some of Carrington's critics make a relatively simple, though quite powerful, point in attacking him. The argument invokes the central commitment of the modern university to the search for truth and to the academic freedom needed to pursue truth. What follows from this view is my unbridled freedom to enunciate whatever truths I discern, however demoralizing and destructive they might be. Speech that is free only within the boundaries of creedal conformity is obviously not genuinely free at all. Paul Brest, for example, stated in a letter to Phillip Johnson that "institutional orthodoxy is inimical to the pursuit of truth."[47]

The predicate of this argument is twofold: a) there exists, in *some* meaningful sense, "truth" that can be pursued; and 2) the professor of truth has a duty to do precisely that, i.e., to profess the truths he or she perceives. There may, of course, also be a third term in this argument, that knowledge of the truth will set one free.

What is so objectionable about Carrington's argument is his presumed willingness to limit membership on a law school faculty to those who believe that certain things are true about the world and to deny membership to those with a different vision of reality. What presumably must be affirmed is the truth that "law matters." Carrington does not want professors to lie by saying what they do not believe; he simply wants to ensure that members of the community will genuinely share a given creed of faith in the law that they can affirm with pride. Some of us respond, though, that the legal academy should be open to multiple visions of the truth, including those which attack the basic premises behind the theology of the civil religion.

Things (or lives) are more complex than the dichotomies laid out in the last paragraph might suggest. The true patron saint of modernity might be said to be Pontius Pilate. Responding to Jesus's claim that his "task [was] to bear witness to the truth," Pilate reasonably asked, "[W]hat is truth?"[48] What gives twentieth-century modernism its particular identity is its brutal washing, in what Holmes called "cynical acid,"[49] of many of the fondest tenets of preceding eras, including a confidence about the ability to grasp "truth."

Can a teachable notion of the Constitution survive the acidic bath? Are there truths that our Constitution teaches? An obvious dilemma within constitutional law, and a major inquiry of my professional life, is our ability, as children of the twentieth century, to take seriously the ideas, intellectual structures, and rhetoric of an earlier time. I noted at the conclusion of Chapter One the irony present in the fact that our culture, "which has experienced a centuries-long 'melancholy, long-withdrawing roar' from religious faith," nonetheless wishes to believe "in the continuing reality of a collectivity of citizens organized around a constitutional faith." The title of Owen Fiss's article, "The Death of the Law?" though couched as an question, nonetheless serves to confirm the earlier suggestion that "the 'death of constitutionalism' may be the central event of our time just as the 'death of God' " dominated the past century.

The relentless repudiation of older modes of thought does not appear to have a self-evident stopping point. Modernist approaches to the world most certainly temper, if indeed they do not "deconstruct," any innocence we might have about the notion of academic vocation and attached concepts of truth.[50] I do not, for example, view my professing of law as the enunciating of *truths*. My ultimate legal views are clearly based on moral—or ideological—premises whose truth cannot be demonstrated. What is evoked in the classroom, including my own classroom, are political visions rather than political truths, and the future will, in some ways, be constructed out of the visions that most persuade our student audiences. This description holds, I believe, not only for my own classroom but for *all* of us who talk about law. I obviously do not believe that I *lie* in talking to my students. I try scrupulously to be absolutely honest in conveying my views. I detest those who are willing to engage in Platonic "royal lies" or who are willing to play the Dostoevskian Grand Inquisitor by enunciating and enforcing creeds that they do not in fact believe. But all of this speaks to sincerity rather than truth. Sincerity—or intellectual honesty—may be a *sine qua non* of professing, but it does not establish a sufficient foundation for the freedom the professor enjoys.

In his important history of academic freedom, Walter Metzger noted that the modern theory of academic freedom developed out of the debate surrounding Darwinian evolution. "[S]cience invested the theory of academic freedom with a special conception of truth and a formula for tolerating error." It was the "concept of scientific competence [that] gave the faculties new leverage against misuses of administrative power."[51] Indeed, one sees "the argument for scientific competence[] used in the Darwinian debate as an answer to clerical presumptuousness."[52] Competence was not a new notion; as we have already seen, it was at the root of the nonreligious definitions of professionalism several centuries ago. Yet the linkage to science gave a new dynamic to the claims for the freedom of academics.

Metzger offers three specific "contributions of science: the formula for tolerating error; the limitation upon administrative power; [and] the set of positive values." Darwinian science confronted an essentially static conception of truth, which carried with it the implication that new thought had to conform with what is already known to be true. What replaced this static notion was a dynamic, evolutionary perspective. Now "all beliefs are [only] tentatively true or tentatively false, and only verifiable through a continuous process of inquiry."[53] There can never be confidence that one's current conception of truth is in fact really true (or, indeed, that one could ever have the means for knowing of absolute truth or falsity).

This was not, however, a formula for "anything goes." Attached to the concept of dynamic development was an "emphasis on disciplined inquiry [establishing] important limits to the permissible tolerance of error." If the *substance* of truth was ultimately "indeterminate," to adopt a recent vogue term, the *process* of ascertaining the best current estimate of truth was quite knowable. According to evolutionists, "every claim to a discovery of truth must submit to open verification," and verification was defined in terms of following given rules of inquiry "best understood by those who qualify as experts." "Hence," says Metzger, "academic freedom does not theoretically justify all kinds of intellectual nonconformity, but only that kind of nonconformity that proceeds according to rules." Similarly, academic freedom defends "not any private belief, but [only] that kind of private belief that allows itself publicly to be tested." The result is "not a perfect competition of ideas, but rather an imperfect competition to which certain opinions come enhanced with a special professional warranty."[54]

As Metzger points out, "science" brought with it commitments to certain values, not exclusive to that enterprise but nonetheless thought to be specially linked to it. These values included "tolerance and honesty, publicity and testifiability, individuality and cooperativeness." He goes on to emphasize two other values. The first is what he calls "universalism," the necessity of judging work on the basis of universal criteria. "Universalism" follows from "the scientific criterion of reliability—the dissociation of a scientific work from the beliefs and associations of its author." The second value is "neutrality" or "disinterestedness." "[S]cience must transcend ideology," and professors are expected to "renounce all commitments that corrupt the passion for truth."[55]

Truth as an ideal is obviously not a nineteenth-century invention. Anthony Kronman, for example, has written a powerful and eloquent article centered rhetorically on the Socratic commitment to truth. Professors, he says, are committed to truth in a way that lawyers—

and therefore students who wish to be lawyers—are not.[56] That is, the practice of law in important aspects is all too similar to what Socrates in the *Gorgias* denounced as mere oratory or rhetoric.[57] Lawyers master techniques of persuasion, and the truly successful advocate is the one who, like the master orator, can make the lesser argument appear the greater. Lawyers are interested not in truth, but in winning. Professors, according to Kronman, are (or should be) different, upholding a commitment to truth.

My own teaching career has included teaching undergraduate and graduate students, and my shift to professing law has not been without anguish, for precisely some of the reasons delineated by Kronman. Law students are often indifferent to, and sometimes contemptuous of, values that do not seem related to what will help them as advocates in the pursuit of victory. Indeed, I have suggested elsewhere that the most important source of nihilism in our culture—far more significant than the writings of a relatively few law professors— is the actual practice of law, and the socialization of students by lawyers operating in a system of unbridled advocacy.[58]

There is undoubtedly something very attractive about the analyses of Metzger and the arguments of Kronman. If I shared their perspectives, I would have no hesitation at all in denouncing Carrington's vision of the law school as dangerously anachronistic. I would also not hesitate to endorse the vision of the law school as a center of detached analysis with truth as the only goal. What prevents such an endorsement?

Contemporary claims for academic freedom, like claims for professional authority in general, often rest on epistemological assumptions concerning truth. These assumptions can be first-order assertions about what in fact is true, or second-order assertions about what particular methods are likely to produce truth. To use an ancient Greek distinction, all professors, including those of professions, claim privileged access to genuine "knowledge" as opposed to mere "opinion." However much we might be modest and disclaim any absolute truth in what we know, the modesty usually stops well short of asserting that ours is simply one among an infinite number of equally possible views. The lives that we actually live involve choosing to credit certain views even as we radically discredit others by labeling them as stupid, insane, or "off-the-wall." None of us genuinely is willing to let even a hundred intellectual flowers bloom, whether in our institutional or more personal lives. Yet the basis for choosing which flowers to nourish, or which gardeners to hire, has become ever more problematic.

To put it mildly, there is a real problem today concerning what law professors, especially those identified with critical legal studies, are willing to say about the notion of truth.[59] In particular, those of us who are classified as nihilists have drunk deeply at the well of those branches of modern thought most skeptical of concepts like truth, neutrality, or disinterestedness, insofar as all of these terms retain a strong barrier between the knowing subject and the object of knowledge. Many of us, instead, view what is professed to be known as itself constituted by the subject that claims to know. "Truth" may continue to be a word within modernist culture, but only as a synonym for culturally shared conventions. At the very least there are, from this perspective, no self-evident, immutable, or eternal truths. And the more local, socially constituted truths of our cultures and everyday lives are, in important ways, up for grabs.

Paul de Man, the late member of the Yale English Department and one of the introducers of "deconstruction" to the American intellectual vocabulary, emphasized "the necessary subversion of truth by rhetoric as the distinctive feature of all language."[60] He quoted Nietzsche's answer to Pilate's question: Truth consists of "[a] moving army of metaphors, metonymies and anthropomorphisms, . . . rhetorically sublimated, transposed, and beautified until, after long and repeated use, a people considers them as solid, canonical, and unavoidable. Truths are illusions whose illusionary nature has been forgotten. . . ."[61]

I have been much influenced by Richard Rorty, probably the most notable contemporary American proponent of a pragmatist theory of truth. Rorty proclaims "that truth is not the sort of thing one should expect to have a philosophically interesting theory about."[62] The philosophical traditions going back to Plato that attempt to say interesting things about truth as such have "outlived [their] usefulness." This view, it should be emphasized, does not argue that truth is necessarily "relative" or "subjective." Indeed, as many people have pointed out, such an assertion would be self-contradictory inasmuch as it would confidently proclaim as "truth" the relativity of truth claims. Instead, Rorty's view is simply that nothing interesting can be said about truth. It is almost literally not worth talking about. "Philosophy, the attempt to say 'how language relates to the world' by saying what *makes* certain sentences true, or certain actions or attitudes good or rational, is, on this view, impossible."[63] Its impossibility derives from its requiring us "to step outside our skins, the traditions, linguisitic and other, within which we do our thinking and self-criticism—and compare ourselves with something absolute" in order to transcend the recognition that our views are " 'merely conventional' and contingent aspects of one's life."[64]

Rorty notes that the view he articulates raises "the question of whether we can give up what Stanley Cavell calls the 'possibility that one among endless true descriptions of me tells me who I am.' " This belief in a single true self—to whom fidelity is then presumably owed—runs deep in our culture. Significantly, Dean Robert McKay, defending new rules of professional conduct promulgated by the American Bar Association, asserted that "the lawyer is not asked—and must not be asked—to be other than true to self, or to be false to any other. . . ."[65] One can understand McKay's desire to reassure his audience without accepting his claim. The unexamined life may not be worth living, but the hope that examination would generate a one true self who could be known—and to whom one could, following Polonius's advice, be "true"—is chimerical. Rorty admits that this view is hard to live with. He quotes Sartre's remark that the establishment of fascism would establish "fascism [as] the truth of man, and so much the worse for us." Rorty goes on to say that this brings together such quintessential Americans as William James and John Dewey and continental thinkers as Nietzsche and Foucault: All portray "the sense that there is nothing deep down inside us except what we have put there ourselves, no criterion that we have not created in the course of creating a practice, no standard of rationality that is not an appeal to such a criterion, no rigorous argumentation that is not obedience to our own conventions."[66]

One can, of course, try to describe the conventions within a given culture, though this in itself raises at least two problems. One is recognizing what "the" conventions are. How, for example, does one warrant to law students what are "good" legal opinions as opposed to bad ones? Many persons, for example, have criticized the "craftsmanship" of Justice Blackmun's opinion in the abortion case *Roe* v. *Wade*.[67] We might, however, adopt Mark Tushnet's suggestion and view it as the inauguration of a "cubist" mode of analysis that we, trained according to more academic standards of aesthetics, have trouble appreciating.[68] It is no less "lawyerly" for all that, though.

How could it be, since a basic source for data on what *counts* as conventional lawyering is the opinions of the Supreme Court?

A second problem, many of us would say, is that the conventions are hopelessly inconsistent and contradictory. There are, as my colleague Philip Bobbitt has argued in his book *Constitutional Fate*,[69] several "modalities" of constitutional argumentation, but there is no ultimate guide as to which modality—say, original meaning as against doctrinal elaboration—should control. What most infuriates Carrington is the presence in the legal academy of those who would quote Rorty's description of an interpreter as one who "simply beats the text into a shape which will serve his own purpose."[70] One can, of course, express outrage about particular beatings. I do not like some of Justice Rehnquist's opinions, for example; but they are not disqualified as examples of the lawyer's conventional arts on that account any more than opinions I admire, say by Justice Brennan, are any less "beatings" of the text merely because I like them.

To be sure, like most members of our legal culture, I can recognize, even if I cannot formalistically analyze, "off-the-wall" legal arguments, and I can advise students that they will very likely be disappointed if they present them; but this represents a relatively modest concession, I suspect, from the perspective of someone like Carrington. For what I do not do is advise my students that there is a given theory of constitutional interpretation that is true or legitimate as against illegitimate contenders. *Every* case, and *every* opinion in every case, studied in a law school classroom is an example of on-the-wall "thinking like a lawyer." This obviously includes such morally egregious cases as *Dred Scott*, with Chief Justice Taney's reminder that in the American constitutional system established in 1787 blacks had "no rights which the white man was bound to respect."[71] I do not treat the opinions as equally attractive; the grounds for preference, though, are the social visions articulated rather than the legal craft revealed.[72] One can indeed pick favorites among them, but not because they genuinely exemplify a content-neutral, nonideological practice of legal thinking.

The fact that I think I am describing what all law professors (and ultimately all of us in general) do helps to explain why I do not believe that *my* academic freedom (or tenure) is any more dubious than that of someone who articulates more traditional notions of truth. No abstract criteria can ultimately define who should—or should not—be hired on a law faculty. A particular conversational community, sometimes called an academic "discipline" or even a "profession" will decide whose conversations it finds interesting, helpful, or illuminating. Those people will be hired, and none others. One might self-consciously try to extend the range within a particular school of conversational options. I believe very strongly that proponents of Critical Legal Studies have performed a real service in expanding the communal conversation. Yet none of us could possibly believe that everyone is a genuine contributor. A proponent of law and astrology would, I am confident, be turned down by every faculty, whether dominated by mainstream or CLS academics. It is a somewhat more complicated issue what we would do if one of our already tenured colleagues converted (and isn't that the appropriate word) to become a proponent of law and astrology. At the very least, one would assume that he or she would not be allowed to continue teaching any required courses.

CONCLUSION

This chapter might strike some readers as rather gloomy. I am therefore tempted to try to lighten the tone by adopting what might be termed a "Holmesian resolution." Justice Holmes tended to undercut the radicalism—indeed intellectual savagery and protonihilism—of some of his remarks by adopting extraordinarily reassuring rhetoric at their conclusion. No better example exists than the final paragraph of his monumental speech on "The Path of the Law." Emphasizing the utility of studying law only from the perspective of a hypothetical "bad man," Holmes spent most of his lecture throwing "cynical acid" on the impressionable minds of his student audience. Yet he concluded his remarks by reminding students that study of "[t]he remoter and more general aspects [of the law]" would not only allow them to become "great master[s] in [their] calling, but connect [their] subject with the universe and catch and echo of the infinite, a glimpse of its unfathomable process, a hint of the universal law."[73]

I cannot do that. I have neither the eloquence nor, just as importantly, the neo-Emersonian optimism (what one might indeed call "faith") of Holmes. One hopes that the study (and professing) of law will serve ultimately as a source of both self-respect and social betterment. It may not, however, and it is simply foolish to pretend otherwise. If one puts faith only in that which guarantees salvation, then, once again, we can conclude only that law is unworthy of our faith, though it always remains worthy of our study.

But let us return to the imagined application of William Schneiderman to join a faculty of law. Although Communists are scarcely "nihilists"—they have far too much faith for any such appellation—they surely do not share Carrington's commitment to the American constitutional structure. My own inclination would certainly be to hire Schneiderman, on the assumption that he presents his ideas in an interesting and stimulating manner. Whatever reservations I have about the model of law school as a secular department of religion, I certainly prefer that model to that of the law school as divinity school, at least so long as the proponents of that latter model demand the level of faith that Carrington seems to require. But the point of this chapter is that cold logic and analysis scarcely resolves Schneiderman's status. Instead, we must choose between two fundamentally different cultural visions of legal study. A leap must be made, whether of faith or of something else.

CONCLUSION:
ADDING ONE'S SIGNATURE
TO THE CONSTITUTION

RETURNING TO PHILADELPHIA

EVEN IF ONE accepts the guiding notion of this book, the Constitution as the focus of a faith community, that does not resolve the question of our own stance regarding "constitutional faith". To leap or not to leap? That is surely the question. To begin formulating an answer, I return to where the main body of this book began, to the Second Bank of the United States and the bicentennial exhibit, "Miracle in Philadelphia," located there. When visitors reached the section relating to the delegates' vote on September 17, 1787, accepting the draft of the Constitution submitted by the Committee on Detail, they were confronted by two endless scrolls, each with the same two questions directed to the viewer: "Will You Sign This Constitution? If you had been in Independence Hall on September 17, 1787, would you have endorsed the Constitution?" Presumably, adding one's signature would serve to transform the experience from a mere remembrance of times past to a renewed dedication to—a continuing ordination of, as it were—the Constitution as an ever-living presence encouraging the establishment of a more perfect Union committed above all to the realization of justice and the blessings of liberty. Every participant in the exhibit was thus asked to make a choice—to sign or not to sign, to ratify or to reject, the Constitution of the United States.[1] The exhibit implicitly directed a question at us: How do *we* stand vis-à-vis the Constitution? Our answer to that question is at the same time a sign of our willingness to join in affirming a "constitutional faith," whatever the attendant difficulties in giving content to the notion.

So what is *our* demeanor as we come to Philadelphia to contemplate the origins of the Constitution. Do *we* celebrate, affirm, renew any previous vows of loyalty? Can we, with an open heart, do ourselves what we require of those who would join the American polity from abroad by becoming naturalized citizens—declare (and celebrate) our status as Americans "attached to the principles of the Constitution"? If we answer "no," is it because some other conception of Americanness offers us a better mode of political self-understanding? Or have we simply become "alienated residents," willing to accept certain political benefits of residence but without the density of felt membership in, and loyalty to, a specifically political order linked in a meaningful way to the Constitution?

We may doubt that the Park Service genuinely intended to put into question the viewer's commitment to the Constitution. And surely the intended meaning of the Bicentennial, at least from the perspective of public officials like Chief Justice Burger and other of its organizers, was to celebrate (and vindicate) the sacred text rather than to mount a challenge to its authority. Yet if modern literary theory has taught us anything, it is the omnipresence within texts of words, signs, or symbols that undercut and subvert the "intended" message. The intended meaning of the Bicentennial may have been to ratify the authority of the Constitution; the invitation to sign, however, raised the possibility of challenging its authority. It served to bring the otherwise absent Jefferson, with his call for repeated constitutional conventions and his skepticism about thoughtless veneration, into the Madisonian presence. And surely it would have been a devastating commentary on the Constitution if most of the visitors made a reasoned decision not to sign.

Consider, for example, a recent report from Israel describing the launching of the celebration of the fortieth anniversary of its independence. Leaders of Israel, both past and present, were gathered at the presidential mansion, and they were asked to "re-sign" the Declaration of Independence as, in the words of the *Jerusalem Post*, "an act of symbolic reaffirmation of that historic document and rededication to its principles." Several persons refused to do so, and others signed only under protest, and the *Post* called this "a cause for worry," a demonstration of the potential fragility of the values presumptively underlying Israel's constitution as a nation-state. One refuser, for example, based his decision on the countenancing by the Declaration of the permanent division of Eretz Yisrael, the Biblical land of Israel, into latter-day Israeli and Arab states. "[U]nity of the Land was, to him, more important than the rise of the state upon it. A septuagenarian who had been one of the original signatories, and who now signed again, nevertheless had second thoughts about equality of rights for the minorities, meaning Arabs. . . ."[2] One would be foolish indeed to treat as inconsequential such decisions.

It would be only slightly less devastating if most visitors dismissed the invitation at the Philadelphia exhibit as trivial gimmickry, for that response would itself be evidence of the distance that had developed between the citizenry and the Constitution. Presumably such a response would indicate that one simply could not take seriously the prospect that the Constitution was worth genuinely grappling with as a potential object either of commitment or of rejection. What Chief Justice Burger implicitly compared to the Torah would have turned into a kind of Santa Claus. It was something to be shown the many schoolchildren being brought to Philadelphia in patriotic exercise, who might themselves be expected to, and did in fact, add *their* signatures in a "hands-on" experience of socialization, but not something to be believed in by more sophisticated adults.

Adult knowledge—and potential disillusionment—is key. One might, for example, try to imagine two golden wedding anniversaries. The first would feature a couple whose marriage is universally recognized as truly fine. Perhaps they choose to ratify that recognition, so to speak, by symbolically re-engaging in their marriage ceremony. As they restate their vows of long ago, or even sign a new marriage "contract," we can all share in the sense of human triumph over what Lincoln might call the "lesser angels" of our nature. But imagine a second event, suffused with a kind of bitter nostalgia, in which the motif is remembrance of the fond hopes of fifty years ago coupled with a recognition that the marriage—though never formally dissolved by divorce—nonetheless in no way lived up to those hopes (and, even worse, its potential). Here, renewal of the wedding vows would be rank sentimentality, the known historical reality contradicting the claims of the words, and the only appropriate response of the participants in this sad spectacle would be embarrassment at the self-delusion of the couple. Bicentennials, like anniversaries, are noncontingent events, dictated by the relentless turn of the calendar; our

responses to them, however, are richly contingent and worth examination for the light they shed on our own commitments.

Perhaps one doubts the legitimacy of the analogy to the wedding
anniversary or to the overall framing question, that is, ought we to
sign the Constitution. I have already tried, through the discussion of
loyalty oaths in Chapter Three, to present an answer to such doubt-
ers. There we examined the peculiarly ideological nature of the very
notion of American identity and its emphasis on what Huntington
identified as the "American creed" to which Fanny Wright suggested
we should "wed" ourselves. I also indicated in that chapter that many
of us had in fact signed loyalty oaths, whether as a condition of becoming a state employee or simply by virtue of applying for a passport.
Still, ironically enough, I suspect that one consequence of the coercive nature of the requirement placed upon us to sign such oaths is
that many of us did not reflect with any great seriousness on their
meaning (other than, perhaps, their signification of the presence of a
too-powerful state). Assuming that we noticed them at all, many of us
probably treated them roughly the same way my law students responded to part of a document that they are required to submit to the
Bar Assocation as part of the process of becoming a lawyer. All applicants must sign a statement indicating that they have read the Code
of Professional Responsibility and pledge their adherence to its demands. The overwhelming majority of my students freely indicated
that they had perjured themselves: They had not in fact read the
Code, and they treated the affirmation that they had as a mere for-
malism, not to be taken seriously. My students, who would surely
take umbrage at being called "nihilists," nonetheless treated the
words they signed as without genuine meaning. They surely provided
no guide either to what the signatories knew about the document in
question (for they had not read it) or about their likely conduct as
lawyers (for they had not reflected on what challenges to their sense
of self might be presented by taking on the role of the lawyer). How
many of us who have taken loyalty oaths are any different?

A decision accepting the invitation proferred by the Philadelphia
exhibit to sign the Constitution was, precisely because of its noncoer-
civeness, perhaps a more significant gesture than the routinized submission to authority signified by the standard loyalty oath. This is not
to say that many visitors did not sign it without reflection, but the
gratuitous nature of the deed—to sign or not to sign—invited a kind
of reflection that the passport oath, for example, does not. From an

ordinary utilitarian perspective, nothing rode on the decision. We did not have to balance the desire to travel abroad or the need for a job against the cost to our personal pride or dignity of signing a notoriously vague set of words. In adding one's name to the Philadelphia scroll one gained nothing; in declining to do so one lost nothing— from one perspective, that is. From another perspective, perhaps, one gained or lost everything, i.e., one's true identity as a member— or rejector—of a peculiar American fellowship. Perhaps the analogy is to the simple box marked "religion" that many of us confronted in some document upon registering for college. It was precisely the ability to mark "none" that made the decision to affirm membership in a particular community potentially significant, especially insofar as that decision occurred at the moment of transformation from the maximally encumbered status of child to the presumably more fluid status of adult charged with shaping one's own identity.

In any event, the designers of the Philadelphia exhibition issued a deceptively simple invitation, to sign the Constitution. So please join me in an imaginative trip back to the Second Bank as we place ourselves in front of the scrolls.

WHICH CONSTITUTION
(IF ANY) DOES ONE SIGN?

What do we do? The first thing *we*—that is, highly self-conscious persons willing to engage in a conversation like the one that is now concluding—must decide is what constitutes the Constitution that we are being asked to sign. In formal terms, we are asked to endorse the specific document that was adopted by the convention on September 17 and ratified by the States. Thus one young man who came over to the exhibit while I was observing it—on May 24, 1987, during a major "bicentennial weekend" taking place in Philadelphia commemorating the opening of the Philadelphia Convention on May 25, 1787—indicated that "I wouldn't have signed it because of no bill of rights." A woman who was signing at the time responded, "It was a beginning."

It is obvious that the 1787 Constitution is not the Constitution that we live with, and not only because that Constitution has been subsequently amended, beginning in 1791 with the Bill of Rights. After all, Paul Brest has spoken of contemporary constitutional law as primarily "the elaboration of the Court's own precedents," and he has referred to the documentary Constitution of 1787 as akin to "a remote ancestor who came over on the Mayflower."[3] In addition, of course, I devoted much of Chapter One to arguing that emphasis on the Constitution as "document" bespeaks a specifically "protestant" notion of constitutionalism. I find more meaningful a "catholic" view of the Constitution that adds to the parchment ratified in 1788 (and formally amended thereafter) not only key decisions of the Supreme Court, Congress, and the president, but also fundamental documents such as the Declaration of Independence and the Gettysburg Address and, beyond that, aspects of the American experience that cannot be reduced to a text at all.

Even if we concede the Constitution's documentary existence, the vital question remains: "Which text captures the Constitution that we are being asked to, and that we would in fact, sign?" The obvious focus of the Philadelphia exhibit is the Constitution drafted in the Philadelphia summer of 1787. Signing *that* document just as obviously raises a number of problems, including that voiced by the man who refused to sign because of the absence of a Bill of Rights. Historically, of course, the failure of the Convention delegates to include a Bill of Rights did not doom their handiwork, but certainly the conventional view is that ratification was purchased only through a de facto agreement that the text would be so supplemented as soon as possible, as was in fact done.

As we make the Bill of Rights more central to our concerns, do we make as well our signature contingent on our knowledge of the way the story turned out in 1791? We may be signing not the text presented to George Washington and his compatriots on September 17, but rather a text that was unavailable to them and one by no means presumed to be likely or even desirable. We might recall, for example, that several of the Philadelphia framers, including Madison, Wilson, and Hamilton, specifically derided complaints about the lack of a Bill of Rights, going so far as to suggest that the addition of a Bill of Rights would actually make the Constitution worse by suggesting that the national government in fact had powers not specifically granted to it that needed specific limitation.

The lack of a Bill of Rights was obviously no small matter, and George Mason, one of the most distinguished members of the Virginia delegation, refused to sign because of this lack. Was he wrong to have done so? Or, at the very least, was it a reasonable decision, one that we ourselves can honor even if we reject it and choose instead to give our maximum praise to those who signed?

Much more serious, for some of us, is the brooding omnipresence of American history—race and, more precisely, slavery. One can immediately try to evade the slavery issue in somewhat the same way that one evades the lack of a Bill of Rights in the 1787 Constitution. That is, just as one can in effect stipulate that the document one is signing is that supplemented by the 1791 Amendments, so can one announce that he or she is signing the post-1868 Constitution.

We can take a rigorously historicist approach and say that it is absurd to try to place ourselves within the context of 1787 and decide whether we would have endorsed the Constitution then or, indeed, whether we applaud the specific outcome of that year now. I am sympathetic to that argument, given that I do not believe that we can shed our historically located skin and engage in a mental equivalent of completely successful time travel. We can engage the past, to be sure, but we cannot rejoin the past. There is one fundamental problem with the historicist strategy, however. Designed, among other things, to save the Constitution—and its framers—from censure, it also has the result of displacing it as an object of esteem. For if we distance ourselves from 1787 by treating it as an essentially "lost world," to adopt the title of Daniel Boorstin's brilliant book on Thomas Jefferson, then it makes little more sense to select out what we like for praise than to focus on what we object to for censure.

In any case, we return to what is surely the most difficult problem presented those who would celebrate the Constitution, chattel slavery. To ignore chattel slavery as a constitutionally legitimized presence in American history is not, to put it mildly, a satisfactory solution, any more than is the mindless celebration of Western humanism (or Christian sensibility) that ignores the Holocaust's arising in a land of unusually high culture and piety. Although the presence of slavery should create qualms for both whites and blacks alike, it is understandable that there might be special reason to wonder how black visitors to Philadelphia respond when invited to sign the Constitution.

Recall the 1974 witness of Barbara Jordan's impassioned "faith in the Constitution" that was "whole, . . . complete, . . . [and] total." Could she possibly have made the same speech in regard to the Constitution of 200 years ago? Indeed, might she not have joined her unmatched eloquence to William Lloyd Garrison's description of the Constitution as a "Covenant with Death and an Agreement with

Hell," with its subversion therefore becoming the heartfelt duty of a moral being? Justice Thurgood Marshall raised some of the questions in a speech on May 6, 1987, where he took sharp issue with the "proud proclamations of the wisdom, foresight, and sense of justice shared by the framers and reflected in a written document now yellowed with age." Instead, Justice Marshall emphasized that "the government they devised was defective from the start." Rectification of those defects "requir[ed] several amendments, a civil war, and momentous social transformation" before our "system of constitutional government" achieved the "respect for the individual freedoms and human rights [that] we hold as fundamental today."[4] The central objects of his concern were compromises made to slave interests during the Convention.

One can, of course, adopt Frederick Douglass's argument discussed in Chapter Two, with its view of the Constitution, correctly understood, as "anti-slavery." As we saw, though, this argument depends on a number of very controversial interpretive premises, including a hyper-textuality coupled with a sweeping dismissal of the relevance of Supreme Court decisions purporting to give an authoritative construction of the Constitution.

However, what if a potential signer—perhaps you yourself—is unwilling to pay that price or, at the very least, is unable to agree with Douglass's reading of the Constitution and accepts instead the more standard reading of the document as significantly protective of slaveholder interests? One might, for example, adopt Justice Story's view that abominations like the Fugitive Slave Clause, not to mention the guaranteed protection of the international slave trade for 20 years and the added representation given the South because of its slaves, were necessary in order to form the Union. At this point inquiry could branch off into at least two directions. The first assumes the desirability of Union and then asks whether in fact achievement of that end required the means chosen in Philadelphia and therefore our retrospective, albeit reluctant, ratification. To ask the question in this way inevitably gives greatest "gravitational weight" to the historical record as it actually developed and the justifications offered at the time, for it indeed seems tendentious to deny the efficacy of the compromises offered to attaining the goal of creating a strengthened United States. We may, however, ask a second question: Do we in fact share the commitment to Union that justifies the compromises?

Once again, one might quickly ask whether we can really ask such questions in a meaningful way. Can we genuinely imagine an alternative history for the last 200 years that would allow us to answer the question as asked? Indeed, as someone like Michael Sandel would remind us, isn't the very self that grapples with the question so much the product of the existence of the Union that we are ultimately asking if we would wish to be radically different selves?

We do know that there were many who opposed ratification of the Constitution because they feared the centralized Union that they saw implied by the document, and it presumably remains open to us to declare our sympathy with or opposition to some of these anti-Federalists, even though they were defeated. Few of the anti-Federalists, of course, focused on the collaboration with slavery as the source of their discontents, though, to their credit, some did, such as Luther Martin in Maryland. Much more important, for most of them, was the fear that popular participation in governance would become attenuated and that government would increasingly be placed in the hands of elites. The most important response to this argument is contained in the 14th Federalist Paper, where Madison delivers his crucial attack on the assumption that republican government can be maintained only in a relatively small territory. Even if we think that Madison was right within his particular context, where he was writing of a country of approximately 3 million people in 13 states, one may doubt that his arguments apply quite so neatly to the country that ultimately developed and within which we live. It is hard to gainsay the feelings of utter marginalization and meaninglessness of participation within the present political order; calls by Professor Sunstein and others for the revival of republican political sensibility, however attractive to some of us, will remain implausible as prescriptions for a polity of such different size and scope as that which we have become.

This being said, it is hard to believe that a "balkanized" United States would necessarily have developed in any more participatory a fashion than the constitutional union. There is no plausible counter-rendering of our history that would leave us with a small—or egalitarian—enough population to make generalized active citizenship a norm. Moreover, one must also ask about the costs imposed by actively attempting to maintain a small, homogeneous social order conducive to such citizenship. Many of us benefitted from generous immigration policies that might well not have survived a stronger emphasis on preserving a republican political order.

Still, one might well turn this argument around and contend that a more balkanized political order divided along northern and southern lines would nonetheless have remained equally hospitable to immigration while not forcing the collaboration with slavery found in the Constitution, if those are indeed one's central concerns. There is no good reason to believe that the northern states, whose economies generated pro-immigrant policies, would have behaved any differently had they not been joined with the southern states, which were historically more skeptical about open immigration. The problem is that we move into the realm of more and more counterfactual history that sends the imagination reeling. Assuming that Napoleon would still have been willing to sell the Louisiana territories, to whom would he have sold them? And so on.

And, of course, the central problem with "disunionist" thinking, as pointed out by some of Garrison's own opponents, is that it focuses more on the immorality of collaboration with slavery than on the question of how one most quickly can bring slavery to an end. We know that with ratification of the Thirteenth Amendment chattel slavery ended by 1865. Is there good reason to believe that it would have ended earlier had the Constitution not been ratified and balkanization followed? I suspect not. But the important point is surely this: Can one who believes that the ratification of the Constitution *did* enhance the prospects (and actuality) of chattel slavery sign the Constitution? What precisely is the value of the Constitution and of the concomitant nation that would justify even an extra week's slavery?

As already suggested, one might try to finesse these difficult, if not excruciating, questions by focusing on what some have called the "second" Constitution—i.e., the post–Civil War document distinguished by the addition of the Thirteenth, Fourteenth, and Fifteenth Amendments. That allows a solution of the chattel slavery problem (though not necessarily other kinds of slavery, such as wage slavery), and it might justify the decision of many blacks to add their signatures to the reformed document. But could Barbara Jordan necessarily sign even the 1868 Constitution? After all, the standard reading of *that* Constitution is that it did not guarantee women the right to vote. Women were not given this most basic attribute of community membership until 1920 and the Nineteenth Amendment, and some partisans of the Equal Rights Amendment would deny that women have been granted full rights of membership even today.

Now, one might argue that the Fourteenth Amendment, correctly read, "in fact" invalidated allocation of the ballot by gender; at the

very least, though, this makes problematic the existence of the Nineteenth Amendment and raises many important issues of constitutional
interpretation. But what of today's Constitution? Is it sufficiently
"perfect" that signing is unproblematic? I assume that no one need
believe that it is truly perfect in order to sign; the question is what
deviation from perfection is tolerable, justifying inevitable compromises.

One's ascriptions of "perfection" might well depend on one's relative position in the various structures of American society. Those who
are well off, for example, might well be more appreciative of the Constitution's protection of so-called "negative" liberties, that is, rights
against oppressive state interference in one's everyday life. In the past
this included a strong component of protection against the development of what we have come to call the welfare state, which involves
at least mild redistribution from the more wealthy to the less wealthy.
But what reason do persons mired in poverty have to be wildly appreciative of negative rights when what they seek are affirmative protections such as food, shelter, and clothing? Should a homeless resident
of Philadelphia, whose interest in the Second Bank of the United
States might be primarily as a shelter from the storm, necessarily sign
any extant version of the Constitution? Might he or she become a
modern George Mason and declare that a Constitution lacking a
strongly affirmative Bill of Rights is not worth signing, whatever its
other strengths might be?

But one need not be radical to find potentially severe imperfections
in our constitutional scheme. A recent report by Lloyd Cutler and
other distinguished citizens suggested that the vaunted system of separation of powers and checks and balances is in fact a recipe for im-
mobilism and a government incapacitated from effective action (or,
what is worse, tempted to achieve "effectiveness" by the surreptitious
practices carried to new heights—or depths—by the Reagan Administration). The answer, according to these analysts, lies in such practices as tightening the connection between presidential and congressional elections, allowing members of Congress to serve in the
Cabinet, and, most radical of all, allowing the calling of new elections
should president and Congress be hopelessly deadlocked.

Perhaps one way of testing whether these would truly be "fundamental" changes in our constitutional system would be by asking
whether a person who shares the premises of this analysis would sign
the Constitution. An affirmative answer could well have two aspects:

1) Even with the defects of the present system of governance, it is still sufficiently protective of liberty and helpful to achieving justice that it deserves our support; and 2) one could emphasize as key to the Constitution the existence of Article V, the amending clause. For Article V is the best possible evidence for the proposition that the framers themselves did not believe that they had created a perfect document and that future changes were completely legitimate, at least so long as they went through Article V procedures. Article V can become the great source of consensus, paradoxically, by legitimizing radical dissension. I hope that Chapter Four, with its extended analysis of *Schneiderman*, demonstrated some of the problems with such a view.

TOWARD A LIMITED AFFIRMATION OF CONSTITUTIONAL FAITH

I have been engaging in a process of repeated deferral, indicating the various ramifications of the question without indicating my own answers. It is time to cease the evasion.

I have certainly been tempted to say that I would not sign the Constitution, whether to indicate a symbolic solidarity with the victims of the American Constitution (including, but not limited to, slaves) or simply to manifest a certain kind of iconoclasm. But, as judges sometimes say, that opinion just won't write, at least for me, though I do regard it as a genuine possibility for others.

The Constitution is a linguistic system, what some among us might call a discourse. It has helped to generate a uniquely American form of political rhetoric that allows one to grapple with every important political issue imaginable. It provides "a common language," Jefferson Powell has noted, "with which to carry on debate about the distribution and use of power in our society."[5] The fact that its teachings are "indeterminate" is quite beside the point; so is any system of language. There is little meaningful "determinacy" to English; it allows the formulation of a literally infinite number of sentences, many of which can be in logical contradiction with one another. But they all count as recognizable sentences of *our* language, which forms us just as much as we purport to form it.

The fact remains that I believe that constitutionalist discourse *can* be a valuable way of addressing crucial public issues. There is nothing that is unsayable in the language of the Constitution, even if some things will sound strange and "off-the-wall." Indeed, on the day that I signed the Philadelphia scroll, I was ultimately compelled to add my signature by the memory of Frederick Douglass and *his* willingness to embrace the Constitution. His ability to speak in the terms of the Constitution—and to stretch the sense of constitutional possibility—helped to overcome my genuine doubts that had been reinforced by Justice Marshall's speech. Justice Marshall is, I think, a better guide to the actual interpretation of the Constitution given by trained adepts in the law, the most important of whom are judges. Yet Douglass is an eloquent guide to the possibilities present in the discourse and the ability to make what first appears "off-the-wall" seem altogether appropriate.

The genealogy of constitutional interpretation quite often follows the path marked by Professor Risinger: "Today's frivolity may be tomorrow's law. . . . [T]he law often grows by an organic process in which a concept is conceived, then derided as absurd (and clearly not the law), then accepted as theoretically tenable (though not the law), then accepted as the law."[6] As Mark Tushnet, among others, has pointed out, there is no bar to someone's speaking "constitution-talk" in order to derive a full program of affirmative welfare rights or, indeed, a thoroughly socialist society, however strange such sentences would sound to most native speakers today. Given the possibilities of this language that we already have, I have no reason to believe that a competing rhetoric is likely to prove more productive, even without considering all the costs attached to learning the new language of any such rhetoric.

One can obviously learn new languages, just as it is helpful to try to become less parochial about the so-called American way of doing things; but it is a radical step indeed when a person consciously repudiates an old language, and the renunciation and abjuration of that language are almost always accompanied by special circumstances. I have been told that there are some Afrikaaner writers who have chosen to stop writing in that language as a sign of their revulsion against the terrible culture linked with it; presumably, some writers did the same with German some fifty years ago. For a writer, no more magnificent, or terrible, gesture can be imagined.

My refusal to sign the Constitution would require a much deeper alienation from American life and politics than I can genuinely feel (or, indeed, have ever felt). The Constitution—or "Constitution-talk"—has in some of its manifestations incarnated what is worst about the United States; but it captures as well what is best about this country. I recognize, of course, that as a definitely privileged member of the American class structure, I may be more genuinely aware of the benefits over the burdens or, more ominously, may be unaware of the extent to which my benefits are structurally dependent on what I purport to find less attractive. To recognize that possibility does not establish it as fact, though; until it is established, I can sign.

Whatever its problems, *Schneiderman* is altogether accurate in evoking a sense of the fluidity of the Constitution, its resistance to any kind of fixity or closure, even though some would seek it either in the text or in the pronouncements of an authoritative institution like the Supreme Court. For me, signing the Constitution—and agreeing therefore to profess at least a limited constitutional faith—commits me not to closure but only to a process of becoming and to taking responsibility for constructing the political vision toward which I strive, joined, I hope, with others. It is therefore less a series of propositional utterances than a commitment to taking political conversation seriously. I would want to distinguish this from an entirely "Article V" view of the Constitution, though, because I do indeed believe that the Constitution is best understood as supportive of such conversations and requiring a government committed to their maintenance. Moreover, as suggested in Chapter Two, what makes my faith assertion only a limited one is the recognition that even my "best" Constitution might at times come into conflict with what I regard as my most important moral commitments; under such circumstances, it would be the Constitution that (I hope) would give way.

That I—a white, male, well-paid law professor—would sign the Constitution surely can evoke little surprise. We (that is, persons with this collection of attributes) have done well under the Constitution. Why shouldn't we pay it the token esteem of "signing" it? It is absolutely vital, though, to recognize that other persons, nonwhite, non–male, non–well off, to name only the most obvious examples, need not share the esteem, and indeed, may understandably share a sense of rage rather than mere indifference when they contemplate the celebrations that have been so much a part of the Bicentennial years. The vital challenge facing the American faith community is the possibility of expanding the relevant "we" in "We the People," who must ultimately endorse the faith if it is to live as anything other than an ideological charade.

It would be essentially misleading to attribute to constitutional faith the longevity that we associate with the great religious faiths that have provided the metaphors for this book, particularly Judaism and Christianity. We might think instead of the great Egyptian, Greek, and Roman religions that today stock museums with their treasures but are otherwise dead as informing visions of how we the living might structure our own lives. Whether constitutional faith maintains itself depends on our ability to continue taking it seriously. I have tried to show that this is no easy task. I also hope that I have demonstrated, at least in part, that the question is worth asking and that answers can emerge, if at all, only out of conversation.

N O T E S

INTRODUCTION

1. The case was Schneiderman v. United States, 320 U.S. 118 (1943), and it will be the central focus of Chapter Four below. All quotations in the following two paragraphs come from *From the Diaries of Felix Frankfurter* (ed. Joseph Lash [New York: W. W. Norton & Co., 1975], pp. 211-12), where Frankfurter included an extensive entry detailing the remarks he had made at the Supreme Court conference.

2. In 1917 Frankfurter wrote a friend about attending Rosh Hashanah services and mentioned that "I'm rather happy that I can go through these symbolic religious events without a sense of discord or disrespect (by my mere presence) to the believers, tho the significance for me is not creedal." Letter to Katherine Ludington, quoted in Michael Parrish, *Felix Frankfurter and His Times: The Reform Years* (New York: The Free Press, 1982), p. 129. And, responding to Walter Lippman's question, "What is a 'Jew' anyway?" Frankfurter could answer only that "[a] Jew is a person whom non-Jews regard as a Jew." Felix Frankfurter to Jerome Frank (May 3, 1946), quoted in ibid.

3. Patriotism was a cardinal value for Frankfurter. When told by Archibald MacLeish that he was writing a patriotic play, Frankfurter replied, "Good. You couldn't make it too patriotic for me." Garson Kanin, "Trips to Felix," in Wallace Mendelson, ed., *Felix Frankfurter: A Tribute* (New York: Reynal & Co., 1964), p. 49. Paul Freund described Frankfurter's patriotism as so "unabashed" that it was "almost childlike." Harvard Law School, "Felix Frankfurter: Talks in Tribute," February 26, 1965, p. 11, quoted in Sanford Levinson, "The Democratic Faith of Felix Frankfurter," *Stanford Law Review* 25 (1973): 430.

4. Both the description of Wright and the quotation come from Werner Sollors, *Beyond Ethnicity: Consent and Descent in American Culture* (New York: Oxford University Press, 1986), p. 152.

5. Whittle Johnson, "Little America—Big America," *Yale Review* 58 (October 1968): 10-11.

6. Irving Kristol, "The Spirit of '87," *The Public Interest*, no. 86 (1987): 5.

7. *Hegel's Political Writings*, trans. T. Knox (Oxford: Oxford University Press, 1964), p. 244.

8. Clifford Geertz, "The Uses of Diversity," in Sterling McMurrin, ed., *The Tanner Lectures on Human Values* (Salt Lake City: University of Utah Press, 1986), p. 271.

CHAPTER ONE

1. Paul Leicester Ford, *Writings of Thomas Jefferson*, vol. 10 (New York: G. P. Putnam's Sons, 1899), p. 42 (letter to Samuel Kercheval, July 12, 1816).

2. Ibid., p. 43.

3. Alexander Hamilton, John Jay, and James Madison, *The Federalist*, ed. Jacob Cooke (Cleveland: Meridian Books, 1961), p. 340.

4. Letter to G. L. Turberville, November 2, 1788, in Max Farrand, ed., *Records of the Federal Convention of 1787*, vol. 3 (New Haven: Yale University Press, 1937), p. 354. James Sundquist quotes this letter on the first page of *Constitutional Reform and Effective Government* (Washington, D.C.: The Brookings Institution, 1986), where he argues that the Framers, with their emphasis on separation of powers and checks and balances, bequeathed us a structure of national government that is "too congenitally divided, too prone to stalemate, too conflict-ridden to meet its immense responsibilities" (p. 16).

5. *Writings of James Madison*, vol. 14, ed. Robert Rutland (Charlottesville: University of Virginia Press, 1983), pp. 191-92. See also *Writings of James Madison*, vol. 9, ed. Gaillard Hunt (New York: G. P. Putnam's Sons, 1910), pp. 429-31, where Madison calls for the "preservation of the [American] system [of government] in its purity, its symmetry, and its authenticity," saying that "this can only be done by a steady attention and sacred regard to the chartered boundaries." I owe these references to Robert Ferguson, " 'We Do Ordain and Establish': The Constitution as Literary Text," *William and Mary Law Review* 29 (1987): 3.

6. Michael Kammen, *A Machine That Would Go of Itself: The Con-

stitution in American Culture (New York: Alfred Knopf, 1986), pp. 70-71.

7. Abraham Lincoln, "The Perpetuation of Our Political Institutions," in Richard Current, ed., *The Political Thought of Abraham Lincoln* (Indianapolis: Bobbs-Merrill Co., 1961), pp. 16-17.

8. See the influential essay by Robert Bellah, "Civil Religion in America," *Daedalus* (Winter 1967), reprinted in Robert Bellah, *Beyond Belief: Essays on Religion in a Post-Traditional World* (New York: Harper & Row, 1970), pp. 168-89. See generally Russell E. Richey and Donald G. Jones, eds., *American Civil Religion* (New York: Harper & Row, 1974). See also two helpful essays by W. Lance Bennett: "Political Sanctification: The Civil Religion and American Politics," *Social Science Information* 14 (1975): 79, and "Imitation, Ambiguity, and Drama in Political Life: Civil Religion and the Dilemmas of Public Morality," *Journal of Politics* 41 (1979): 106. Bennett describes civil religion "as the collection of myths and rituals that explain and dramatize the origins, guiding principles, rules of order, and destiny of a political culture" ("Imitation," p. 109).

9. Irving Kristol, "The Spirit of '87," *The Public Interest*, no. 86 (1987): 5. See also E. D. Hirsch, Jr., *Cultural Literacy: What Every American Needs to Know* (Boston: Houghton Mifflin Co., 1987), pp. 98-101.

10. Alexander Bickel, *The Morality of Consent* (New Haven: Yale University Press, 1975), p. 24.

11. Kent Newmyer, *Supreme Court Justice Joseph Story: Statesman of the Old Republic* (Chapel Hill: University of North Carolina Press, 1985), p. 387.

12. Kristol, "Spirit of '87," p. 5.

13. Anne Norton, *Alternative Americas: A Reading of Antebellum Political Culture* (Chicago: University of Chicago Press, 1986), p. 18.

14. Ibid., p. 25.

15. Ibid., p. 19.

16. Max Lerner, "Constitution and Court as Symbols," *Yale Law Journal* 42 (1937): 1294-95.

17. Quoted in Ben A. Franklin, "Burger Made Chancellor at William and Mary," *The New York Times*, February 8, 1987, p. 26, col. 4.

18. Kammen, *Machine*, p. 45, quoting L. H. Butterfield, *The Letters of Benjamin Rush* (Princeton: Princeton University Press, 1951), 1: 475.

19. *The Federalist*, p. 238.

20. Thomas Jefferson to John Adams, August 30, 1787, in *The Adams-Jefferson Letters*, ed. Lester J. Cappon, vol. 1 (Chapel Hill: University of North Carolina Press, 1959), p. 196.

21. Quoted in Kammen, *Machine*, p. 264.

22. Edward Corwin, "The 'Higher Law' Background of American Constitutional Law," *Harvard Law Review* 42 (1928): 153. Corwin is writing specifically about the relationship of the Constitution to "natural law," but his point would hold equally for the positing of the Constitution's origins in the will of a divine providence.

23. Edward Corwin, "The Worship of the Constitution," *Constitutional Review* 4 (January 1920): 3, republished in Richard Lass, ed., *Corwin and the Constitution* (Ithaca: Cornell University Press, 1981), pp. 47-55. Michael Kammen's important study of the Constitution and American culture includes a substantial index entry under the heading "worship of Constitution." Kammen, *Machine*, p. 532.

24. Kammen, *Machine* p. 235.

25. Ibid., pp. 470-71 n. 17.

26. Barbara Jordan and Shelby Hearon, *Barbara Jordan, A Self-Portrait* (Garden City, N.Y.: Doubleday & Co., 1979), p. 187.

27. Theodore H. White, *Breach of Faith: The Fall of Richard Nixon* (New York: Atheneum/Reader's Digest Press, 1975).

28. See Jean Jacques Rousseau, *The Social Contract*, bk. 4, ch. 8 (trans. Maurice Cranston [Baltimore: Penguin Books, 1968], pp. 176-87. Rousseau, who believed that "everything that destroys social unity is worthless" (p. 181), saw one of the sovereign's functions as the creation of "a profession of faith which is purely civil" that would serve to outline those "sentiments of sociability, without which it is impossible to be either a good citizen or a loyal subject" (p. 186).

29. Robin Williams, *American Society: A Sociological Interpretation* (1951), quoted in Will Herberg, "America's Civil Religion: What It Is and Whence It Comes," in Richey and Jones, *American Civil Religion*, p. 76.

30. Alpheus T. Mason, "The Supreme Court: Temple and Form," *Yale Review* 48 (1959): 526.

31. Kammen, *Machine*, p. 264.

32. William Yandell Elliott, "The Constitution as the American Social Myth," in Conyers Read, ed., *The Constitution Reconsidered*, rev. ed. by Richard B. Morris (New York: Harper & Row, 1968), p. 219.

33. "And I say this to you: You are Peter, the Rock; and on this rock I will build my church, and the forces of death shall never overpower it. I will give you the keys of the kingdom of Heaven; what you forbid on earth shall be forbidden in heaven, and what you allow on earth shall be allowed in heaven." Matthew 16:18-19.

34. Henry Adams, *The Education of Henry Adams* (New York: The Modern Library, 1931), p. 277.

35. F. F. Bruce and E. G. Rupp, *Holy Book and Holy Tradition* (Manchester: Manchester University Press, 1968), p. 70.

36. *Cambridge History of the Bible: The West from the Reformation to the Present Day*, ed. S. L. Greenslade, vol. 3 (Cambridge: Cambridge University Press, 1963), p. 175, quoting William Chillingworth, *The Religion of Protestants: A Safe Way to Salvation* (1638).

37. *Cambridge History of the Bible*, 3: 94-174.

38. Ibid., 3: 193-94.

39. Ibid., 3: 201.

40. Frank Kermode, "Institutional Control of Interpretation," *Salmagundi* 43 (Winter 1979): 78.

41. Quoted in Quentin Skinner, *The Foundations of Modern Political Thought: The Age of Reformation*, vol. 2 (Cambridge: Cambridge University Press, 1978), p. 146.

42. Ibid., 2: 148-66.

43. Ibid., 2: 3-6.

44. See Thomas Grey, "The Constitution as Scripture," *Stanford Law Review* 37 (1984): 7, citing Geo Widengren, "Holy Book and Holy Tradition in Islam," in Bruce and Rupp, *Holy Book*, pp. 210-27; F. Rahman, *Islam*, 2d ed. (Chicago: University of Chicago Press, 1979), p. 219.

45. F. E. Peters, *The Children of Abraham: Judaism/Christianity/Islam* (Princeton: Princeton University Press, 1982), pp. 12-13.

46. Marcel Simon, "The Ancient Church and Rabbinical Tradition," in Bruce and Rupp, *Holy Book*, p. 94.

47. See, generally, Jacob Neusner, *The Oral Torah, The Sacred Books of Judaism* (San Francisco: Harper & Row, 1986).

48. See Isadore Twersky, ed., *A Maimonides Reader* (New York: Behrman House, 1972), pp. 35-41.

49. Midrash Exod. rabba, 47, quoted in Simon, "The Ancient Church," p. 110.

50. David Biale, *Gershom Scholem: Kabbalah and Counter-History* (Cambridge, Mass.: Harvard University Press, 1979), p. 97.

51. Gershom Scholem, *The Messianic Idea in Judaism and Other Essays in Jewish Spirituality* (New York: Schocken Books, 1971), p. 290, quoted in Biale, *Gershom Scholem*, p. 98.

52. Biale, *Gershom Scholem*, pp. 98, 251 n. 79.

53. See Ellen Flesseman-Van Leer, "Present-day Frontiers in the Discussion about Tradition," in Bruce and Rupp, *Holy Book*, pp. 154-70, which is an excellent discussion of the differences between the 1965 "dogmatic constitution De divina revelatione of the second Vatican Council, promulgated on 18 November 1965, and the report of the second section of the Fourth World Conference on Faith and Order, Montreal 1963, entitled *Scripture, Tradition and Traditions*" (p. 155).

54. Grey, "Constitution as Scripture," pp. 10-11, quoting Avery Dulles, *Revelation and the Quest for Unity* (1968), pp. 85-86.

55. Robert M. Grant with David Tracy, *A Short History of the Interpretation of the Bible* (Philadelphia: Fortress Press, 1984), p. 176.

56. Grey, "Constitution as Scripture," p. 11, citing David Kelsey, *The Uses of Scripture in Recent Theology* (1975), 56-88.

57. David Hartman, *The Living Covenant* (New York: Macmillan, 1985).

58. S.G.F. Brandon, "The Holy Book, the Holy Tradition and the Holy Ikon: A Phenomenological Survey," in Bruce and Rupp, *Holy Book*, p. 3.

59. See Frank Kermode, "The Canon," in Robert Alter and Frank Kermode, eds., *The Literary Guide to the Bible* (Cambridge, Mass.: Harvard University Press, 1987), pp. 600-609. See also David Stern, "Sacred Text and Canon," in Arthur A. Cohen and Paul Mendes-Flohr, eds., *Contemporary Jewish Religious Thought* (New York: Charles Scribner's Sons, 1987), pp. 841-47.

60. Christopher Arthur, "Gadamer and Hirsch: The Canonical Work and the Interpreter's Intention," *Cultural Hermeneutics* 4 (1977): 185.

61. Grant with Tracy, *Short History*, p. 177.

62. *Cambridge History of the Bible*, 3: 1.

63. Quoted in Grant and Tracy, *Short History*, p. 75.

64. Avery Dulles argues that "strongly institutionalist development occurred" within the Catholic Church only in the late Middle Ages and the period of the Counter-Reformation, "when theologians and canonists, responding to attacks on the papacy and hierarchy, accented precisely those features that the adversaries were denying." Until then, he says, "Catholic theology . . . was relatively free of

institutionalism." Avery Dulles, *Models of the Church: A Critical Assessment of the Church in All Its Aspects* (Garden City, N.Y.: Doubleday & Co., 1974), p. 33. I am obviously not competent to adjudicate such historical disputes, and nothing in my argument depends on accurately dating the emergence of what all agree is a strongly institutionalist theory now undergirding the Roman Catholic Church.

65. Moses ben Nahman [Nachmanides], *Commentary on the Torah*, trans. Charles Chavel, vol. 5 (New York: Shilo Publishing House, 1976), pp. 206-7.

66. Martin Luther, *Three Treatises* (Philadelphia: The Muhlenberg Press, 1943), p. 13.

67. Ibid., p. 21.

68. The text from which I am quoting omits the bracketed word, but it seems clear that this is a mistake. See, e.g., the texts of the so-called Apostles Creed and of the Constantinopolitan Creed, popularly known as the Nicene Creed, both reprinted in John H. Leith, ed., *Creeds of the Churches: A Reader in Christian Doctrine from the Bible to the Present*, 3rd ed. (Atlanta: John Knox Press, 1982), pp. 24-25, 33.

69. Luther, *Three Treatises*, pp. 21-22.

70. Ibid., p. 23. Emphasis added.

71. See Skinner, *Foundations*, 2: 10-15. "The true church becomes nothing more than an invisible *congregatio fidelium*, a congregation of the faithful gathered together in God's name. . . . While introducing . . . later concessions [in regard to visible embodiment of the Church], however, Luther continued to insist that the true Church has no real existence except in the heart of its faithful members. His central conviction was always that the Church can simply be equated with *Gottes Volk*, 'the people of God living from the word of God' " (2: 10-11).

72. Hans Küng, *Infallible? An Inquiry* (Garden City, N.Y.: Doubleday & Co., 1971), p. 142, quoting Steck, "Die Autorität der Offenbarung. Das Erst Vatikanum im Urteil evangelischer Theologie," *Publik* (January 16, 1970).

73. Quoted in Daniel Jeremy Silver, *A History of Judaism*, vol. 1, *From Abraham to Maimonides* (New York: Basic Books, 1974), p. 335; a general discussion of Karaism can be found on pp. 333-41 there. See also L. Nemoy, ed., *A Karaite Anthology* (New Haven: Yale University Press, 1952).

74. *Cambridge History of the Bible*, 3: 186.

75. See generally Julian Franklin, ed., *Constitutionalism and Resistance in the Sixteenth Century: Three Treatises by Hotman, Beza, and Mornay* (New York: Pegasus, 1969).

76. Christopher Goodman, *How Superior Powers Ought to Be Obeyd of Their Subjects: And Wherein They May Lawfully by Gods Worde Be Disobeyed and Resisted. Wherein Also Is Declared the Cause of All This Present Miserie in England, and the Only Way to Remedy the Same* (Geneva, 1558), in Edmund Morgan, ed., *Puritan Political Ideas* (Indianapolis: Bobbs-Merrill Co., 1965), p. 10. See also Skinner, *Foundations*, 2: 235-38, for a discussion of Goodman's radicalism.

77. Goodman, *How Superior Powers* . . . , p. 9.

78. Quoted in Mark DeWolfe Howe, *Justice Oliver Wendell Holmes*, vol. 2, *The Proving Years* (Cambridge, Mass.: Harvard University Press, 1963), p. 156.

79. Louis Hartz, *The Liberal Tradition in America* (New York: Harcourt, Brace, 1955).

80. This is not to say that constitutional ambiguity alone accounts for potential instability. A perfectly unambiguous constitution, assuming that such an entity can exist, could easily generate instability if it protected some interest deemed fundamentally immoral by a critical mass of the population. See, for example, the prohibition in Article V of the Constitution of congressional outlawing of American participation in the international slave trade before 1808.

81. See "Report on the Virginia Resolution," in Marvin Meyers, ed., *The Mind of the Founder: Sources of the Political Thought of James Madison* (Indianapolis: Bobbs-Merrill Co., 1973), pp. 303-6.

82. Joseph Story, *Commentaries on the Constitution of the United States*, vol. 1, 3rd ed. (Boston: Little, Brown & Co., 1858), p. 271. Webster adds the qualification "subject, always, like other popular governments, to its responsibility to the people," but clearly the bulk of his remarks aims to legitimize "government" becoming the judge of its own powers.

83. See Charles Black, *The People and the Court: Judicial Review in a Democracy* (Englewood Cliffs, N.J.: Prentice-Hall, Inc., 1960), pp. 56-86. Black built his own analysis in part on the earlier work of Robert Dahl, "Decision-Making in a Democracy: The Supreme Court as a National Policy-Maker," *Journal of Public Law* 6 (1957): 279. See also David Adamany, "Legitimacy, Realigning Elections,

and the Supreme Court," *Wisconsin Law Review* (1973): 790; Richard Funston, "The Supreme Court and Critical Elections," *American Political Science Review* 69 (1975): 795; and Jonathan Casper, "The Supreme Court and National Policymaking," *American Political Science Review* 70 (1976): 50.

84. See Book 3, Chapter 4: "Who is Final Judge or Interpreter in Constitutional Controversies?"

85. 14 U.S. (1 Wheat.) 304 (1816).

86. Robert Cover, "The Supreme Court, 1982 Term—Foreword: Nomos and Narrative," *Harvard Law Review* 97 (1983): 53.

87. Samuel I. Rosenman, ed., *The Public Papers and Addresses of Franklin D. Roosevelt*, vol. 6 (New York: Dodd, Mead Co., 1941), p. 124, quoted in Michael Kammen, *The Origins of the American Constitution: A Documentary History* (New York: Viking Publishing Co., 1986), p. vii. Roosevelt's reference to "the Bible" is scarcely unproblematic; one might well ask, "Whose Bible?" As Robert Davidson notes, not only is the "Hebrew Bible" different from the "Protestant Bible," which of course includes the so-called New Testament that transforms the Hebrew Bible into an "Old Testament," but also the "Roman Catholic Bible" is different from the Protestant version, for the former includes books of the Apocrypha whose canonical status was rejected by later Protestants. See Robert Davidson, "Moses' Ghostwriters," *The New York Times Book Review*, August 10, 1987, p. 9 (review of Richard Friedman, *Who Wrote The Bible?* [New York: Summit Books, 1987]).

88. Marbury v. Madison, 5 U.S. (1 Cranch) 137, 178 (1803).

89. Ibid., at 175-76.

90. Jonathan Culler, *Structuralist Poetics* (Ithaca: Cornell University Press, 1975), pp. 131, 134.

91. Roland Barthes, *Writing Degree Zero*, trans. A. Lavers and C. Smith (New York: Hill and Wang, 1978), pp. 19-20.

92. "The Constitution of the United States: Is It Pro-Slavery or Anti-Slavery?" in Philip Foner, ed., *Writings of Frederick Douglass*, vol. 2 (New York: International Publishers, 1950), pp. 467-80.

93. Ibid., pp. 467, 468.

94. Ibid., pp. 468, 469.

95. Ibid., p. 469.

96. Hugo Black, *A Constitutional Faith* (New York: Alfred Knopf, 1968), p. 1.

97. See Hugo Black, Jr., *My Father: A Remembrance* (New York: Random House, 1975), pp. 10-14.

98. Quoted in Philip Bobbitt, *Constitutional Fate* (New York: Oxford University Press, 1982), p. 33.

99. Gerrard Winstanley, *The Law of Freedom in a Platform or, True Magistracy Restored* [1649] (New York: Shocken Publishers, 1973), p. 49. See T. Wilson Hayes, *Winstanley the Digger: A Literary Analysis of Radical Ideas in the English Revolution* (Cambridge, Mass.: Harvard University Press, 1979).

100. Griswold v. Connecticut, 381 U.S. 479 (1966).

101. Black, *A Constitutional Faith*, p. 9.

102. Edwin Meese, "The Law of the Constitution," *Tulane Law Review* 61 (1987): 981.

103. I have lost my reference to the source of this quotation, but I have no doubt of its accuracy.

104. 4 Wheat. 316, 407 (1819)

105. Felix Frankfurter, "The Constitutional Opinions of Mr. Justice Holmes," in Philip B. Kurland, ed., *Felix Frankfurter on the Supreme Court: Extrajudicial Essays on the Court and the Constitution* (Cambridge, Mass.: Harvard University Press, 1970), p. 25.

106. Felix Frankfurter, "Taft and the Supreme Court," in Kurland, *Felix Frankfurter*, p. 61.

107. Christopher G. Tiedman, *The Unwritten Constitution of the United States: A Philosophical Inquiry into the Fundamentals of American Constitutional Law* (New York: G. P. Putnam's Sons, 1890).

108. William B. Munro, *The Makers of the Unwritten Constitution* (New York: The Macmillan Co., 1930).

109. Thomas Grey, "Do We Have an Unwritten Constitution?" *Stanford Law Review* 27 (1975): 703.

110. Frankfurter, "Taft," p. 61.

111. Frankfurter, "Constitutional Opinions," p. 30.

112. Poe v. Ullman, 367 U.S. 497, 522 (1961).

113. Ibid., at 542.

114. Black, *A Constitutional Faith*, p. 36.

115. 367 U.S. at 542. This is the sentence omitted by the ellipsis in the text at note 113.

116. Calder v. Bull, 3 U.S. (3 Dall.) 386, 387-89 (1798).

117. Ibid., at 399.

118. See Ronald Dworkin, *Taking Rights Seriously* (Cambridge,

Mass.: Harvard University Press, 1978), especially "Constitutional Cases," pp. 131-49, as well as his more recent discussion in *Law's Empire* (Cambridge, Mass.: Harvard University Press, 1986), pp. 359-69. The most prolific advocate of "intentionalism" is Raoul Berger; see especially his *Government by Judiciary: The Transformation of the Fourteenth Amendment* (Cambridge, Mass.: Harvard University Press, 1977). Attorney General Edwin Meese has presented what he terms "The Jurisprudence of Original Intent" in two speeches reprinted in *The Great Debate: Interpreting Our Written Constitution* (Washington, D.C.: The Federalist Society, 1986), pp. 1-10, 31-42.

119. See especially two important articles by Thomas Grey: "Do We Have an Unwritten Constitution?" (cited in n. 109 above); and "Origins of the Unwritten Constitution: Fundamental Law in American Revolutionary Thought," *Stanford Law Review* 30 (1978): 843. See also Suzanna Sherry, "The Founders' Unwritten Constitution," *University of Chicago Law Review* (1987): 1124.

120. See Peter Chirico, *Infallibility: The Crossroads of Doctrine* (Kansas City: Sheed Andrews and McMeel, Inc., 1977), and Küng, *Infallible? An Inquiry*, for a defense and attack respectively on the question of papal infallibility.

121. See, e.g., Cooper v. Aaron, 358 U.S. 1, 18 (1958); Powell v. McCormack, 395 U.S. 486, 521 (1969); United States v. Nixon, 418 U.S. 683, 704 (1974).

122. I should note that one distinguished strain of Roman Catholic thought strongly attacked any argument that the pope was absolutely sovereign and unchallengeable. As Quentin Skinner points out, an important source of constitutionalist argument is the conciliarist tradition within the Catholic Church. See Skinner, *Foundations*, 2: 36-47. And Harold Berman, in *Revolution in Law* (Cambridge, Mass.: Harvard University Press, 1984), persuasively argues that conventional legal history tends to ignore the Catholic contribution to the Western constitutionalist tradition. If it is grossly inaccurate to summarize Catholicism as emphasizing strictly papal authority, it is nevertheless true that even the conciliarist tradition is institutionalist, representing a way for the organized Church to correct the errors of a renegade pope. I am grateful to Walter F. Murphy for education on this point. The analogy asserted in this book does not require a resolution of the dispute between papalists and conciliarists, since both are distinguished by their in-

stitutionalism from the radical implications found in some of Luther's ideas.

123. *The New York Times*, February 16, 1978, p. A22. Pfeffer, as special counsel to the American Jewish Congress, had prevailed in a number of Supreme Court cases striking down legislation aiding parochial schools.

124. See generally, Walter F. Murphy, "Who Shall Interpret the Constitution?" *The Review of Politics* 48 (1986): 401-423, for a good overview of the problem.

125. William Nelson, "The Eighteenth-Century Background of John Marshall's Constitutional Jurisprudence," *Michigan Law Review* 76 (1978): 911-13.

126. Ibid., p. 916, quoting *Legal Papers of John Adams*, ed. L. Kinvin Wroth and Hiller Zobel, vol. 1 (Cambridge, Mass.: Harvard University Press, 1965), p. 230.

127. See Morton Horwitz, *The Transformation of American Law* (Cambridge, Mass.: Harvard University Press, 1977), p. 228.

128. The classic arguments of both Jackson and Calhoun, as well as Webster's vigorous defenses of judicial supremacy, are reprinted in Robert Remini, ed., *The Age of Jackson* (New York: Harper & Row, 1972).

129. 17 U.S. (4 Wheat.) 316 (1819).

130. Andrew Jackson, Veto Message, July 10, 1832, in *Messages and Papers of the Presidents*, ed. James Richardson, vol. 2 (Washington, D.C.: Government Printing Office, 1896), p. 582.

131. Prigg v. Pennsylvania, 16 Pet. 359 (1842).

132. In the Matter of Booth, 3 Wis. 1, 91 (1858), rev'd, 21 How. 506 (1859); on remand, 11 Wis. 517 (1859). I owe this reference to my colleague Philip Bobbitt.

133. William M. Wiecek, *The Sources of Antislavery Constitutionalism in America, 1760-1848* (Ithaca: Cornell University Press, 1977), p. 7.

134. Quoted in Herbert Aptheker, ed., *Documentary History of the Negro People*, vol. 1 (New York: Citadel Press, 1951), p. 318.

135. Paul Angle, ed., *Created Equal? The Complete Lincoln-Douglas Debates of 1858* (Chicago: University of Chicago Press, 1958), p. 36. (Chicago, July 10, 1858.)

136. Ibid., pp. 78-79. (Springfield, Ill., July 17, 1858.)

137. *Messages of the Presidents*, ed. Richardson, vol. 6 (1897), p. 9. I should note Lincoln's 1857 statement that Supreme Court decisions

"on Constitutional questions, when fully settled, should control, not only the particular cases decided, but the general policy of the country, subject to be disturbed only by amendments of the Constitution. . . . More than this would be revolution." Roy Basler, ed., *The Collected Works of Abraham Lincoln*, vol. 2 (New Brunswick, N.J.: Rutgers University Press, 1953), p. 401, quoted in Paul L. Colby, "Two Views on the Legitimacy of Nonacquiescence in Judicial Opinions," *Tulane Law Review* 61 (1987): 1059 n. 89. Left dangling by Lincoln, of course, is what counts as a "fully settled" constitutional question.

138. Meese, "Law of the Constitution," p. 983.

139. Ibid., pp. 982, 983, quoting Charles Warren, *The Supreme Court in United States History*, vol. 3 (Boston: Little, Brown and Co., 1922), pp. 470-71.

140. Meese, "Law of the Constitution," p. 983.

141. 163 U.S. 537 (1896).

142. Meese, "Law of the Constitution," p. 983.

143. 347 U.S. 483 (1954).

144. Meese, "Law of the Constitution," p. 985.

145. Ibid., p. 988.

146. The issue of the *Tulane Law Review* that contains the attorney general's speech follows it with a symposium on "Perspectives on the Authoritativeness of Supreme Court Decisions." Among the articles in the symposium is mine, "Could Meese Be Right This Time?" pp. 1071-78, originally published in *The Nation* 243 (December 20, 1986): 689, 704-7.

147. Stuart Taylor, "Liberties Union Denounces Meese," *The New York Times*, October 24, 1986, p. A17, col. 1.

148. Ibid. See also Ronald Ostrow, "Meese: View That Court Doesn't Make Laws Is Scored," *Los Angeles Times*, October 24, 1986, p. 27, col. 1.

149. Taylor, "Liberties Union." *The Wall Street Journal*, which was almost unique among major newspapers in supporting Meese (see "The Irrepressible Mr. Meese," October 29, 1986, p. 28, col. 1) can be forgiven a certain joy in quoting Tribe's landmark 1979 treatise, *American Constitutional Law*, against himself:

Despite the growth of federal judicial power, the Constitution remains a fundamentally democratic document, open to competing interpretations limited only by the values which inform the Constitution's provisions themselves, and by the complex political process that the Constitution creates—a process which on various occasions gives the Supreme Court, Congress, the President, or the states, the last word in constitutional debate.

(Laurence Tribe, *American Constitutional Law* [Mineola, N.Y.: Foundation Press, 1978], p. 33.) It is noteworthy that Professor Tribe did not include "the people," either individually or collectively, in his enumeration.

150. Anthony Lewis, "Law or Power," *The New York Times*, October 27, 1986, p. A23, col. 1.

151. Taylor, "Liberties Union."

152. *F.D.R.: His Personal Letters*, vol. 3 (New York: Duell, Sloan and Pearce, 1950), p. 459. See also Arthur Schlesinger, Jr., *The Age of Roosevelt*, vol. 3, *The Politics of Upheaval* (Boston: Houghton Mifflin, 1960), p. 258. Schlesinger there quotes Roosevelt as commenting, "Joe Kennedy thinks the statement is so strong they will burn the Supreme Court in effigy."

153. Radio Address by President Roosevelt, March 9, 1937, quoted in Walter F. Murphy, James Fleming, and William Harris, *American Constitutional Interpretation* (Mineola, N.Y.: Foundation Press, 1986), p. 233.

154. Lincoln had refused to honor a writ of habeas corpus issued by Taney in regard to the military detention of John Merryman, a Southern sympathizer in Maryland. Taney, sitting as circuit justice, wrote an opinion denouncing Lincoln's unilateral suspension of habeas corpus in the absence of congressional authorization, as arguably required by Article I, Section 9 of the Constitution. See Ex parte *Merryman*, 17 Fed. Cases 145 (U.S. Cir. Ct. 1861). Lincoln's suspension of habeas corpus is further discussed in Chapter Four below.

155. Francis Biddle, *In Brief Authority* (Garden City, N.Y.: Doubleday & Co., 1962), p. 331, quoted in Robert Scigliano, *The Supreme Court and the Presidency* (New York: Free Press, 1971), p. 49. The threat was mooted by the Supreme Court's decision in In re *Quirin*, 317 U.S. 1 (1942).

156. *Washington Post*, October 29, 1986, p. A18, col. 1.

157. Dworkin, *Taking Rights Seriously*, p. 211.

158. Ibid., pp. 214-15.

159. Graves v. New York, 306 U.S. 466, 491-92 (1939)(Frankfurter, J., concurring). Meese quotes this passage in "Law of the Constitution," p. 986.

160. Dworkin, *Taking Rights Seriously*, pp. 214-15.

161. Candor requires that I acknowledge not only the overly schematic use of terms like "protestant" and "catholic," but also the fact that my own predelictions toward what I am calling a "catholic–protestant" perspective—the joinder of a non-text-identified Constitution with a rejection of judicial supremacy—undoubtedly come from its similarity to the historical development of what I find the most attractive aspects of Judaism.

162. See Wiecek, *Sources of Antislavery Constitutionalism*, pp. 242-43.

163. Wendell Phillips, *Can Abolitionists Vote or Take Office under the United States Constitution?* (1845), p. 14.

164. Wendell Phillips, *Review of Lysander Spooner's Essay on the Unconstitutionality of Slavery . . .* (1847), p. 93.

165. See, e.g., Burt Neuborne, "The Binding Quality of Supreme Court Precedent," *Tulane Law Review* 61 (1987): 991.

166. Katzenbach v. Morgan, 384 U.S. 641 (1966).

167. Lassiter v. Northampton County Board of Elections, 360 U.S. 45 (1959).

168. 384 U.S., at 659.

169. Oregon v. Mitchell, 400 U.S. 112 (1970).

170. Ibid., at 209.

171. 388 U.S. 307 (1967).

172. See the description of the episode in David Garrow, *Bearing the Cross: Martin Luther King, Jr., and the Southern Christian Leadership Conference* (New York: William Morrow, 1986), pp. 231-58.

173. Letter from Anthony Lewis to author, February 20, 1987.

174. 401 U.S. 437 (1971). See Kent Greenawalt, "All or Nothing at All: The Defeat of Selective Conscientious Objection," *Supreme Court Review* (1971): 31.

175. Dworkin, *Taking Rights Seriously*, p. 215.

176. Brown v. Allen, 344 U.S. 443, 540 (1953)(Jackson, J., concurring).

177. See Paul Brest and Ann Vandenberg, "Politics, Feminism, and the Constitution: The Anti-Pornography Movement in Minneapolis," *Stanford Law Review* 39 (1987): 607-61.

178. The letters are quoted in Sanford Levinson, "What Do Lawyers

Know (And What Do They Do With Their Knowledge)? Comments on Shauer and Moore," *Southern California Law Review* 58 (1985): 454 n. 52. Tribe's letter to Alice Rainville, the president of the City Council, is reprinted in David Bryden, "Between Two Constitutions: Feminism and Pornography," *Constitutional Commentary* 2 (1985): 180. Compare Tribe's letters with the passage from his treatise quoted in note 149 above.

179. Charles Black, *Structure and Relationship in Constitutional Law* (Baton Rouge: University of Louisiana Press, 1969), pp. 88-89.

180. Ibid. See also Black, *The People and the Court*, p. 15: "We entrusted the task of constitutional interpretation to the courts because we conceived of the Constitution as law, and because it is the business of courts to resolve interpretative problems arising in law. A law which is applied by a court, but is not to be interpreted by a court, is a solecism simply unknown to our conceptions of legality and the legal process."

181. See Paul Brest, "The Conscientious Legislator's Guide to Constitutional Interpretation," *Stanford Law Review* 27 (1975): 585; idem, "Congress as Constitutional Decisionmaker and Its Power to Counter Judicial Doctrine," *Georgia Law Review* 21 (1986): 57.

182. E. D. Hirsch, *Validity in Interpretation* (New Haven: Yale University Press, 1967), p. 123 n. 53.

183. E. D. Hirsch, "Book Review," *New York Review of Books*, June 14, 1979, p. 20. My former colleague, Walter Murphy of Princeton, informs me that Hirsch is incorrect. The institution he presumably means to refer to is the Congregation for the Sacred Doctrine of the Faith, but even it operates under the authority of the pope and does not share the pope's undelegable power as ultimate authority. In practice, though, the Congregation apparently can be said to have the last word.

184. E. D. Hirsch, *The Aims of Interpretation* (Chicago: University of Chicago Press, 1976), p. 20.

CHAPTER TWO

1. American Bar Association, Model Code of Professional Responsibility, Ethical Consideration 9-6. "Ethical considerations" are goals toward which all lawyers should aspire, though only the violation

of "disciplinary rules" found elsewhere in the Model Code can serve as the basis of professional discipline.

2. Thomas Grey, "The Constitution as Scripture," *Stanford Law Review* 37 (1984): 18 (emphasis in original).

3. J. Elliot, ed., *The Debates in the Several State Conventions on the Adoption of the Federal Constitution*, vol. 2, 2nd ed. (Washington, D.C.: 1836), p. 202.

4. Philip Kurland and Ralph Lerner, eds., *The Founders' Constitution*, vol. 4 (Chicago: University of Chicago Press, 1987), p. 645. I discovered both of these last quotations in Philip Kurland, "The Origins of the Religion Clauses of the Constitution," *William and Mary Law Review* 27 (1986): 849.

5. Davis v. Beason, 133 U.S. 333 (1890)

6. Ibid., at 334.

7. Ibid.

8. "The Church taught that not only was it necessary for men to be married in order to reach the highest degree of heavenly glory, but that the greater the number of wives a man had, the greater his reward would be." Orma Linford, "The Mormons and the Law: The Polygamy Cases, Part I," *Utah Law Review* 9 (1964): 310.

9. Jeffrey Leeds, "A Life on the Court," *The New York Times Magazine*, October 5, 1986, p. 79. Justice Brennan made similar comments in a television interview with Bill Moyers. In this latter interview, moreover, the justice stated that he viewed every part of the Constitution to be "holy."

10. Quoted in Kent Newmyer, *Supreme Court Justice Joseph Story: Statesman of the Old Republic* (Chapel Hill: University of North Carolina Press, 1985), p. 377.

11. Quoted in Christopher Lasch, "What's Wrong with the Right," *Tikkun*, no. 1 (1986): 28.

12. "Kahane Is Deprived of Right to Sit in Israel's Parliament," *The New York Times*, June 9, 1987, p. 10, col. 5. (Kahane subsequently agreed to take the oath.) One might similarly consider the behavior by a group of so-called ultra-Orthodox Jews upon being sentenced for attacking bus stops that they viewed as violating Jewish law by displaying advertising featuring "immodest" women. According to the *Wall Street Journal*, the miscreants, who clearly violated Israeli law, "burst into a happy song as they were led into a municipal court [in Jerusalem]. 'God is our king, and only to him [*sic*] are we slaves,' they sang as friends joined in." Gerald Seib, "Religious Dis-

cord Rises Among Israeli Jews, Spurs Intense Debate," *Wall Street Journal*, June 18, 1986, p. 12, col. 1.

13. Owen Fiss, "Objectivity and Interpretation," *Stanford Law Review* 34 (1982): 753 (emphasis added).

14. See, e.g., Paul Brest, "The Misconceived Quest for the Original Understanding," *Boston University Law Review* 60 (1980): 204.

15. Fiss, "Objectivity," p. 753.

16. Douglass to C. H. Chase, *The North Star*, February 9, 1849, in P. Foner, ed., *The Life and Writings of Frederick Douglass*, vol. 1 (New York: International Publishers, 1950), p. 353.

17. Fiss, "Objectivity," p. 754.

18. Ibid.

19. Ibid., p. 755

20. Stephen Macedo, *The New Right v. The Constitution* (Washington, D.C.: Cato Institute, 1986), p. 4.

21. William Connolly, "Thomas Hobbes: The Politics of Divine Containment" (unpublished manuscript), p. 7.

22. Ibid., p. 8.

23. Fletcher v. Peck, 10 U.S. (6 Cranch) 87 (1810), at 143 (Johnson, J. concurring).

24. Connolly, "Thomas Hobbes," p. 7.

25. Quoted in Robert Bellah, "The Normative Framework for Pluralism in America," *Soundings* 61 (1978): 68.

26. Cass Sunstein, "Interest Groups in American Public Law," *Stanford Law Review* 38 (1985): 41-42. See also Frank Michelman, "The Supreme Court 1985 Term—Foreword: Traces of Self-Government," *Harvard Law Review* 100 (1986): 59.

27. Jacob Cooke, ed., *The Federalist* (Cleveland: The World Publishing Co., 1961), p. 59.

28. See Clifford Geertz, "Anti Anti-relativism," *American Anthropologist* 86 (1984): 263.

29. See, e.g., Martin Redish, *Freedom of Expression: A Critical Analysis* (Charlottesville, Va.: The Michie Company, 1984), p. 48. I criticize Redish, who embraces the notion of "self-realization" as the central value of the First Amendment, in "First Amendment, Freedom of Speech, Freedom of Expression: Does It Matter What We Call It?" *Northwestern University Law Review* 80 (1985): 767.

30. See Ian Shapiro, *The Evolution of Rights in Liberal Theory* (New Haven: Yale University Press, 1986), p. 60.

31. Quoted in Robert Leiter, "Unorthdox Leftist," *Present Tense* 14 (January/February 1987): 31.
32. Sunstein, "Interest Groups," pp. 30-31.
33. Robert N. Bellah, "Religion and Legitimation in the American Republic," in Robert N. Bellah and Phillip E. Hammond, *Varieties of Civil Religion*, 12-13 (New York: Harper & Row, 1980).
34. Michael Perry, *The Court, the Constitution, and Human Rights* (New Haven: Yale University Press, 1982), pp. 98-101.
35. Gillette v. U.S., 401 U.S. 437, 457 (1971).
36. Alasdair MacIntyre, *After Virtue: A Study in Moral Theory* (Notre Dame: University of Notre Dame Press, 1982), p. 146.
37. R. Booth Fowler, Book Review, *Journal of American History* 73 (1986): 252.
38. Max Farrand, *Records of the Federal Convention*, vol. 2 (New Haven: Yale University Press, 1927), p. 73.
39. See William Wiecek, "The Witch at the Christening: Slavery and the Constitution's Origins," in Leonard Levy and Dennis Mahoney, eds., *The Framing and Ratification of the Constitution* (New York: Macmillan, 1987), pp. 167-84; Paul Finkelman, "Slavery and the Constitutional Convention: Making a Covenant with Death," in Richard Beeman, Stephen Botein, and Edward Carter II, eds., *Beyond Confederation: Origins of the Constitution and American National Identity* (Chapel Hill: University of North Carolina Press, 1987), pp. 188-225.
40. Fairness requires pointing out that the South would have been delighted had each slave been counted as a full person. It was the North that insisted on the "three-fifths" clause, given that the issue was the strength of Southern representation, which would increase the more the slaves were recognized as full persons, and not the actual moral status of the slaves.
41. See Walter Merrill, *Against Wind and Tide: A Biography of Wm. Lloyd Garrison* (Cambridge, Mass.: Harvard University Press, 1963), p. 205. The phrase appeared in a resolution that Garrison had introduced at a meeting of the Massachusetts Anti-Slavery Society in January 1843: "That the compact which exists between the North and the South is a 'covenant with death, and an agreement with hell'—involving both parties in atrocious criminality; and should be immediately annulled" (ibid.).
42. 10 U.S. (6 Cranch) 87 (1810).
43. Ibid., at 139.

44. Ibid., at 143.
45. Calder v. Bull, 3 U.S. (3 Dall.) 386 (1798), at 388. Chase supplied

> [a] few instances . . . to explain what I mean. A law that pun-
> ished a citizen for an innocent action, or, in other words, for
> an act, which, when done, was in violation of no existing law;
> a law that destroys, or impairs, the lawful private contracts of
> citizens; a law that makes a man a judge in his own cause; or a
> law that takes property from A. and gives it to B. It is against
> all reason and justice, for a people to intrust a Legislature with
> such powers; and, therefore, it cannot be presumed that they
> have done it.

We were introduced to Chase in the previous chapter, where he was
identified as a participant in the "catholic" strain of American constitutional theory. And we saw there as well the author of a quite
different opinion in *Calder*, Justice Iredell, who noted that "[t]he
ideas of natural justice are regulated by no fixed standard" and that
it therefore follows that "the Legislature [is] possessed of an equal
right of opinion" as to what justice requires (ibid. at 399), which
entails, of course, that the legislature might come to a conclusion
that strikes the outside observer not as justice at all but rather as
tyranny.
46. The Antelope, 23 U.S. (10. Wheat.) 66 (1825).
47. See generally John T. Noonan, Jr., *The Antelope: The Ordeal of
the Recaptured Africans in the Administrations of James Monroe
and John Quincy Adams* (Berkeley: University of California Press,
1977).
48. 23 U.S., at 114. Compare Captain Vere's comment in Billy Budd:
"Our vowed responsibility is in this: That however pitilessly that
law may operate in any instances, we nevertheless adhere to it and
administer it" (Herman Melville, *Billy Budd*, ed. Harrison Hayford
and Merton M. Sealts [Chicago: University of Chicago Press, 1962]
p. 111). Robert Cover, who points out that Melville's father-in-law
was an important Massachusetts judge who on occasion ruled
against the claims to freedom of slaves, uses *Billy Budd* as a foundation for understanding the rhetoric of the judiciary in *Justice Accused: Antislavery and the Judicial Process* (New Haven: Yale University Press, 1975). For a very different reading of Captain Vere
that views his claims of legal accountability as being in bad faith,

see Richard Weisberg, *The Failure of the Word* (New Haven: Yale University Press, 1984), p. 147.

49. United States v. La Jeune Eugenie, 26 F. Cas. 832 (C.C. Mass. 1822).

50. 23 U.S., at 115, 120.

51. Ibid., at 114-15.

52. 41 U.S. (16 Pet.) 536 (1842).

53. H. Jefferson Powell, "Joseph Story's *Commentaries on the Constitution*: A Belated Review," *Yale Law Journal* 94 (1986): 1311.

54. Ibid., pp. 1311-12, quoting *Commentaries*, 1: 374.

55. Ibid., p. 1312.

56. Ibid., p. 1312 n. 176. Powell quotes from *Commentaries*, 1: 374-75, where Story argues that the sole remedy against constitutional oppression is "a remedy never provided for by human institutions. It is by a resort to the ultimate right of all human beings . . . to apply force against ruinous injustice."

57. Oliver Wendell Holmes, "Introduction to *Spirit of the Laws*," *Collected Legal Papers* (New York: Harcourt, Brace and Holt, 1920), p. 258.

58. "The Holmes-Cohen Correspondence," *Journal of the History of Ideas* 9 (January 1948): 27.

59. Lochner v. New York, 198 U.S. 45, 75 (1905)(Holmes, J., dissenting).

60. Bailey v. Alabama, 219 U.S. 219 (1911).

61. Dennis v. United States, 341 U.S. 494, 556 (1951)(Frankfurter, J., concurring).

62. Ibid., at 556 (emphasis added).

63. Alexis de Tocqueville, *Democracy in America*, vol. 1 (New York: Vintage Books, 1945), p. 185.

64. Alexander M. Bickel, *The Least Dangerous Branch* (Indianapolis: Bobbs-Merrill Co, 1962).

65. Alexander M. Bickel, *The Morality of Consent* (New Haven: Yale University Press, 1975).

66. Ibid., p.25, quoting Lochner v. New York, 198 U.S. 45, 76 (1905).

67. Ibid. Elsewhere he states that "we do need, individually and as a society, some values, some belief in the foundations of our conduct, in order to make life bearable" (p. 77).

68. Ibid., p. 24.

69. Ibid., p. 25.

70. 198 U.S. at 76.

71. Bickel, *Morality of Consent*, p. 120.
72. Ibid., p. 104.
73. See Jeffrey Stout, "Liberal Society and the Languages of Morals," *Soundings* 69 (1986): 32.
74. H.L.A. Hart, *The Concept of Law* (Oxford: Oxford University Press, 1961), pp. 55-60.
75. Ronald Dworkin, *Law's Empire* (Cambridge, Mass.: Harvard University Press, 1986), p. 47. Dworkin is specifically discussing the social practice of "courtesy," but the point of his discussion is to analogize the social practice of "law" to that of "courtesy."
76. Ibid.
77. Ibid., pp. 227-28.
78. Sotirios Barber, *On What the Constitution Means* (Baltimore: Johns Hopkins Press, 1984), p. 57. Michael Perry also makes an extended "aspirational" argument in Chapter 7 of his forthcoming book on constitutional interpretation.
79. "The Constitution of the United States: Is It Pro-Slavery or Anti-Slavery?" *Life and Writings of Frederick Douglass*, vol. 2 (New York: International Publishers, 1950), pp. 467-80. Randall Kennedy has reminded me that this reversal may not be so "remarkable" after all, when one realizes that most blacks rejected as too despairing the Garrisonian conception of a proslavery Constitution. Douglass was in fact "catching up" with predominant black opinion rather than leading it into a new realization of constitutional possibilities. Too, Douglass was building on an important body of anti-slavery constitutional theory developed by radicals like Lysander Spooner. Still, Douglass's speech analyzed in the text remains a remarkable rhetorical performance, even if it is not "original."
80. Ibid., p. 468.
81. Ibid.
82. Ibid., p. 476.
83. It is worth noting that Dworkin presents a somewhat similar reading of the Constitution in "The Law of the Slave-Catchers," *The Times Literary Supplement*, December 5, 1975, p. 1437 (reviewing Robert Cover, *Justice Accused*).
84. Ibid., p. 1473.
85. Ibid.
86. Robert Bork, "Tradition and Morality in Constitutional Law," in Mark Cannon and David O'Brien, eds., *Views from the Bench: The*

Judiciary and Constitutional Politics (Chatham, N.J.: Chatham House Publishers, 1985), p. 171.

87. See Sotirios Barber, "Epistemological Skepticism, Hobbesian Natural Right and Judicial Self-Restraint," *Review of Politics* 48 (1986): 379.

88. Ronald Dworkin, *Taking Rights Seriously* (Cambridge, Mass.: Harvard University Press, 1977), pp. 133-35. See also Barber, *On What the Constitution Means*, pp. 117-19.

89. Max Weber, *Letter to Edgar Jaffe*, quoted in Carl Schneider, "Moral Discourse and the Transformation of American Family Law," *Michigan Law Review* 83 (1985): 1819.

90. See James Fishkin, *The Limits of Obligation* (New Haven: Yale University Press, 1982), for a consideration of this example.

91. Bork, "Tradition and Morality," p. 171.

92. Ronald Dworkin delivers a devastating attack on Bork's "philosophy" in "The Bork Nomination," *The New York Review of Books*, August 13, 1987, pp. 3-10. I put the word in quotation marks because Dworkin's argument is that Bork's "constitutional philosophy is empty: not just impoverished and unattractive but no philosophy at all" (p. 10).

93. The reader might consider whether it matters if the tornado is completely unprecedented or only an extremely rare event in the history of Johnny's particular town.

94. Article I, Section 10.

95. Keystone Bituminous Coal Association v. DeBenedictis, 107 S.Ct. 1232, 1251 (1987).

96. 290 U.S. 398 (1934).

97. Ibid., at 442.

98. Ibid., at 444. Justice Sutherland wrote a strong dissent, joined by the remaining three justices. He argued that the historical intention of the Constitution's drafters was precisely to prevent debtor-relief legislation like that upheld. "If the provisions of the Constitution," he concluded, "be not upheld when they pinch as well as when they comfort, they may as well be abandoned" (p. 438).

99. See, for a review of some of the relevant case law, Paul Brest and Sanford Levinson, *Processes of Constitutional Decisionmaking*, 2d ed. (Boston: Little Brown & Co., 1983), pp. 1111-34.

100. Hugo Black, "The Bill of Rights," *New York University Law Review* 35 (1960): 865; idem and Edmund Cahn, "Justice Black and First Amendment 'Absolutes': A Public Interview," *New York Uni-*

versity Law Review 37 (1962): 549. See also, e.g., Black's concurring opinion in New York Times v. Sullivan, 376 U.S. 254, 293-297 (1964).

101. One of the few exceptions is Justice Hans Linde of the Oregon Supreme Court. See Linde, " 'Clear and Present Danger' Reexamined: Dissonance in the *Brandenburg* Concerto," *Stanford Law Review* 22 (1970): 1163.

102. See Mark Tushnet, "A Note on the Revival of Textualism in Constitutional Theory," *Southern California Law Review* 58 (1985): 700; Bruce Ackerman, "Discovering the Constitution," *Yale Law Journal* 93 (1984): 1066-78.

103. See, for example, Judge Bork's concurring opinion in Ollman v. Evans, 750 F.2d 970, 993 (1984), where he defended the notion of "evolving constitutional doctrine" protective of the press against the attack of Judge Scalia, who viewed such judicially mandated evolution as, in Judge Bork's words, "anathema to judges who adhere to a philosophy of judicial restraint" (p. 995).

104. See Bennett B. Patterson, *The Forgotten Ninth Amendment* (Indianapolis: The Bobbs-Merrill Co., 1955).

105. For a recent review of the literature and a persuasive argument of the thesis mentioned, see Michael Kent Curtis, *No State Shall Abridge: The Fourteenth Amendment and the Bill of Rights* (Durham, N.C.: Duke University Press, 1986). See also Robert J. Kaczorowski, "Revolutionary Constitutionalism in the Era of the Civil War and Reconstruction," *New York University Law Review* 61 (1986): 863; *idem*, "To Begin the Nation Anew: Congress, Citizenship, and Civil Rights after the Civil War," *American Historical Review* 92 (1987): 45.

106. Quoted in Sherry, "Founders' Unwritten Constitution," p. 1163.

107. See Douglas Laycock, "Taking Constitutions Seriously: A Theory of Judicial Review," *Texas Law Review* 59 (1981): 349.

108. Irving Kristol, "The Spirit of '87," *The Public Interest*, no. 86 (1987): 9.

CHAPTER THREE

1. Thus one modern prayerbook prefaces the "Sh'ma"—"Hear, O Israel: The Lord our God, the Lord is One"—with the comment, "We formally affirm God's sovereignty, freely pledging Him our

loyalty." *Siddur Sim Shalom*, ed. Jules Harlow (New York: Rabbinical Assembly, 1985), pp. 284-85. And the song "Yigdal" that often concludes Sabbath religious services "is based upon thirteen principles of faith articulated by Maimonides" (ibid., p. 327). See Menachem Kellner, "Dogma," in Arthur Cohen and Paul Mendes-Flohr, eds., *Contemporary Jewish Religious Thought: Original Essays on Critical Concepts, Movements, and Beliefs* (New York: Charles Scribner's Sons, 1987), pp. 141-45. Kellner argues that the articulation of propositional faith commitments developed only in medieval Judaism, partly in response to Christianity and Islam. See also the essay in the same book by Ze'ev Gries, "Heresy," pp. 339-51. Gries notes that the *cherem* ("ban"), the principal means of law enforcement used by the Jewish community against those who rebelled against religious authorities, applied not to "slips of faith, but only [to] scorn or insult for the principal bearers of the faith—the scholars" (ibid., p. 341).

2. See Werner Sollors, *Beyond Ethnicity: Consent and Descent in American Culture* (New York: Oxford University Press, 1986), p. 6.

3. "[C]onversion to Judaism is existentially joining a community defined as a people, which acts as a body politic rather than a congregation of believers. . . ." (Jochanan H. A. Wijnhoven, "Convert and Conversion," in Cohen and Mendes-Flohr, *Contemporary Jewish Religious Thought*, p. 104.)

4. John H. Leith, ed., *Creeds of the Churches: A Reader in Christian Doctrine from the Bible to the Present*, 3rd ed. (Atlanta: John Knox Press, 1982), p. 8. The asking of such a commitment, and the intensity of feeling surrounding its affirmation, may vary, of course, not only among the particular denominations of Christianity, but also across the time embraced within the history of a given denomination. See, e.g., a recent description by Lief Carter of the local Episcopal church that he attends and in which he "actively participate[s]": "It has become crystal clear to me that *no* shared theological or ideological basis constitutes this community or permits smooth mediation of disputes. . . . My church community is constituted of and mediated by symbols, rituals, musical and rhetorical performances, displays of good character and, above all, affection expressed through conversation. Theology is rarely mentioned outside the service. When it comes up, it is as likely to start a fight as it is to mediate one" (Lief Carter, "Jumping: Mashaw on Due Process in the Administrative State" [book review], *American*

Bar Foundation Research Journal [1986]: 148-49). What, then, does it mean to call oneself an "Episcopalian"? Is a "conversational community" the same as a "faith community"?

5. McCulloch v. Maryland, 17 U.S. (4 Wheat.) 316, 407 (1819).

6. Marbury v. Madison, 5 U.S. (1 Cranch) 137, 178, 180 (1803). A remarkable adaptation of Marshall's argument can be found in a suggestion by H.W.R. Wade that oath-taking provides the solution to the British dilemma of establishing an entrenched bill of rights within the structure of a parliamentary system that seemingly prevents one parliament from binding its successor. According to Wade there is an "easy way out" of this dilemma, and it lies through the institution of the judicial oath. "All that need be done in order to entrench any sort of fundamental law is to secure its recognition in the judicial oath of office. The only trouble at present is that the existing form of oath gives no assurance of obedience to statutes binding later Parliaments. But there is every assurance that if the judges undertake upon their oath to act in some particular way they will do so. If we should wish to adopt a new form of constitution, therefore, all that need be done is to put the judges under oath to enforce it. An Act of Parliament could be passed to discharge them from their former oaths, if that were thought necessary, and to require them to be resworn in the new terms. All the familiar problems of sovereignty then disappear: a fresh start has been made; the doctrine that no Parliament can bind its successors becomes ancient history; and the new fundamental law is secured by a judiciary sworn to uphold it." Wade goes on to cite Article VI of the United States Constitution, as well as the Indian and Malaysian constitutions. H.W.R. Wade, *Constitutional Fundamentals* (London: Stevens & Sons, 1980), pp. 37-38.

7. Consider the symbolism involved when the Senate Foreign Relation Committee forced Assistant Secretary of State Elliott Abrams to take an oath to tell the truth upon the disclosure that he had previously misled the Senate in testimony concerning United States policy in Nicaragua. Some senators indicated that they no longer trusted Abrams to tell the truth in the absence of an oath. Presumably the oath served a dual purpose: Not only did it put greater moral pressure on Abrams not to lie (or even mislead), but it also served to establish the basis for a later indictment for perjury should it be determined that he failed to comply with his promise. And the *Washington Monthly*, in September 1987, reported Lieu-

tenant Colonel Oliver North's attempt to reassure someone who, because North had previously lied to Congress, questioned the trustworthiness of his testimony before the congressional joint committee on the Iran-Contra episode. Said Col. North: "But I was not under oath then."

8. John Locke, *Treatise on Civil Government and a Letter Concerning Toleration*, ed. C. L. Sherman (New York: Irvington, 1979), p. 212.

9. Merrill D. Peterson, *Thomas Jefferson and the New Nation* (New York: Oxford University Press, 1970), p. 132. See also the much more critical analysis in Leonard Levy, *Jefferson and Civil Liberties: The Darker Side* (Cambridge, Mass.: Harvard University Press, 1963), pp. 30-31. According to Levy, "The chief purposes of the oath were to coerce loyalty and to identify for purposes of punishment every person who, in Jefferson's phrase, was 'a traitor in thought, but not in deed.' " Levy goes on to describe the various oaths that all of the new states had adopted by 1778 as " 'weapons of savage coercion' that failed to distinguish between loyalty itself and the ritual of swearing it" (ibid., p. 30).

10. *Writings of James Madison*, vol. 14, ed. Robert Rutland (Charlottesville: University of Virginia Press, 1983), p. 191 (article on "Charters," published in the *National Gazette* on January 19, 1792).

11. Karl Barth, "The Christian Community and the Civil Community," in *Community, State and Church* (1960), pp. 149, 151, quoted in Robert Cover, "Nomos and Narrative," *Harvard Law Review* 97 (1984): 14.

12. Sollors, *Beyond Ethnicity*, p. 6.

13. One should note that not all political systems allow voluntary emigration, and most are less willing than the United States to embrace immigrants. No country, including the United States, leaves the decision to enter solely to the discretion of the would-be immigrant.

14. Sollors, *Beyond Ethnicity*, p. 112. See also ibid., p. 151: "To say it plainly, American identity is often imagined as volitional consent, as love and marriage, ethnicity as seemingly immutable ancestry and descent."

15. Samuel P. Huntington, *American Politics: The Promise of Disharmony* (Cambridge, Mass.: Harvard University Press, 1981), pp. 22-23.

16. Whittle Johnson, "Little America—Big America," *Yale Review* 58 (October 1968): 10-11.

17. Huntington, *American Politics*, p. 24.

18. Ibid., p. 25.

19. Hans Kohn, *American Nationalism: An Interpretive Essay* (New York: Macmillan, 1957), p. 8.

20. Huntington, *American Politics*, p. 30.

21. The "perhaps" acknowledges the possibility, as we shall see manifested later in the thought of Abraham Lincoln, that the Declaration, one of Kristol's "trinity," takes precedence.

22. Gary Jacobsohn, *The Supreme Court and the Decline of Constitutional Aspiration* (Totowa, N.J.: Rowman and Littlefield, 1986), p. 136.

23. Anne Norton, *Alternative Americas: A Reading of Antebellum Political Culture* (Chicago: University of Chicago Press, 1986), p. 74.

24. Michael Walzer, *Spheres of Justice* (New York: Basic Books, 1984), pp. 31, 39.

25. See, e.g., Cass Sunstein, "Interest Groups in American Public Law," *Stanford Law Review* 38 (1986): 30-31 ("the purpose of this article is to help revive aspects of an attractive conception of governance—we may call it republican . . .").

26. See Peter Schuck and Rogers Smith, *Citizenship Without Consent: Illegal Aliens in the American Polity* (New Haven: Yale University Press, 1985).

27. Some writers have expressed dissent from the notions expressed in this paragraph. Thus Joseph Carens argues, in "Aliens and Citizens: The Case for Open Borders," *The Review of Politics* 49 (1987): 251, that liberal states committed to the priority of individual rights cannot limit immigration in order to protect homogeneity (or, for that matter, economic status). See generally Alan Dowty, *Closed Borders: The Contemporary Assault on Freedom of Movement* (New Haven: Yale University Press, 1987). See also Bruce Ackerman, *Social Justice in the Liberal State* (New Haven: Yale University Press, 1980), 89-95; J. Lichtenberg, "National Boundaries and Moral Boundaries: A Cosmopolitan View," in *Boundaries: National Autonomy and Its Limits*, ed. P. Brown and H. Shue (Totawa, N.J.: Rowman and Littlefield, 1981); Roger Nett, "The Civil Right We Are Not Ready For: The Right of Free Movement of People on the Face of the Earth," *Ethics* 81 (1971): 212.

28. Garry Wills, *Inventing America: Jefferson's Declaration of Independence* (New York: Doubleday & Co., 1978), p. xxii.

29. Huntington, *American Politics*, p. 25.

30. Wills, *Inventing America*, p. 28.

31. Leith, *Creeds of the Churches*, p. 9. See Joseph Berger, "Vatican Orders a Theologian to Retract Teachings on Sex," *The New York Times*, March 12, 1986, at p. A17, col. 1. This article concerned the disciplining of Catholic University professor Charles Curran and will be considered below in Chapter Five.

32. Robert Post, "The Social Foundations of Defamation Law: Reputation and the Constitution," *California Law Review* 74 (1986): 736-37. See Emile Durkheim, *The Division of Labor in Society*, trans. George Simpson (Glencoe, Ill.: The Free Press, 1933), pp. 108-9; Kai Erikson, *Wayward Puritans: A Study in the Sociology of Deviance* (New York: John Wiley, 1966), p. 13.

33. See Arthur Leff's proposed definition of "seal" as a "way of saying 'this counts,' 'this is for keeps,' 'we're not kidding around any more' and similar things. Seals are not the only mechanism of that kind; the archaic language and ceremony of a marriage . . . has something of the same intent. . . ." "A Letter from Professor Leff to a Prospective Publisher," *Yale Law Journal* 94 (1985): 1852.

34. Luke 17:33 (New English Bible): "Whoever seeks to save his life will lose it; and whoever loses it will save it, and live." See also Matthew 10:39; Mark 8:35. Sollors notes the frequency with which such "conversion" imagery appears in autobiographical narratives of immigrants detailing their becoming "Americans." He offers as an example the beginning of Mary Antin's *The Promised Land*: "I was born, I have lived, and I have been made over. Is it not time to write my life's story? I am just as much out of the way as if I were dead, for I am absolutely other than the person whose story I have to tell." Sollors, *Beyond Ethnicity*, p. 32.

35. Quoted in Harold Hyman, *To Try Men's Souls: Loyalty Tests in American History* (Berkeley: University of California Press, 1959), p. 15. Hyman's is the standard history of loyalty oaths.

36. See Bernard Bailyn, *The Ideological Origins of the American Revolution* (Cambridge, Mass.: Harvard University Press, 1967); Gordon Wood, *The Creation of the American Republic* (Chapel Hill: University of North Carolina Press, 1969). See also Forrest McDonald, *Novus Ordo Seculorum: The Intellectual Origins of the Constitution* (Lawrence: University of Kansas Press, 1985), for a

magnificent portrayal of the mixture of views contending with one another in the post-Revolutionary United States.

37. Wade, *Constitutional Fundamentals*, p. 38.
38. Hyman, *To Try Men's Souls*, pp. 74, 75. See also Charles Royster, *A Revolutionary People at War: The Continental Army and American Character, 1775-1783* (Chapel Hill: University of North Carolina Press, 1979), pp. 105-6, on the importance of extracting oaths of allegiance, even though "[o]aths alone proved nothing about the oath-takers" (ibid., p. 106).

A contemporary illustration of the perceived importance of oaths in revolutionary situations is provided by the recommendation by Philippine Justice Minister Neptali Gonzales that charges of rebellion, a capital offense under Philippine law, be dropped in regard to those members of the military who would swear loyalty to the Aquino government. The news report indicated that "oath-taking ceremonies were held at camps throughout the country" ("Marcos Running Mate, 40 Others Are Charged in Revolt," *Boston Globe*, July 29, 1986, p. 4, col. 5). There were also mass oath-taking ceremonies of fidelity to the new Philippine constitution following its ratification by the people in January 1987.

39. Hyman, *To Try Men's Souls*, pp. 82-84.
40. This point was made many years ago by Cecelia Kenyon in *The New York Review of Books*, November 14, 1963, pp. 22-23, where she was reviewing Leonard Levy's *Jefferson and Civil Liberties: The Darker Side*, in which he severely criticized Jefferson for supporting a loyalty oath in Virginia.
41. See Harold M. Hyman, *Era of the Oath: Northern Loyalty Tests during the Civil War and Reconstruction* (Philadelphia: University of Pennsylvania Press, 1954). A major issue following the conclusion of that clash, reflected in the text of the Fourteenth Amendment quoted at the start of this chapter, involved so-called test oaths that would be extracted from those who had (or were thought to have) supported the dissolution of Union. A slim majority of the Supreme Court struck down a requirement that no attorney could practice before a federal court without having sworn an "ironclad" oath that he had not, among other things, "yielded a voluntary support to any pretended government, authority, power, or constitution within the United States, hostile or inimical thereto." Ex parte *Garland*, 4 Wallace 333 (1867). The same majority struck down a Missouri oath in Cummings v. Missouri, 4 Wallace 277 (1867). See

Hyman, *Era of the Oath*, pp. 107-120. The cases are also discussed and analyzed in Charles Fairman, *History of the Supreme Court of the United States*, vol. 6, *Reconstruction and Reunion 1864-88, Part One* (New York: Macmillan, 1971), pp. 240-48.

42. The issue was especially salient within the academic community. See, e.g., Ellen Shrecker, *No Ivory Tower: McCarthyism and the Universities* (New York: Oxford University Press, 1986), pp. 114-25 (detailing the University of California loyalty oath controversy).

43. 319 U.S. 624 (1943).

44. Ibid., at 642.

45. See Jerold Israel, "*Elfbrandt* v. *Russell*: The Demise of the Oath?" *Supreme Court Review* (1966): 193.

46. Cole v. Richardson, 405 U.S. 676, 677-678 (1972).

47. Ibid., at 680.

48. It is also worth mentioning that one other common occasion for the swearing of a loyalty oath is in applying for a passport entitling one to leave and enter the United States. Why an oath should be required for a passport, but not for a ballot, is not self-evident.

49. 8 U.S.C. § 1427(a)(1983). Requirements for naturalization are summarized in David Wiessbrodt, *Immigration Law and Procedure in a Nutshell* (St. Paul, Minn.: West Publishing Co., 1984), excerpted in T. Alexander Aleinikoff and David Martin, *Immigration: Process and Policy* (St. Paul, Minn.: West Publishing Co., 1985), pp. 859-69.

50. In Aleinikoff and Martin, *Immigration*, p. 863.

51. See 8 U.S.C. § 1424 (1983).

52. 8 U.S.C. § 1448.

53. Kent Greenawalt, "Promise, Benefit, and Need: Ties That Bind Us to the Law," *Georgia Law Review* 18 (1984): 737, 739.

54. See the materials collected in Aleinikoff and Martin, *Immigration*, pp. 834-49.

55. Gerald Rosberg, "Aliens and Equal Protection: Why Not the Right to Vote?" *Michigan Law Review* 75 (1977): 1127-35.

56. See Robert Reinhold, "Flow of 3d World Immigrants Alters Weave of U.S. Society," *The New York Times*, June 30, 1986, p. 1, col. 6 (late city final ed.), which notes that only 5 percent of the 570,000 legally admitted immigrants arriving in the United States in 1985 came from Europe; nearly half came from Asia, and migration from Latin America constituted another 40 percent. Moreover, in absolute numbers, more immigrants will arrive legally during

the 1980s, approximately six million, than during any other decade in our history save for 1901-1910, when 8.8 million immigrants arrived. If illegal immigration, estimated at 300,000-500,000 per year, is added, then the numbers could surpass even that earlier high point. (Immigrants, however, constituted a significantly higher *percentage* of the population during these earlier periods. Indeed, today the United States's percentage of foreign-born residents [7 percent] is substantially less than Australia's [20 percent], Canada's [16 percent], or France's [11 percent].)

57. For the emphasis on "content-neutrality" as a major foundation of contemporary first amendment doctrine, see, e.g., Members of the City Council v. Taxpayers for Vincent, 466 U.S. 789 (1984); Widmar v. Vincent, 454 U.S. 263 (1981).

58. See Roger Lowenstein, "Immigration Aides Base Big Decisions on 15-Minute Chats," *Wall Street Journal*, June 5, 1986, p. 1, col. 4.

59. Michael Sandel, *Liberalism and the Limits of Justice* (Cambridge: Cambridge University Press, 1982).

60. Sollors, *Beyond Ethnicity*, p. 6.

61. Ibid., p. 151, quoting "Democracy *versus* the Melting Pot," in Horace Kallen, *Culture and Democracy in the United States: Studies in the Group Psychology of the American Peoples* (1924), p. 122 (essay originally published in 1915). Kallen later elaborated some of the implications of this distinction between what Sollors terms "blood" (grandfathers) and "law" (wives):

> The citizen of America may become one of England, the Baptist a Methodist, the lawyer a banker, the Elk a Mason, the Republican a Socialist, the capitalist a proletarian. But the son, father, uncle, cousin cannot cease to be these; he cannot reject the relationships these words express, nor alter them. . . . Natural groups, like the Irish, the Jews, or any nationality, cannot be destroyed without destroying their members. Artificial groups, like states, churches, professions, castes, can. These are social organizations; natural groups are social organisms.

(ibid., quoting Horace Kallen, *The Structure of Lasting Peace* [1918], p. 31.)

62. Joanna Kates, "Hers," *The New York Times*, October 9, 1986, p. C2, col. 3. One may doubt whether family relationships are quite

so binding (or quite so "natural") as Kallen and Kates portray them, but surely anyone with such a view would find it unnecessary, perhaps even bizarre, to suggest applying the same kinds of procedures to the family as to "artificial" entities like the state. A true "nation-state," involving a perfect overlap between the social and the political, would present an interesting test case of Kallen's categories, but there are few such states; the United States is most definitely not one of them.

63. See John Gillis, *For Better, For Worse: British Marriage 1600 to the Present* (New York: Oxford University Press, 1985), p. 16. Gillis points out that more informal traditions exist, both in other societies and within our own. For Trobrianders the sharing of food apparently performed the same function as the articulation of words, and our own history has included "common-law marriage," where there is no formal exchange of vows.

64. Ibid., p. 20. The seventeenth-century political theorist Samuel Pufendorf referred to the "common maxim of the lawyers that *consenting and not bedding, makes a marriage.*" S. Pufendorf, *Of the Law of Nature and Nations* (1672), bk. 6, ch. 1, § 14, quoted in Robert Goodin, *Protecting the Vulnerable: A Reanalysis of Our Social Responsibilities* (Chicago: University of Chicago Press, 1985), p. 72.

65. Gillis, *For Better, For Worse*, pp. 38, 44, 45.

66. The comments made about marriage do not depend on rejection of bigamy or other forms of polygamy. Presumably a bigamist has a different level of commitment to his wives than to others.

67. I am informed by Ellen Kandoian of wedding ceremonies in Maine during the 1970s that pledged durability of the marriage "as long as love shall last."

68. Letter from Donald Herzog to author, June 5, 1986.

69. David Hartman, *The Living Covenant: The Innovative Spirit in Traditional Judaism* (New York: Macmillan, 1985), p. 5.

70. G.W.F. Hegel, *The Philosophy of Right* (1821), secs. 75, 161 additions, quoted in Goodin, *Protecting the Vulnerable*, p. 91.

71. A breaching party, to be sure, has a duty to pay damages, so that the victim of the breach gets the benefit of the bargain; but a presumption exists against requiring "specific performance." The most famous statement of this view is surely Justice Holmes's: "The duty to keep a contract at common law means a prediction that you must

pay damages if you do not keep it,—and nothing else." Holmes, "The Path of the Law," *Harvard Law Review* 10 (1897): 462.

72. See Sandel, *Liberalism and the Limits of Justice*.

73. See Judith Shklar, *Men and Citizens: A Study of Rousseau's Social Theory* (Cambridge: Cambridge University Press, 1969), p. 57.

74. Emile Durkheim, *The Elementary Forms of Religious Life*, quoted in Anthony Giddens, ed., *Durkheim on Politics and the State* (Stanford: Stanford University Press, 1986), p. 163.

75. Michael Walzer, "Political Alienation and Military Service," in *Obligations* (Cambridge, Mass.: Harvard University Press, 1970), pp. 99-100, 112-13. Walzer notes that their status is a function of their being "alienated residents" (ibid., p. 114).

76. I am grateful to Jim Fishkin for emphasizing this point to me in conversation.

77. Once within the polity, though, naturalized citizens presumably acquire the same freedom of belief that we have and may repudiate the propositional oaths earlier taken.

78. See generally Morton Grodzins, *The Loyal and the Disloyal: Social Boundaries of Patriotism and Treason* (Chicago: University of Chicago Press, 1956), pp. 7-8.

79. Walzer, "The Problem of Citizenship," in *Obligations*, p. 205.

80. Lewis Coser, *Greedy Institutions: Patterns of Undivided Commitment* (New York: The Free Press, 1974).

81. James Kettner, *The Development of American Citizenship, 1608-1870* (Chapel Hill: University of North Carolina Press, 1978), p. 218.

82. See U.S. Const. Art. I, § 8: "The Congress shall have the power . . . to establish a uniform rule of naturalization . . . throughout the United States."

83. Act of Mar. 26, 1790, ch. 3, 1 Stat. 103.

84. James Morton Smith, *Freedom's Fetters: The Alien and Sedition Laws and American Civil Liberties* (Ithaca: Cornell University Press, 1956), p. 23.

85. Kettner, *Development*, p. 240.

86. Act of Jan. 29, 1795, ch. 20, 1 Stat. 414.

87. Kawakita v. United States, 343 U.S. 717 (1952).

88. Ibid., at 720.

89. Ibid., at 721.

90. Ibid., at 734-36.

91. Douglas Laycock, for example, notes that citizenship "is the defin-

itive indication of *the* polity with which one is affiliated"; Douglas Laycock, "Taking Constitutions Seriously: A Theory of Judicial Review," *Texas Law Review* 59 (1981): 388 (emphasis added). Laycock quite naturally seems to assume that the proper article is "the" rather than "a," though dual citizenship requires the use of the latter.

92. See Perkins v. Elg, 307 U.S. 325, 329 (1939); Aleinikoff and Martin, *Immigration*, pp. 917-31.

93. See Sanford Levinson, "Testimonial Privileges and the Preferences of Friendship," *Duke Law Journal* (1984): 631.

94. John H. Howe, *The Changing Political Thought of John Adams* (Princeton: Princeton University Press, 1966), pp, 45-46, quoting Lyman Butterfield, ed., *Adams Family Correspondence*, vol. 2 (Cambridge, Mass.: Harvard University Press, 1963), pp. 96-97. (John Adams to Abigail Adams, August 14, 1776.)

95. Jean Starobinski, *1789: The Emblems of Reason* (Charlottesville: University of Virginia Press, 1982), pp. 101-124, particularly pp. 105-110.

96. Ibid., p. 102.

97. Garry Wills, *Cincinnatus: George Washington and the Enlightenment* (Garden City, N.Y.: Doubleday & Co., 1984), p. 186.

98. Stanley Hauerwas, "Freedom of Religion: A Subtle Temptation" (unpublished manuscript), pp. 2, 19.

99. Nicholas Capaldi, "Explication Versus Exploration: The Nature of Constitutional Interpretation: Morgan's *Disabling America*," *American Bar Foundation Research Journal* (1987): 245.

100. Amos 3:3.

101. Cf. Lief Carter, *Contemporary Constitutional Lawmaking: The Supreme Court and the Art of Politics* (New York: Pergamon Press, 1985), p. 14: "Communities *are* those networks of people who believe their past communications had meaning and who have faith that future communications will also have meaning. Community members do *not* necessarily share substantive beliefs. Good friends who disagree strongly about ideologies, scientific propositions, and questions of taste remain good friends as long as they continue to use the same communicative framework." However, Carter also writes that "[e]ven in normal times the conversations that build communities need authoritative and hence undisputed starting points" (ibid., pp. 51-52).

102. J. Anthony Lukas, *Common Ground: A Turbulent Decade in the Lives of Three American Families* (New York: Alfred Knopf, 1985).
103. Fowler, Book Review, *Journal of American History* 73 (1986): 252-53.
104. Starobinski, *1789*, p. 102.
105. See ibid., p. 104.

Chapter Four

1. Eakin v. Raub, 12 S.&R. 330, 353 (Pa. 1825) (Gibson, J., dissenting).
2. Ibid., at 353-54.
3. Ibid., at 354.
4. Youngstown Sheet and Tube Co. v. Sawyer, 343 U.S. 579 (1952).
5. For an example of the Court's willingness to shield perpetrators of constitutional wrongdoing from personal liability for the damages inflicted when the wrongdoers have exhibited "good faith," see Scheuer v. Rhodes, 416 U.S. 232, 247 (1974). More troublesome is such shielding even in the absence of good faith. See Nixon v. Fitzgerald, 457 U.S. 731 (1982).
6. William E. Connolly, *The Terms of Political Discourse*, 2nd ed. (Princeton: Princeton University Press, 1983), p. 10.
7. Ibid., quoting W. B. Gallie, "Essentially Contested Concepts," reprinted in Max Black, ed., *The Importance of Language* (Englewood Cliffs, N.J.: Prentice-Hall, 1962), p. 123.
8. *Mahzor for Rosh Hashanah and Yom Kippur*, ed. Rabbi Jules Harlow, 2nd ed. (New York: The Rabbinical Assembly, 1978), p. 256.
9. 320 U.S. 119. Government attorneys, however, responding to an initiative from Sumner Welles, the undersecretary of state, had suggested to Chief Justice Stone in an informal letter that the Court postpone consideration of the appeal and thus free the government from an embarrassment in regard to its new ally. See J. Woodford Howard, *Mr. Justice Murphy: A Political Biography* (Princeton: Princeton University Press, 1968), p. 310. Howard has a very illuminating discussion of *Schneiderman* at pp. 309-322, as does Sidney Fine in *Frank Murphy: The Washington Years* (Ann Arbor: University of Michigan Press, 1984), pp. 408-421.
10. 320 U.S., at 123.
11. Ibid., at 122.

12. Howard, *Mr. Justice Murphy*, p. 309.

13. Ibid., p. 311.

14. 320 U.S., at 133.

15. Ibid., at 134.

16. It is thus easily possible to dismiss the relevance of *Schneiderman* for contemporary litigation, given this change of language. This would only serve to underscore the peculiar position of the case in our constitutional firmament.

17. See, e.g., Charles Taylor, "Interpretation and the Sciences of Man," in idem, *Philosophic Papers: Philosophy and the Human Sciences*, vol. 2 (Cambridge: Cambridge University Press, 1985), pp. 15-57.

18. Howard, *Mr. Justice Murphy*, p. 311.

19. Georg Lukács, *History and Class Consciousness: Studies in Marxist Dialectics* (Cambridge, Mass.: M.I.T. Press, 1971), p. 263.

20. The reference is to Paul's second letter to the Corinthians 3:4-6 (King James Version).

21. Robert M. Grant with David Tracy, *A Short History of the Interpretation of the Bible* (Philadelphia: Fortress Press, 1984), p. 176.

22. Max Farrand, ed., *Records of the Federal Convention of 1787*, vol. 3 (New Haven: Yale University Press, 1937), p. 14.

23. See Bruce Ackerman, "The Storrs Lectures: Discovering the Constitution," *Yale Law Journal* 93 (1984): 1017 n. 6. These lectures comprise the introduction to a much more extensive project, under the general title "Discovering the Constitution," on which Ackerman is currently engaged. The central topics of Ackerman's project include the legitimacy of the Reconstruction Congress and its actions leading to the adoption of the Fourteenth Amendment to the Constitution, as well as the constitutional propriety of the actions of the Supreme Court during the constitutional "revolution" of 1937, when it abandoned wholesale the jurisprudence of the previous half-century regarding the powers of Congress and the states to regulate the economy. I am very grateful to Professor Ackerman for his willingness to share his unpublished materials, and I regret that I have not had the time to work them thoroughly into the analysis presented in this chapter.

24. Richard Kay, "The Illegality of the Constitution," *Constitutional Commentary* 4 (1987): 57. Kay is not registering a criticism; he argues that "[e]very legal system is governed, at the end, by principles whose authority cannot be found in law" (ibid., p. 58).

25. Ackerman, "Discovering the Constitution," p. 1017 n. 6.

26. Farrand, *Records of the Federal Convention*, 1: 262 (speech of June 16, 1787, Yates transcription).

27. Emphasis in original.

28. John Locke, *Two Treatises on Government*, ed. Peter Laslett (Cambridge: Cambridge University Press, 1963), p. 424.

29. Letter to John Colvin, September 20, 1810, in Gerard Stourzh, *Alexander Hamilton and the Idea of a Republican Government* (Stanford: Stanford University Press, 1970), p. 34. Representative Henry Hyde of Illinois quoted this passage in his remarks to (and about) Lieutenant Colonel Oliver North on July 13, 1987, during the hearings of the joint congressional committee investigating the presumptively illegal behavior of the Reagan Administration in financing the efforts of Nicaraguan "Contras."

30. Locke, *Two Treatises*, pp. 425-26.

31. *The Political Thought of Abraham Lincoln*, ed. Richard Current (Indianapolis: Bobbs-Merrill Co., 1967), p. 262. Howard indicates that Murphy was much influenced by the invocation of Lincoln (along with Jefferson and Taney) by Wendell Willkie, Schneiderman's lawyer, in his argument (Howard, *Mr. Justice Murphy*, p. 313). Murphy noted to his law clerk that it was "very doubtful" that the government had failed to show that the party (and Schneiderman) had "advocated the overthrow of the government by force and violence," but he went on to classify such advocacy as "doctrinal utterances and academic or theoretical exhortations," which must be protected lest one "conclude that Jefferson and Lincoln had not behaved as one attached to the Constitution" (ibid., p. 314).

32. 365 U.S. 265 (1961).

33. Ibid., at 270.

34. Act of 1906 § 4.

35. U.S. v. De Francis, 50 F.2d 497, 498.

36. United States v. Mirsky, 17 F.2d 275, 276 (1926).

37. 320 U.S., at 135.

38. Ibid.

39. Ibid., at 139-40.

40. Ibid., at 140 n. 20, quoting Brief for the United States, p. 105.

41. Ibid., at 136. This sets up an interesting question in its own right: How exactly does the Constitution differ from a (national) party platform or "asserted [national] principles"? Should we expect that judges, or presidents, who swear fidelity to the Constitution nec-

essarily "subscribe unqualifiedly to all of its platforms or asserted principles"?

42. Ibid., at 154-55, citing vol. 2 of Lord Bryce's *The American Commonwealth* (1915), p. 334.

43. Ibid., at 137.

44. Ibid.

45. Ibid., at 138.

46. Ex parte *Sauer*, 81 F. 355, quoted in William Preston, Jr., *Aliens and Dissenters: Federal Suppression of Radicals, 1903-1933* (Cambridge, Mass.: Harvard University Press, 1963), p. 63. Chapter Three of this valuable book is devoted to naturalization cases that occurred throughout the period. One should recall, moreover, that the majority in *Schneiderman* itself emphasized that the case involved *de*naturalization; they left the clear impression that the case might have come out differently had Schneiderman been seeking initial entry to American citizenship.

47. Act of 1906, § 4.

48. Preston, *Aliens and Dissenters*, p. 72.

49. Ibid., p. 69.

50. 320 U.S., at 139.

51. Ibid., at 140.

52. Ibid., at 141, quoting 119 F.2d at 504.

53. Ibid., at 141.

54. George Will, "What to Read? Start with Genesis," *Washington Post*, June 28, 1984, p. 15, col. 1, quoted in Gene Nichol, "Children of Distant Fathers: Sketching an Ethos of Constitutional Liberty," *Wisconsin Law Review* (1985): 1322. Nichol treats Lincoln as one "of the United States' principal political architects" (ibid., p. 1310), and he attempts to draw from Lincoln's political vision a justification for the protection by the Supreme Court of a high measure of personal autonomy as revealed, e.g., in such cases as Griswold v. Connecticut, 381 U.S. 479; Roe v. Wade, 410 U.S. 113 (1973); and Moore v. East Cleveland, 431 U.S. 494 (1977).

55. This way of putting it is designed to reject the simpler narrative that puts the onus of the 1861 war entirely on the South as its "initiator." Lincoln had an independent choice to make once the *fait accompli* of declarations of independence from the union had occurred. He, like the Charlestonians who fired on Fort Sumter, chose war.

56. Prigg v. Pennsylvania, 41 U.S. (16 Pet.) 536 (1842), at 611 (emphasis added).
57. Nichol, "Children," p. 1323 (emphasis added).
58. Owen Fiss and Charles Krauthammer, "The Rehnquist Court," *The New Republic* (March 10, 1982): 20.
59. *Collected Works of Abraham Lincoln*, ed. Roy Basler, vol. 4 (New Brunswick, N.J.: Rutgers University Press, 1953), p. 169.
60. Anne Norton, *Alternative Americas: A Reading of Antebellum Political Culture* (Chicago: University of Chicago Press, 1986), p. 298.
61. Ibid.
62. Allen Nevins and Milton H. Thomas, eds., *The Diary of George Templeton Strong*, vol. 4 (New York: Macmillan, 1952), pp. 20-21 (entry of July 15, 1865). I owe this reference to Daniel Aaron.
63. 320 U.S. at 142.
64. Ibid., at 143.
65. Ibid., at 143-44.
66. Ibid., at 144-45.
67. Ibid., at 148.
68. Ibid., at 153.
69. Ibid., at 157.
70. Ibid., at 157-58.
71. Ibid., at 158-59.
72. Ibid., at 154.
73. Howard, *Mr. Justice Murphy*, p. 315.
74. Minersville School District v. Gobitis, 310 U.S. 586 (1940).
75. 320 U.S., at 176.
76. Ibid., at 177.
77. Ibid., at 181.
78. Ibid., at 186.
79. Ibid., at 184.
80. Ibid., at 197.
81. Ibid., at 196.
82. Ibid., at 196-97.
83. Ibid., at 193.
84. Ibid., at 195.
85. Ibid.
86. Ibid., at 193-94.
87. Ibid., at 195.
88. Ibid., at 135.
89. 322 U.S. 665 (1944). See Fine, *Frank Murphy*, pp. 421-22.

90. Ibid., at 669.
91. Ibid., at 669 n. 2.
92. Ibid., at 673.
93. Ibid., at 674.
94. Ibid., at 676.
95. Ibid., at 677. Justice Murphy, joined by Justices Black, Douglas, and Rutledge, wrote a separate opinion agreeing that the facts delineated certainly did not justify a finding under the *Schneiderman* standard that Baumgartner "did not bear or swear true allegiance to the United States at the time of naturalization . . ." (ibid., at 680).
96. 341 U.S. 494 (1951).
97. See, e.g., Michel Foucault, *Discipline and Punish* (New York: Pantheon Books, 1978), for a menu of possibilities.
98. Walter Murphy, "An Ordering of Constitutional Values," *Southern California Law Review* 53 (1980): 754-57. See also Douglas Linder, "What in the Constitution Cannot Be Amended," *Arizona Law Review* 23 (1981) 717.
99. Murphy, "An Ordering," p. 757 n. 255, citing the West German *Grundgesetz* art. 79.
100. Ibid., p. 756 (emphasis in original).
101. 71 U.S. (4 Wall.) 120 (1866).
102. Murphy, "An Ordering," p. 756 n. 254.
103. Ibid., p. 787. See also the very rich argument by William Harris in Chapter 4 of *The Interpretable Constitution* (unpublished manuscript, 1987), to which I am much indebted.
104. Article III, Section 2, Clause 2.
105. The Francis Wright, 205 U.S. 381 (1881).
106. See Henry Hart, "The Power of Congress to Limit the Jurisdiction of Federal Courts: An Exercise in Dialectic," *Harvard Law Review* 66 (1953): 1364-65.
107. The major exception among American religions is the Mormons. Thus the ruling elder of the Church several years ago announced that new revelation (rather than interpretation of existing Mormon doctrine) required changing the status of blacks within the Church. A similar revelation in the late-Nineteenth Century brought polygamy to an end as an official doctrine of the Church.
108. Peter Chirico, *Infallibility: The Crossroads of Doctrine* (Kansas City: Sheed Andrews and McMeel, Inc., 1977), p. 195.

109. See Shmuel Shilo, "Circumvention of the Law in Talmudic Literature," *Israel Law Review* 17 (1982): 151-68.
110. Robert Goldenberg, "Halakhic Creativity" (Book Review), *Tikkun* 2 (November-December 1987): 80.
111. Joel Roth, *The Halakhic Process: A Systemic Analysis* (New York: Jewish Theological Seminary of America, 1986), quoted in Goldenberg, "Halakhic Creativity," p. 80.
112. Gershom Scholem, "Judaism," in Arthur Cohen and Paul Mendes-Flohr, eds., *Contemporary Jewish Religious Thought: Original Essays on Critical Concepts, Movements, and Beliefs* (New York: Charles Scribner's Sons, 1987), pp. 505-6. See also David Biale, *Gershom Scholem: Kabbalah and Counter-History* (Cambridge, Mass.: Harvard University Press, 1979).

CHAPTER FIVE

1. See Clifford Geertz, *The Interpretation of Cultures* (New York: Basic Books, 1973).
2. See the discussion of "Autonomy and Community," in Mark Yudof, "Library Book Selection and the Public Schools: The Quest for the Archimedean Point," *Indiana Law Review* 59 (1984): 530-33.
3. Paul Carrington, "Of Time and the River," *Journal of Legal Education* 34 (1984): 222. Since a genuine "nihilist" would scarcely be expected to recognize as obligatory such a duty—that recognition would obviously be a refutation of the description of the person as a "nihilist"—a question raised by at least some of Carrington's readers is whether he would push from the legal academy those who will not jump. See, e.g., the correspondence about Carrington's article collected in " 'Of Law and the River,' and of Nihilism and Academic Freedom," *Journal of Legal Education* 35 (1985): 1. I have no reason to doubt Carrington's assurance that he would not be a pusher, however much he encourages the jumping.
4. See Gary Peller, "The Metaphysics of American Law," *California Law Review* 73 (1985): 1219-40, for an excellent analysis of strands within Realism.
5. Owen Fiss, "The Death of the Law?" *Cornell Law Review* 72 (1986): 16.
6. Carrington, "Of Time," p. 226.
7. Ibid., pp. 227-28 (emphasis added).

8. Ibid., p. 227.

9. "Nihilism and Academic Freedom," p. 10 (letter from Carrington to Robert W. Gordon).

10. Carrington, "Of Time," p. 226.

11. Ibid., p. 228

12. See Model Code of Professional Responsibility, Ethical Consideration 9-6 (1981).

13. Carrington, "Of Time," p. 227.

14. "Nihilism and Academic Freedom," p. 10.

15. Ibid.

16. Ibid., p. 26.

17. See, e.g., Ted Finman, "Critical Legal Studies, Professionalism, and Academic Freedom: Exploring the Tributaries of Carrington's River," *Journal of Legal Education* 35 (1985): 180. Finman is not affiliated with CLS. For an excellent critique of Carrington's confused notions of nihilism by one of the most distinguished scholars associated with CLS, see Robert Gordon's letters to Carrington, "Nihilism and Academic Freedom," pp. 1-9, 13-16.

18. See *Oxford English Dictionary*, vol. 8 (1933), pp. 1426-29, from which all of the following examples are taken.

19. John H. Leith, ed., *Creeds of the Churches: A Reader in Christian Doctrine from the Bible to the Present*, 3rd ed. (Atlanta: John Knox Press, 1982), p. 5.

20. Ibid., p. 9.

21. Obviously we might object to the creed itself.

22. See Frederick E. Blumer, "Academic Freedom and Church-Related Institutions," *Academe* 72 (January-February 1986): 51.

23. Joseph Berger, "Vatican Orders a Theologian to Retract Teachings on Sex," *The New York Times*, March 12, 1986, p. A17, col. 1. See also a fascinating set of letters in the London *Times* regarding the call by the Vatican for the Dutch theologian Edward Schillebeeckx to come to Rome in order to discuss the fidelity of his writings to Catholic doctrine. A group of some 70-odd English "holders of academic chairs of theology" signed a letter to *The Times* criticizing the Vatican and endorsing Schillebeeckx's "freedom of interpretation." *The Times*, December 1, 1979. On December 6, additional letters considered the matter. Dom Betet Innes, after reminding his readers that "most heretics have been theologians," went on to endorse the "safest rule of faith [as] the *sensus fidelium*, even that of the unlearned." The "faithful" have "the right" to "reliable guid-

ance and that, for Roman Catholics at least, comes from the Pope and the Bishops acting together" (*The Times*, December 6, 1979, p. 15).

24. Ari Goldman, "Vatican Curbs U.S. Theologian Over Liberal Views on Sex Issues," *The New York Times*, August 19, 1986, p. A1, col. 2. The chancellor of the university, Archbishop James Hickey, stated that he "fully support[ed] this judgment of the Holy See. The Holy Father and the bishops have the right and the duty to insure that what is taught in the name of the church be completely faithful to its full and authentic teaching. The faithful have a right to sound teaching and the church's officially commissioned teachers have a particular responsibility to honor that right."

25. Blumer, "Academic Freedom," p. 22.

26. See generally Walter Metzger, *Academic Freedom in the Age of the University* (New York: Columbia University Press, 1961), pp. 24-29.

27. Jonathan Z. Smith, *Imagining Religion: From Babylon to Jonestown* (Chicago: University of Chicago Press, 1982), p. xi.

28. Alan Freeman and John Henry Schlegel, "Sex, Power and Silliness: An Essay On Ackerman's *Reconstructing American Law*," *Cardozo Law Review* 6 (1985): 850 n. 10 (personal communication from David Engel to Alan David Freeman and John Henry Schlegel).

29. Arthur Green, "Jewish Studies and Jewish Faith," *Tikkun*, no. 1 (1986): 84-90.

30. Ibid., p. 86.

31. "Nihilism and Academic Freedom," p. 26.

32. But see as well the elaboration of American law regarding slavery, especially such cases as State v. Mann, 13 N.C. (2 Dev.) 263 (1824), discussed in Mark Tushnet, *The American Law of Slavery 1810-1860: Considerations of Humanity and Interest* (Princeton: Princeton University Press, 1981), pp. 54-65.

33. Jay M. Feinman, "Priests and Prophets," *Saint Louis University Law Journal* 31 (1986): 53.

34. Ibid., pp. 58, 59. Compare the description that Raymond Geuss gives of (his favorite notion of) critical theory: "A critical theory is addressed to members of *this* particular social group . . .[,] it describes *their* epistemic principles and *their* idea of the 'good life' and demonstrates that some belief they hold is reflectively unacceptable for agents who hold their epistemic principles and a source

of frustration for agents who are trying to realize this particular kind of 'good life.' " Raymond Geuss, *The Idea of a Critical Theory: Habermas and the Frankfort School* (Cambridge: Cambridge University Press, 1981), p. 63, quoted in Michael Walzer, *Interpretation and Social Criticism* (Cambridge, Mass.: Harvard University Press, 1987), p. 89 n. 21.

35. Walzer, *Interpretation*, p. 73. Walzer notes that this social immersion is not true of all of the Biblical "prophets." Thus Jonah's mission is to go to a society—Nineveh—distinctly not his own. He is "an alien voice, a mere messenger, unconnected to the people of the city" (ibid., pp. 77-78). His message of impending doom and the need for repentance may, of course, be altogether correct; the Ninevans in fact believed him and repented, but the point is that Jonah's prophecy was stripped down to its bare essentials. His "is prophecy without poetry, without resonance, allusion, or concrete detail" (ibid., p. 77). See also p. 80: "Jonah, by contrast [to Amos], has no personal interest in Nineveh and no knowledge of its moral history." The importance of the book of Jonah is its self-reference, not its narrative ordering of Nineveh's own self-understanding.

36. Ibid., p. 78.

37. Ibid., p. 81.

38. Charles Fried, "The Lawyer as Friend: The Moral Foundations of the Lawyer-Client Relation," *Yale Law Journal* 85 (1976): 1060. Fried assumes the basic justice of the American social order, so perhaps he would not be so reassuring to those lawyers who used their skills in behalf of the property rights of slaveholders. Fried never indicates exactly *when* we became a sufficiently just society to justify lawyers in a belief that they would be good persons however they chose to use their legal talents.

39. W. Forsythe, *Hortensius the Advocate* (1879), p. 379.

40. John Mortimer, *Clinging to the Wreckage: A Part of Life* (New York: Penguin Books, 1982), pp. 95-96.

41. Michael Sandel, *Liberalism and the Limits of Justice* (Cambridge: Cambridge University Press, 1982).

42. 23 U.S. (10 Wheat.) 66 (1825).

43. Ibid., at 114.

44. Ibid., at 120-21.

45. See John Noonan, *The Antelope: The Ordeal of the Recaptured Africans in the Administrations of James Monroe and John Quincy Adams* (Berkeley: University of California Press, 1977), for a mar-

velous analysis of this case. Like Noonan's equally impressive predecessor volume, *The Persons and Masks of the Law* (New York: Farrar, Straus and Giroux, 1976), the book explores the ways that "thinking like a lawyer" can blind one to moral implications and become a device for justifying the ways not of God to man but of the powerful to those who suffer under what Carrington rightly calls their lash.

One may regard it as a genuine irony befitting modern times that Noonan, one of the most sensitive critics of orthodox legal culture, has been appointed to the United States Court of Appeals for the Ninth Circuit, presumably in part because of his opposition to *Roe* v. *Wade*. One suspects that Judge Noonan will surprise certain members of the Reagan Administration when in areas other than abortion they posit the stern duty of the "jurist" as overwhelming any "merely" moralistic analysis. See especially Noonan's eloquent conclusion to *The Antelope*, p. 159:

> Those who think in terms of power, of abstract national interests, of human beings in bulk, will always have a major role in governments. Those who suppose that the legal system is a self-subsistent set of rules existing outside of its participants and constraining lawyers and judges to act against their consciences will always be prevalent among lawyers, judges and legal historians. Those who think that every human action can be explained by the necessities of the prevailing social environment, the requirements of role-playing, the demands of national security will always be common among anthropologists, political scientists and sociologists. But every so often in a human heart the ice will crack, and a human person will acknowledge his responsibility for other human persons he has touched.

46. Model Code of Professional Responsibility, Ethical Consideration 7-5 (1981).
47. "Nihilism and Academic Freedom," p. 17. See also the comments of Guido Calebresi and Owen Fiss to Carrington, pp. 23-26; and Ted Finman's exploration of what he calls "The Carrington Thesis and the University's Commitment to the Search for Truth," in Finman, "Critical Legal Studies," pp. 187-92.
48. John 18:37-38.

49. Holmes, "The Path of the Law," in O. W. Holmes, *Collected Legal Papers* (New York: Harcourt Brace, 1920), p. 17.
50. "[D]econstruction used as a French word, means not 'destroying' but 'undoing,' while analyzing the different layers of a structure to know how it has been built. Everything which is not natural has a structure, and has been built; and deconstruction is, to some extent, a way of analyzing the structure. . . . Deconstruction . . . emphasized the history of the construction and the different layers which have built this construction." Jacques Derrida, in "Deconstruction: A Trialogue in Jerusalem," *Mishkenot Sha'ananim Newsletter*, no. 7 (December 1986): 2.
51. Metzger, *Academic Freedom*, p. 89.
52. Ibid., p. 91.
53. Ibid., p. 90.
54. Ibid.
55. Ibid., pp. 91-92.
56. Anthony Kronman, "Foreword: Legal Scholarship and Moral Education," *Yale Law Journal* 90 (1981): 955.
57. See James Boyd White, "The Ethics of Argument: Plato's *Gorgias* and the Modern Lawyer," *University of Chicago Law Review* 50 (1983): 849.
58. See my article, "What Do Lawyers Know (And What Do They Do with Their Knowledge)? Comments on Schauer and Moore," *Southern California Law Review* 58 (1985): 458. See also "Frivolous Cases," *Osgoode Hall Law Journal* 24 (1986): 353, where I examine the willingness of the practicing bar to present "frivolous" arguments when it is in the client's interest to do so.
59. See David Trubek, "Where the Action Is: Critical Legal Studies and Empiricism," *Stanford Law Review* 36 (1984): 595-600 (CLS scholars "have not yet produced their own theory of truth value"). See also the letter from Phillip Johnson to Paul Brest, *Journal of Legal Education* 35 (1985): 18-19, in which he takes Brest, sometimes identified with CLS, to task for invoking the rhetoric of pursuit of truth in support of the presence within law school of professors who deny the very meaningfulness of that pursuit.
60. Paul de Man, *Allegories of Reading: Figural Language in Rousseau, Nietzsche, Rilke, and Proust* (New Haven: Yale University Press, 1979), p. 110.
61. Ibid., quoting Friedrich Nietzsche, *On Truth and Lie in an Extra-Moral Sense*. I should note that Richard Weisberg has recently lev-

eled a strong attack on my reading of Nietzsche. Weisberg argues that Nietzsche is far from being a source of comfort to theorists labeled by Weisberg "ultramodernists." Nietzsche is said to be far more respectful of texts than most of this new breed, including myself. Weisberg argues that Heidegger rather than Nietzsche is the origin of many of the approaches (and errors) of ultramodernism. See Richard Weisberg, "Text into Theory: A Literary Approach to the Constitution," *Georgia Law Review* 20 (1986): 939. Even if I were to change my view about the latitude allowed interpreters by Nietzsche, and I leave open such a change of mind as a real possibility, it would not affect the more important point that skepticism about truthful interpretation is rife in the contemporary academy. (On this point, Weisberg does not disagree.)

62. Richard Rorty, "The Fate of Philosophy," *New Republic* (October 18, 1982): 28. Rorty's major writings are *Philosophy and the Mirror of Nature* (Princeton: Princeton University Press, 1979); and his collection of articles in *Consequences of Pragmatism* (Minneapolis: University of Minnesota Press, 1982).

63. Rorty, "Fate of Philosophy," p. 30 (emphasis in original).

64. Ibid., p. 32.

65. Robert McKay, "In Support of the Proposed Model Rules of Professional Conduct," *Villanova Law Review* 26 (1980-81): 1137.

66. Rorty, "Fate of Philosophy," p. 33. One might compare this argument with that made by Allan Bloom in *The Closing of the American Mind* (New York: Simon and Schuster, 1987). I think it is safe to say that Bloom views the arguments made by Rorty (and popularized by nonphilosophers like myself) as the enemy who must be overcome by the reaffirmation of the classical tradition's absolute, nonrelativistic values that Bloom proclaims.

67. 410 U.S. 113 (1973).

68. Mark Tushnet, "Following the Rules Laid Down: A Critique of Interpretivism and Neutral Principles," *Harvard Law Review* 96 (1983): 821.

69. Philip Bobbitt, *Constitutional Fate: Theory of the Constitution* (New York: Oxford University Press, 1982).

70. Rorty, *Consequences of Pragmatism*, p. 151.

71. Dred Scott v. Sandford, 60 U.S. (19 How.) 393, 407 (1857).

72. Candor requires that I acknowledge that I *do* occasionally label specific arguments clearly incorrect, such as Marshall's argument in *Marbury* v. *Madison* that Article III, Section 2, Clause 2 of the

Constitution has only one, unequivocal meaning (i.e., that the grant of original jurisdiction should be read as including "only" rather than "at least"). Similarly, I have no hesitation in denouncing either as outrageous hyperbole or simple lying Justice Taney's assigning a unified desire to exclude blacks from citizenship to the 1787 framers.

73. Holmes, "The Path of the Law," p. 202.

CHAPTER SIX

1. Similarly, the National Conference of Christians and Jews has prepared a handbill, with the words "Put Your Name on the Line" in boldface, suggesting that the best way to celebrate the Bicentennial would be for the nation's schoolchildren to sign their names to the handbills and mail them to the national office for some appropriate ultimate destination.

2. "Reaffirmations," *The Jerusalem Post International Edition*, October 3, 1987, p. 24 (reprinting editorial from daily *Jerusalem Post*, September 22, 1987).

3. Paul Brest, "The Misconceived Quest for the Original Understanding," *Boston University Law Review* 60 (1980): 204.

4. Thurgood Marshall, "Commentary: Reflections on the Bicentennial of the United States Constitution," *Harvard Law Review* 101 (1987): 1, 2.

5. H. Jefferson Powell, "What the Constitution Means for Your Town, and for You," *Des Moines Register*, December 18, 1986, p. 13a.

6. D. M. Risinger, "Honesty in Pleading and Its Enforcement: Some 'Striking' Problems with Federal Rule of Civil Procedure 11," *Minnesota Law Review* 61 (1976): 57. Compare Ronald Dworkin's recent statement that "questions considered easy during one period become hard before they again become easy questions—with the opposite answers." Ronald Dworkin, *Law's Empire* (Cambridge, Mass.: Harvard University Press, 1986), p. 354.

INDEX

Library of Congress
Library of Congress Cataloging-in-Publication Data

Levinson, Sanford, 1941-
Constitutional faith / Sanford Levinson.
p. cm.   Includes index.
ISBN 0-691-07769-X (alk. paper)
1. United States—Constitutional law—Moral and ethical aspects.
2. United States—Constitutional history. I. Title.
KF4552.L48 1988
342.73′029—dc19
[347.30229]   88-435
CIP